Solving Transport Problems

Series Editor
Patrick Siarry

Solving Transport Problems

Towards Green Logistics

Edited by

Walid Besbes
Diala Dhouib
Niaz Wassan
Emna Marrekchi

WILEY

First published 2019 in Great Britain and the United States by ISTE Ltd and John Wiley & Sons, Inc.

ISTE Ltd
27-37 St George's Road
London SW19 4EU
UK

www.iste.co.uk

John Wiley & Sons, Inc.
111 River Street
Hoboken, NJ 07030
USA

www.wiley.com

Library of Congress Control Number: 2019947447

British Library Cataloguing-in-Publication Data
A CIP record for this book is available from the British Library
ISBN 978-1-78630-389-9

Contents

Chapter 5. An Overview of the Recent Solution Approaches in the Green Vehicle Routing Problem.   115
Emna MARREKCHI, Walid BESBES and Diala DHOUIB

Chapter 6. Multi-Criteria Decision Aid for Green Modes of Crude Oil Transportation Using MACBETH: The Sfax Region Case   135
Nouha HAMMAMI, Mohamed Haykal AMMAR and Diala DHOUIB

Chapter 9. Optimization in Multilevel Green Transportation Problems with Electrical Vehicles   203
Marcos R. LEITE, Heder S. BERNANDINO, Luciana B. GONÇALVES and
Stênio SOARES

Preface

Optimization of Green Transportation Problems: Fundamentals and Applications

Achieving a greener environment is a challenging issue despite recent substantial advancements on the subject from environmental agencies, governments, academics, practitioners, and some other concerned quarters such as civil societies. In recent years, academic research is increasingly motivated by practically transferable applications and managerial implications, inspired by real business operations. Nowadays, it is even more important to address and incorporate green issues in research. These are times in which we must make conscious efforts to bridge the gap between academia and industry. Any advances achieved in academia can directly influence company operations and policy and vice versa, and this can act as a conductor of shared knowledge and experience. As a part of the ongoing greening efforts, we believe this book will positively contribute toward providing new dimensions to all relevant stakeholders (e.g. researchers, governments, transport practitioners, green organizations, etc.) to develop new, better and greener models and make strategies to help achieve a cleaner environment. By highlighting various topics related to greenhouse gases, this book also aims to increase general public awareness about the importance of this issue.

Traditionally, academia and transport practitioners have mainly concentrated on efficient fleet management to achieve economic benefits and better-quality service. The green benefits are perceived as secondary objectives achieved as a by-product in academic studies and industry practices. However, more recently, due to growing environment public concerns and the industry appreciation of the issue, the academic community has started to address the green issues. A good deal of literature is available in the area of green transportation and supply chains. Some interesting books and articles have been published in the subject area. We believe that the published research has contributed to identifying the problem areas, enhanced public awareness, suggested solutions, and helped mobilized pressure on certain governments for green legislations and on companies for corporate social responsibilities. However, despite such ample efforts from various researchers around the globe, the area of optimizing green transportation problems appears to be in its infancy. As a part of continued efforts, this book is oriented toward implanting fundamentals and practice in the optimization of green transportation problems that would trigger incitement for further research in the subject area by providing readers with new knowledge and grounds for integrated models and solution methods. The existing research in this book clearly indicates that incorporating green issues in optimization problems can lead to significant improvements in CO_2 emissions and that this is a fruitful emerging area of research with great potential.

Focusing on green transportation, this book is comprised of diverse content. It includes presentations of the green dial-a-ride problem with alternative fuel vehicles for public transportation; the role of green technologies in helping to reduce carbon emissions; a conceptual framework modeling transport pooling in the case of urban and inter-urban distributions and analyzed through various scenarios to minimize traveling distances and greenhouse gases emission; a vehicle routing problem modeling approach with new integrated features such as park-and-loop and car sharing to minimizing adverse environmental impacts by avoiding use of heavy vehicles; an overview of solution approaches used recently for the GVRP and related extensions; a case study based on the MACBETH multi-criteria decision analysis approach using economic, environmental, and social criteria to find the appropriate mode of transport for hazardous materials; a green reverse logistics case of the vehicle routing problem with delivery and collection demands in freight transportation; a synchronized multi-modal transportation model for greener transportation options to decrease the environmental footprint associated with urban logistics; the optimization of multi-level green transportation problems considering aspects such as charging stations and routing; and direct torque control technique approaches suitable for electric vehicle momentum.

As can be seen from the above brief account of the chapters, the studies in this book incorporate diverse aspects related to green transportation. In particular, these studies show the significance of optimization in tackling green transport logistic problems, emphasize the importance of the role of technology and alternative fuel-based transport systems, and provide knowledge for greater environmental awareness.

We believe the studies of green transportation compiled in this edited book have identified certain areas of interest such as references, viewpoints, algorithms, and ideas for researchers, environmental planners, and other concerned quarters to start discussion on developing optimized technology and alternative fuel-based integrated models for environmentally cleaner transport systems.

Walid BESBES
Diala DHOUIB
Niaz WASSAN
Emna MARREKCHI
September 2019

Acknowledgments

The editors of the book would like to thank the reviewers for their useful comments and suggestions that improved the presentation as well as the content of the book chapters. We would also like to thank the publishers ISTE and Wiley for providing a chance to edit a book in the area of green transportation optimization, which is one of the contemporary subjects of interest for researchers and organizations.

An Adaptive Large Neighborhood Search Heuristic for the Green Dial-a-Ride Problem

This chapter studies the Green Dial-a-Ride Problem (G-DARP) which represents an extension of the classical Dial-a-Ride problem by considering a limited driving range of vehicles in combination with limited refueling infrastructure. In the G-DARP, a vehicle is allowed to refuel from any alternative fuel station with partial fill-up to eliminate the risk of running out of fuel during a route. This problem particularly arises for agencies and companies that employ a fleet of Alternative Fuel Vehicles (AFVs) to transport people. We present a linear mixed-integer mathematical programming formulation and propose an effective Adaptive Large Neighborhood Search (ALNS) algorithm to solve the G-DARP. Computational experiments confirm that the proposed algorithm produces high-quality solutions in a cost-effective and green manner. Moreover, the analysis shows the benefit of using partial refueling in terms of reducing the total fuel and CO_2e emissions costs compared to the use of full refueling.

1.1. Introduction

Public transportation has an overwhelming volume within the centers of today's dynamic cities, making it increasingly difficult to manage and plan. In this respect, customers' satisfaction is one of the major factors that should be considered in the transport planning process. Unfortunately, people with disabilities often do not have equal opportunities to benefit from the services, due to accessibility and mobility complications. In practice, their circumstances should be carefully considered during the design and execution of public transportation. Recently, the spread in awareness of the rights and needs of disabled people has spurred the demand for specialized

Chapter written by Mohamed Amine MASMOUDI, Manar HOSNY and Emrah DEMIR.

transportation services that accommodate their needs. This type of specialized transportation has thus been investigated in several contemporary studies, producing interesting insights.

The reduced mobility transportation problem involves planning the routes for a fleet of vehicles, where each vehicle is responsible for transporting a number of disabled persons from certain pickup points to certain destination points. This problem is named as the Dial-a-Ride Problem (DARP) in the literature. Generally, the objective of the DARP is to minimize both transportation costs and the customers' inconvenience (e.g. waiting time).

In traditional DARP studies, Internal Combustion Engine Vehicles (ICEVs) with gasoline or diesel fuel are used to serve the user' requests (see Braekers *et al.* 2014; Masmoudi *et al.* 2016, 2017, 2018b). However, such vehicles are the main source of emissions such as greenhouse gases (GHGs) and air pollutants. In the European Union (EU), the total amount of carbon dioxide-equivalent emissions (CO_2e) emitted by the buses and mini-buses involved in transportation routing actually represents about 22% of the total amount of EU emissions (Eurostat 2018). Up to now, road transport emissions have remarkably increased as indicated by the European Environment Agency (EEA). Therefore, Regulation (EC) No. 443/2009, whose objective is to attain 95 g of CO_2e per kilometer for the vehicles near the year 2020 – instead of 118 g in 2016 – encourages investment in new technologies in the car industry, in order to reduce fuel consumption and CO_2e emissions. Indeed, the most essential defiance that the European lawmaker is facing is to make certain that vehicles' emissions are sufficiently decreased by using renewable energy sources (Tsokolis *et al.* 2016). Aiming to overcome the environmental problems, along with the insufficient preoccupation with energy resources, various organizations such as governmental non-profit companies, agencies, and private establishments have resorted to transforming their ICEVs' fleets by incorporating Alternative Fuel Vehicles (AFVs), such as flexible fuel vehicles, fuel cell vehicles, and hybrid and plug-in vehicles (US Department of Energy (DOE) 2018). These vehicles use various types of alternative fuels (e.g. biodiesel, ethanol, propane, or hydrogen). Thus, this solution can readily help to limit the environmental impacts of transportation and fulfill new governmental regulations.

A conventional diesel engine can run on biodiesel or on a mixture of both types of fuel. In fact, to use biodiesel instead of petroleum-based diesel necessitates no engine adjustments (Masmoudi *et al.* 2018a). Thus, the new diesel-powered vehicles are manufactured to run on biodiesel without any alterations needed. The most common biodiesel types are B20 and B5 (US DOE 2018). Therefore, within the context of the DARP, it was motivating to consider using AFVs (with biodiesel) instead of ICEVs, in order to keep up with the latest technological advancements.

Moreover, due to several advantages, AFVs have become very attractive in recent transport applications (see Adler and Mirchandani 2016; Erdoğan and Miller-Hooks 2012). As a real application, the Société de transport de Montréal (STM) announced the replacement of their fleet with biodiesel vehicles to increase their service capacity.

However, despite the advantages of AFVs, one of their limitations is their limited driving range that necessitates frequent refueling from any Alternative Fuel Stations (AFSs). Thus, another motivation of the current study is to impose the requirement of refueling of vehicles during their service, in order to guarantee that the vehicle will be routed through a given day without being stranded due to lack of fuel, which may cause dissatisfaction of users (e.g. violation of time windows). In reality, the vehicle starts its route every day with different levels of remaining fuel, and during the journey, the vehicle must be refueled with partial or full capacity in order to continue to its target. In this context, our work is closely related to the treatment of the Green Vehicle Routing Problem (G-VRP) by Erdoğan and Miller-Hooks (2012), where the refueling of vehicles is integrated. In addition, in our study, we consider heterogeneous vehicles in terms of their capacity resources and users, which is inspired by the DARP studied by Braekers *et al.* (2014) and Masmoudi *et al.* (2016, 2017). To sum up, the DARP with refueling is considered as a combination of the HDARP (Heterogeneous Dial-a-Ride Problem) and the G-VRP. We call our problem the Green Dial-a-Ride Problem (G-DARP).

The contributions of this chapter are as follows: i) a linear mixed-integer mathematical formulation of the G-DARP is introduced; ii) an efficient Adaptive Large Neighborhood Search (ALNS) heuristic algorithm is proposed; and iii) numerical experiments are applied to demonstrate that the solution approach provides high-quality solutions for newly generated instances.

The remaining sections of the chapter are organized as follows. Section 1.2 provides a brief literature review. Section 1.3 presents a mathematical formulation of the G-DARP. Section 1.4 defines the metaheuristic approach. Section 1.5 reports the numerical experiments. Finally, conclusions are summarized in section 1.6.

1.2. Literature review

This section presents a literature review on Dial-a-Ride Problems and green vehicle routing problems.

1.2.1. *The Dial-a-Ride Problem*

In reality, the transportation of people with reduced mobility is often complicated by the presence of several types of users with specially-needed equipment, such as patient seats, wheelchairs, and stretchers (Masmoudi 2016). Consequently, vehicles with a special space for such equipment are needed to satisfy different users' requests. Parragh (2011) considered the DARP where a patient can be transported by a seat, a stretcher, or a wheelchair. In addition, an accompanying person could be present in the vehicle. The authors considered two types of vehicles and four different resources (i.e. staff seat, patient seat, stretcher, and wheelchair). They proposed Branch-and-Cut (B&C) and Variable Neighborhood Search (VNS) algorithms and solved 36 instances with up to four vehicles and 48 requests. In the study by Braekers *et al.* (2014), multiple depots of heterogeneous vehicles and users are considered to reduce the total routing costs. The authors proposed B&C and Deterministic Annealing (DA) metaheuristic to solve instances containing 2–8 vehicles and 16–96 requests. Braekers and Kovacs (2016) considered a multi-period DARP with a limited number of drivers to serve the users. The authors proposed two mathematical formulations based on 3-index and 4-index and developed a B&C and LNS to solve the multi-period DARP. The algorithms were tested on a real-life case in Belgium as well as on the benchmark DARP instances of Cordeau and Laporte (2003).

Masmoudi *et al.* (2017) developed a hybrid Genetic Algorithm (GA) to solve the heterogeneous and homogeneous DARP. The proposed method was tested on 13 vehicles and 144 requests based on the benchmark DARP instances of Parragh (2011) and Braekers *et al.* (2014). In another study, Masmoudi *et al.* (2016) proposed a new DARP variant by considering a coffee break and multi-depot concepts. They proposed three metaheuristic methods, namely, hybrid Bees Algorithm With Simulated Annealing (BA-SA), hybrid Bees Algorithm With Deterministic Annealing (BA-DA), and ALNS. More recently, Masmoudi *et al.* (2018b) considered a fleet of Electric Vehicles (EVs) instead of the ICEVs in the DARP. The vehicles are allowed to be recharged by swapping their depleted battery for a full one from any battery-swap station. To solve this problem, three Evolutionist Variable Neighborhood Search (EVO-VNS) variants were proposed and compared on newly generated instances with up to 13 vehicles and 144 requests. The results show that the proposed approach provides high-quality solutions for the newly generated instances and for the standard benchmark DARP instances of Masmoudi *et al.* (2017).

For other DARP variants that consider realistic concepts, the readers can find several DARP applications in Liu *et al.* (2015), Amirgholy and Gonzales (2016), and Lim *et al.* (2016). For more details, interested readers are referred to the excellent survey papers of Molenbruch *et al.* (2017) and Ho *et al.* (2018).

1.2.2. *The green vehicle routing problem*

In recent years, there was a trend of research on VRPs that made the problem more practical by taking into consideration more relevant constraints (e.g. intermediate refueling stops). In fact, one of the most interesting problems which was studied and introduced in this respect is the Green-VRP (G-VRP) by Erdoğan and Miller-Hooks (2012), in which refueling stops were incorporated. The authors proposed a mixed-integer linear model in order to minimize the travel distance considering AFSs and also the number of tours and their limited duration. Erdoğan and Miller-Hooks (2012) developed two efficient heuristics and tested them on instances with up to 500 users. Recently, Andelmin and Bartolini (2017) proposed an exact solution approach based on a set partitioning formulation by adding a new valid inequality to solve the traditional G-VRP. The results show that the method is able to solve to optimality several instances with up 110 users. Other G-VRP with refueling studies can be found in Demir *et al.* (2015, 2016), Xiao and Konak (2017), and Demir (2018).

A similar problem to the G-VRP with refueling is the Electric Vehicle Routing Problem With Time Windows and recharging stations (E-VRPTW). This kind of problem has received much interest from the researchers in recent years (see Hof *et al.* 2017; Liao *et al.* 2016; Montoya *et al.* 2017; Schneider *et al.* 2014). For more details about the G-VRP and other green vehicle variety problems, readers are referred to the recent surveys of Demir *et al.* (2015) and Bektaş *et al.* (2019).

1.3. Problem definition

The G-DARP can be formally described as follows. We have a graph G = (V, A). Let $N = 1, \ldots, 2n$ be the set of origin and destination of n users. Each request has a pickup and delivery node pair $\{i, n + i\}$ and has to be served. The subset of pickup nodes is denoted by $P = 1, \ldots, n$ while the subset of delivery nodes is given by $D = n + 1, \ldots, 2n$. Thus, we obtain $N = P \cup D$. $F = 2n + 1, \ldots, 2n + f$ is the set of AFS nodes. Nodes 0 and $2n + 1 + f$ correspond to the origin depot and end of route depot, respectively. The set of nodes is $V = N \cup F \cup \{0, 2n + 1 + f\}$, while $A = (i, j): i, j \in V, i \neq j$ represents the set of arcs connecting each pair of nodes. An arc (i, j) in set A has an associated non-negative travel cost c_{ij} and a non-negative distance d_{ij}. In addition, it is assumed that vehicles travel each arc (i, j) with different speeds between v^l and v^s. Moreover, we assume that the number of stops that the vehicle can make for refueling is unlimited. At the time of refueling, we assume that the tank must be filled with a quantity g. Regarding visits to vertices, we assume that some vertices can have multiple visits, while others are visited only once. To allow this, we augment a set of f' dummy vertices, $F' = \{2n + f + 2, ... , 2n + f + f' + 1\}$ on the graph G, where each dummy node corresponds to a potential visit to an AFS node or a depot that serves as an AFS. Accordingly, we obtain the graph $G' = (V', A')$, where $V' = V \cup F'$. The time window to visit any AFS node is set to $[0,T]$, where T is the length of the planning horizon. In addition, we have a fleet of heterogeneous vehicles $K = 1, ... , K$ in terms of their capacity resources to serve the n users.

The vehicle capacity $|Q^{rk}|$ gives the amount of resource r available on each vehicle k. We assume that there are four types of resources that are available: i) an accompanying person $|Q^{0,k}|$; ii) a handicapped person's seat $|Q^{1,k}|$; iii) a stretcher $|Q^{2,k}|$; and iv) a wheelchair $|Q^{3,k}|$. The fuel tank capacity for each vehicle is H, which is consumed at a rate e in each traveled arc (i,j). Each user i is associated with a time window $[T_i^-, T_i^+]$ and a demand requirement d_i^r for each resource r, where a positive demand is assumed for pickup and a negative for delivery. For the convenience of the users, we implicitly set a limit on the maximum allowed user ride time L_{max}. Finally, a service time s_i is needed when visiting a pickup or delivery node i ($\forall i \in N$), and a refueling time s_f when visiting an AFS node $f \in F$. Since each vehicle is assumed to have only one driver, we use the terms (vehicles and drivers) interchangeably. For each driver, the maximum allowed working time per day is T_{max}.

In most studied VRPs, a Comprehensive Modal Emission Model (CMEM) from Barth and Boriboonsomsin (2009) is applied to estimate the fuel consumption and CO_2e emissions. The fuel conception rate $FR_{ij}(u_j)$ over the course of an arc (i,j) with an amount that is equivalent to the remaining users' requests can be expressed as $FR_{ij}(u_j) = d_{ij}(\alpha_{ij} m(u_j) + \beta v_{ij}^2)$, where $\beta = 0.5 C_d \rho A_f$ and $m(u) = m_v + m_u u$. It should be noted that u_j is the available users' number in the vehicle when arriving at the next user j (Masmoudi et al. 2018b). Based on the fuel consumption function, the total cost of the fuel and CO_2e emissions cost can be expressed as $TC_{ij} = CO. FR_{ij}(u_j)$. Since the fuel consumption is a linear function, we can estimate the CO_2e emissions on each arc (i,j) that can be calculated as $EM_{ij} = FC. FR_{ij}(u_j)$. The description of the most used parameters and values, based on Demir et al. (2012) and on a specific vehicle equipped with wheelchair places, the *Nissan NV400 L2H2* (Nissan 2018), is given in Table 1.1.

Notation	Description	Value
ρ	Air mass density (kg/m^3)	1.25
α_{ij}	Angle of the terrain between nodes i and j	0.9–0.15
m_u	Average weight of user (with wheelchair) in	70(80)[a]
v^l	Lower vehicle speed (km/h)	20
v^s	Upper vehicle speed (km/h)	90
FC	Biodiesel fuel emission factor	2.62
CO	Fuel and CO$_2$ emissions cost per liter (£)	1.4
A_f	Frontal surface (m^2)	4.24[b]
C_d	Coefficient of aerodynamic drag	0.347[b]
m_v	Curb weight (kg)	3,500[b]

Table 1.1. *Parameters and technical specifications of the vehicle.* [a]*Average value estimated from Centers for Disease Control and Prevention (2012);* [b]*specified value of the vehicle* Nissan NV400 L2H2

The G-DARP is concerned with planning a set of routes to serve a number of users while minimizing the total fuel and CO_2e emission costs. The following constraints apply in the G-DARP: i) the vehicle must visit the pickup node before its corresponding delivery; ii) the total collected demand of the nodes must not exceed the capacity of the vehicle; iii) each node must be visited within its allocated time window; iv) the maximum allowed ride time of the user must not be exceeded; v) the pickup and delivery nodes of the same user must be visited by the same vehicle; vi) the vehicle must refuel in an AFS node, if the amount of remaining fuel is not sufficient to serve the next customer; vii) each vehicle route should start and end at the same depot; and viii) the total duration of the route must not exceed the maximum allowed working time.

We present a linear mixed-integer programming formulation for the G-DARP, which is inspired by the formulations of the DARP by Masmoudi *et al.* (2018b). The main difference is that in Masmoudi *et al.* (2018b), the authors assumed that the battery will be fully recharged at each visiting of a recharging station. However, in our case, we allow the tank to be partially refueled as expressed in constraints [14]–[17].

A binary variable x_{ij}^k is equal to 1 if arc (i, j) is included in the solution and 0 otherwise. Continuous variable B_i^k represents the time at which vehicle k starts servicing node i. Continuous variable Q_i^{rk} indicates the load of resource r on vehicle k immediately after visiting node i. Continuous variable l_i^k represents the ride time of user $i \in P$ on vehicle k. Continuous variable y_i^k represents the remaining fuel level in the tank of vehicle k upon arrival to node i. Finally, continuous variable z_i^k represent the fuel state on departure from an AFS node.

$$minimize \sum_{k \in K} \sum_{i \in V'} \sum_{j \in V'} CO[d_{ij}(\alpha_{ij}m(u_j) + \beta v_{ij}^2)]x_{ij}^k \qquad [1.1]$$

subject to

$$\sum_{k \in K} \sum_{j \in N} x_{ij}^k = 1 \qquad \forall i \in P \qquad [1.2]$$

$$\sum_{k \in K} \sum_{j \in N} x_{ji}^k = 1 \qquad \forall i \in D \qquad [1.3]$$

$$\sum_{j \in N} x_{ij}^k = \sum_{j \in N} x_{j,n+i}^k \qquad \forall k \in K, \forall i \in P \qquad [1.4]$$

$$\sum_{j \in V'} x_{0j}^k = 1 \qquad \forall k \in K \qquad [1.5]$$

$$\sum_{i \in V'} x_{i,2n+f+1}^k = 1 \qquad \forall f \in F', \forall k \in K \qquad [1.6]$$

$$\sum_{i \in V'} x_{ij}^k = \sum_{i \in V'} x_{ji}^k \qquad \forall k \in K, \forall j \in V' \qquad [1.7]$$

$$Q_j^{rk} \geq (q_j^r + Q_i^{rk}) \sum_{k \in K} x_{ij}^k \qquad \forall (i,j) \in A, \forall r \in \{0,1,2,3\} \qquad [1.8]$$

$$0 \leq Q_i^{rk} \leq Q^{rk} \qquad \forall k \in K, \forall i \in N, \forall r \in \{0,1,2,3\} \qquad [1.9]$$

$$l_i^k = B_{n+1}^k - (B_i^k + s_i) \qquad \forall k \in K, \forall i \in N, \forall r \in \{0,1,2,3\} \qquad [1.10]$$

$$t_{i,n+i} \leq l_i^k \leq L_{max} \qquad \forall k \in K, \forall i \in P \qquad [1.11]$$

$$B_j^k \geq B_i^k + (s_i + t_{ij})x_{ij}^k - M(1 - x_{ij}^k) \qquad \forall k \in K, \forall i,j \in V' \qquad [1.12]$$

$$T_i^- \leq B_i^k \leq T_i^+ \qquad \forall k \in K, \forall i \in V' \qquad [1.13]$$

$$y_j^k \leq y_i^k - FC_{ij}(u_j)x_{ij}^k + H(1 - x_{ij}^k) \quad \forall j \in V', \forall i \in V, i \neq j, \forall k \in K \qquad [1.14]$$

$$y_j^k \leq z_j^k - FC_{fj}(u_j)x_{fj}^k + H(1 - x_{fj}^k) \quad \forall j \in V', \forall f \in F', i \neq j, \forall k \in K \qquad [1.15]$$

$$y_f^k \leq z_j^k \leq H \qquad\qquad \forall f \in F', \forall k \in K \qquad [1.16]$$

$$y_j^k \geq \min\{FC_{ij}(u_j)t_{j0}, FC_{ij}(u_j)(t_{if} + t_{f0})\} \quad \forall j \in N, \forall f \in F', \forall k \in K \qquad [1.17]$$

$$B_{2n+f+1}^k - B_0^k \leq T_{max} \qquad\qquad \forall k \in K, \forall f \in F' \qquad [1.18]$$

$$x_{ij}^k \in \{0,1\} \qquad\qquad \forall k \in K, \forall (i,j) \in A' \qquad [1.19]$$

The objective function [1.1] minimizes the total fuel and CO_2 emissions costs. Constraints [1.2]–[1.4] guarantee that the pickup and delivery pair are served by the same vehicle. Constraints [1.5] and [1.6] guarantee that each vehicle k starts at the origin depot and ends at the corresponding destination depot, while constraint [1.7] ensures flow conservation. Constraints [1.8] and [1.9] enforce capacity limitations. Constraint [1.10] defines the ride time of each user in each route, which is bounded by constraint [1.11]. These constraints also enforce the precedence constraint between the pickup and delivery nodes of a user. Constraint [1.12] defines the beginning of service at each node and the consistency of the time variables. Also, these constraints ensure subtour elimination. Constraint [1.13] imposes obedience of time windows. Constraints [1.14] and [1.15] make sure that the remaining fuel does not become negative after each visit while constraint [1.16] guarantees that the remaining tank fuel does not surpass the capacity of the tank after each refueling by any AFS node. Constraint [1.17] ensures that each vehicle will be routed without being stranded due to insufficient fuel in the tank. Constraint [1.18] defines the time duration of the route of each vehicle, which is strictly limited by T_{max}. Finally, constraint [1.19] guarantees that the decision variables are binary. It should be noted that constraints [1.8], [1.12], [1.14], [1.15], and [1.17] are not in integer linear form; however, using the big M-method, they can be easily linearized. Also, constraint [1.8] can be linearized as done for constraint [1.20] with $M_i \geq \min\{Q_{max}^r, Q_{max}^r + q_i^r\}$ and $Q_{max}^r = max_{k \in K} Q^{rk}$, following Desrochers and Laporte (1991).

$$Q_j^{rk} \geq Q_i^{rk} + q_i^r - M_i(1 - \sum_{k \in K} x_{ij}^k) + (M_i - q_i^r - q_j^r)\sum_{k \in K} x_{ji}^k \qquad \forall i, j \in N, r \in \{0,1,2,3\} \qquad [1.20]$$

1.4. An Adaptive Large Neighborhood Search for the G-DARP

This section describes an Adaptive Large Neighborhood Search (ALNS) algorithm to solve the G-DARP. This method was first proposed by Ropke and Pisinger (2006) and is considered an extension of the (Adaptive) Large Neighborhood Search suggested by Shaw (1998). The ALNS was used in solving a variety of VRPs including DARPs (see Braekers and Kovacs 2016; Demir *et al.* 2012; Masmoudi *et al.* 2016; Ropke and Pisinger 2006). However, several features are proposed to diversify and intensify the search in our ALNS compared to the traditional ALNS.

1.	**Input:** N: set of users (with their time windows, maximum ride times, demands), K:set of vehicles (with their characteristics), F: set of AFS nodes, $d_{i,i}$:distance between each node $i, i \in V'$.
2.	**Initialize:** The weights and scores of removal, insertion, and local search operators, $x_{best} = x$, $TE = TE_{max}$;
3.	**Repeat**
4.	Choose removal and insertion operators
5.	Apply the selected removal and insertion operators on x to obtain x';
6.	Performs the RS and IS operators in a random order on x';
7.	If x' is feasible **Then**
8.	If $f(x') < f(x)$ OR x' satisfies the acceptance criterion **Then**
9.	$x \leftarrow x'$;
10.	**End If**
11.	If $f(x') < f(x_{best})$ **Then**
12.	$x_{best} \leftarrow x'$;
13.	**Else If** $f(x') < f(x_{best})*1.02$ **Then**
14.	$x' \leftarrow$ local search(x');
15.	If $f(x') < f(x_{best})$
16.	$x_{best} \leftarrow x'$;
17.	**End If**
18.	**End If**
19.	$TE \leftarrow \alpha \times TE$;
20.	**End If**
21.	Adjust the weights and probabilities of the removal, insertion and local searches operators
22.	**Until** n_{ALNS} is reached
23.	**Output** the solution corresponding to x_{best}

Algorithm 1.1. *The ALNS algorithm*

The structure of our ALNS algorithm is shown in Algorithm 1.1. We describe the details of each element of our ALNS in the following sections. The algorithm runs for n_{ALNS} iterations to find the best solution x_{best}. Let x be the initial solution as proposed by Masmoudi *et al.* (2018b), to which also the current best solution x_{best} is initialized. The temperature TE is initialized to its maximum value TE_{max} and the weights and scores of the removal and insertion operators are also initialized. The weights and scores of the removal and insertion operators are updated during the search. At each iteration in our algorithm, one removal and one insertion operator are selected based on their past performances and applied to the current solution x to obtain a new solution x'. After applying the removal and insertion operators, the current solution may become infeasible due to the fuel constraints. In this case, the RS (Remove Station) and IS (Insert Station) operators are applied to ensure the feasibility of the solution. Thus, a new solution x' is obtained. If x' is feasible based on the evaluation function of Masmoudi *et al.* (2018b), there are two possibilities to accept or reject this new solution. If the objective function of x' is better than that of the current solution, x' is accepted and becomes the current solution. Otherwise, x' is accepted only if it satisfies the SA acceptance criterion $e^{(f(x)-f(x')/TE)}$, where the temperature TE is reduced after each iteration by multiplying TE by a cooling factor α.

The new solution x' is improved by a local search operator from (I1, I2, I3, or I4), selected randomly if x' is no more than 2% worse than x_{best}. The improved solution is then accepted, only if its objective value is better than that of the current best solution x_{best}. In fact, one of the main features of our ALNS algorithm is applying a second acceptance function ($f(x') < f(x_{best})*1.02$, which produces another component of diversification of search, where a promising solution x' is given a chance to become the new best solution. Another characteristic of our ALNS is applying a local search operator on the current new solution x', which permits the algorithm to perform a more extensive search in the neighborhood of the current solution and also enforces, if possible, finding a new best solution at each iteration.

1.4.1. *Adaptive weight adjustment procedure*

The roulette wheel mechanism governs the way we choose the removal, insertion, and local search operators in the ALNS algorithm. We have adopted five removal operators and four insertion operators. We select the appropriate operator at each iteration in order to obtain a feasible balance between the solution's quality and the running time. The probability of choosing operator d at iteration t is defined by $P_d^{t+1} = P_d^1(1 - r_p) + r_p \pi_i / \omega_i$, where r_p is the roulette wheel parameter, π_i is the score of an operator i, and ω_i is the number of times that the operator has been used in the last 100 iterations. Moreover, we determine the score of an operator by the following procedure: the score of an operator is increased by π_1, if the existing pair of destroy–repair finds a new best solution; otherwise, if it locates a better solution than the current, the score is enhanced by π_2. On the other hand, if the current pair of operators finds an acceptable solution, which is non-improving, the operators' scores are increased by π_3. After 100 iterations, the new weights are adjusted using the scores obtained and the scores of the removal and insertion operators are reset to zero.

1.4.2. *Removal and insertion operators*

At each ALNS iteration, a set of nodes is selected from the current solution x and added to a list L by using a set of removal operators in order to re-insert them using several insertion operators, to obtain a new solution x'. In our ALNS, we have adopted five removal (R1–R5) and four insertion (P1–P4) operators from Masmoudi *et al.* (2016). The removal operators are: random-users removal (R1), path-removal (R2), time-oriented removal (R3), related removal (R4), and distance-oriented removal (R5). The insertion operators are: the basic greedy insertion (P1), best position inter-route insertion (P2), sorting time insertion (P3), and best position intra-route insertion (P4). For more details about these operators, refer to Masmoudi *et al.* (2016).

1.4.3. *Local search operators*

To improve the solution, several well-known local search operators with different inter and intra-route moves based on the literature are developed. These operators are the relocate operator (I1) of Savelsbergh (1992) and the 2-opt operator (I2) of Lin (1965) for the intra-route moves, whereas the relocate operator (I3) of Savelsbergh (1992) and the 2-opt* operator (I4) of Potvin and Rousseau (1995) are used for the inter-route moves.

After applying the local search operators, the solution may have some unnecessary AFS nodes or it may require additional AFS node(s). In these cases, two operators for inserting and removing an AFS, adopted from Masmoudi *et al.* (2018b) and called Insert Station (IS) and Remove Station (RS), are applied at each ALNS iteration:

– Remove Station (RS): this operator works as follows: for any pair of nodes (i, j), if the fuel level at node i is sufficient to reach node j, the AFS node between them is removed.

– Insert Station (IS): this operator works as follows: for each node $i \in N$ visited by vehicle k, if the remaining fuel level in the tank is not enough to directly reach node $j \in N$ and then the nearest AFS to j, the nearest station of i is visited. In other words, we assume that, at node i, there is always enough fuel to reach the nearest AFS to i. The IS operator then inserts the AFS with a minimum required fuel from i. This way the IS operator ensures that the vehicle will not get stranded due to lack of fuel during its service.

1.5. Computational experiments

In this section, we present the details of the results obtained by our proposed algorithm. The algorithm is coded in C language and performed using the following configuration: Intel processor 4 GHz, 4 GB RAM, and operating Windows 8 with 64 bits. On the other hand, the mathematical model defined in section 1.3 is solved using the CPLEX 12.6.1 solver, with a time limit of four hours imposed, using a personal Dell computer with Intel Core i7-3770 at 2.8 GHz and 8 GB of RAM.

1.5.1. *Data and experimental setting*

To test our algorithm, we generated new data instances based on the generic idea of Masmoudi *et al.* (2018b). In the original data set, different homogeneity levels of users, different geographical users' locations, as well as recharging station locations, are considered. The number of vehicles ranges between 2 and 12, with four resources identified for each vehicle: staff seats, users' seats, stretchers, and wheelchair places. In this context, the way in which the passenger should be transported was already determined, i.e. whether it is preferable for the user to take a seat, a stretcher, or otherwise a wheelchair. Moreover, in case accompanying persons are taking the vehicle, they have the possibility to sit on the stretcher and also they are able to use staff seats or patients' seats. However, patients have the right to use either a patient seat or a stretcher. Therefore, the passengers should use the same identical places that they used before, whether these places are stretchers or wheelchairs.

The number of requests is between 10 and 100 in these instances. The maximum duration of the working day for each vehicle (depending on the instance) T_{max} ranges between 240 and 720 min, and the maximum ride time of each user is set to $L_i^{max} = \max\{60, 2 \times t_{i,n+i}\}$. The time window is set to 15 min, and the number of recharging stations in each instance is assumed to be $0.3*|n|$, where all coordinates of AFSs are randomly generated in a specific square area (i.e. $[10,10]^2$). The readers can find more details in Masmoudi *et al.* (2018b).

In our case, since we consider a fleet of AFVs, the tank capacity of each vehicle H is equal to 30 gallons (*Nissan NV400 L2H2*). On each arc (i,j), the vehicle is assumed to run at a constant speed value selected randomly from the set [20, 30, 40, 50, 60, 70, 80, 90].

1.5.2. *Parameters setting*

This section explains the sensitivity analysis that we did to set the parameters for our algorithm. Following the findings in Masmoudi *et al.* (2016) in the context of DARP using ALNS, we have applied the same parameter values that they used: n_{ALNS}=25,000 iterations, $r_p = 0.7$, $\pi_1 = 15$, $\pi_2 = 5$, $\pi_3 = 10$, $TE_{max} = 100$, $\alpha = 0.99975$, $p_d^0 = 0.10$ for the removal operators, and 0.125 for the insertion operators.

Similar to the tuning methodology of Demir *et al.* (2012) for the study of the performance of different removal and reinsertion operators of the ALNS, Table 1.2 shows the frequency of use of each operator in the algorithm as a percentage of 25,000 iterations. Also, this table shows in the parentheses the total time taken by each operator. The results are calculated using a small data set of instances. We note that, for example, the instance "a0_25_7"; "a0" refers to the type of family class in the benchmark instances of Masmoudi *et al.* (2018b). The second number in the instance name corresponds to the number of users and the last number shows the number of vehicles.

Inst.	Removal operators					Insertion operators			
	R1	R2	R3	R4	R5	P1	P2	P3	P4
a0_25_7	22.43(0.0)	23.01(0.0)	15.88(0.0)	21.19(0.0)	17.51(0.0)	29.77(0.2)	22.33(0.1)	21.61(0.0)	26.28(0.1)
a0_35_13	16.84(0.0)	14.78(0.0)	19.46(0.0)	22.34(0.0)	26.57(0.1)	35.31(0.3)	17.14(0.7)	17.31(0.2)	30.24(1.0)
a0_40_14	20.02(0.0)	25.6(0.0)	18.18(0.0)	20.39(0.0)	15.82(0.0)	27.81(0.9)	26.06(0.1)	24.66(0.1)	21.47(0.6)
a0_45_17	18.71(0.0)	16.8(0.0)	23.92(0.0)	20.24(0.0)	20.33(0.0)	31.42(0.7)	22.75(0.1)	12.67(0.1)	**33.16(0.5)**
a0_50_22	15.22(0.0)	19.3(0.0)	19.81(0.0)	22.84(0.0)	22.83(0.0)	29.36(2.2)	21.85(0.3)	18.22(0.2)	**30.58(0.8)**
a0_75_26	23.54(0.0)	13.03(0.0)	26.62(0.0)	22.6(0.0)	14.2(0.0)	**32.11(0.2)**	17.87(0.0)	21.55(0.0)	28.48(0.1)
a0_100_28	18.02(0.0)	20.11(0.0)	25.72(0.0)	21.66(0.0)	14.5(0.0)	**30.73(0.8)**	22.03(0.3)	18.89(0.1)	28.35(0.6)
a0_100_29	24.87(0.0)	9.6(0.0)	19.31(0.0)	21.97(0.3)	24.23(0.0)	**28.48(1.2)**	22.2(0.2)	27.09(0.2)	22.22(0.8)
Avg	*19.96(0.0)*	*17.78(0.0)*	*21.11(0.0)*	*21.65(0.0)*	*19.5(0.0)*	*30.62(0.8)*	*21.53(0.2)*	*20.25(0.1)*	*27.6(0.6)*

Table 1.2. *Frequency of use as a percentage of 25,000 iterations and the computational time needed by each operator*

As far as the insertion operators are concerned, the results reported in Table 1.2 show that P1 and P4 operators are applied to some extent more than the other two operators. Hence, compared to the rest of the operators, P1 and P4 consume more CPU. In addition, in the majority of cases, we can observe that the removal operators have a similar frequency.

Table 1.3 presents the number of times an operator has found the best and a better solution than the current one, respectively. At this point, the number of times in which the actual solution has probably been improved but did not become the best solution is shown by the number between parentheses. Similarly, it is illustrated by the obtained results that, to some extent, all removal operators may take part in generating better solutions.

Inst.	Removal operators					Insertion operators			
	R1	R2	R3	R4	R5	P1	P2	P3	P4
a0_25_7	11(171)	6(183)	5(200)	16(57)	9(180)	19(36)	9(386)	3(304)	16(64)
a0_35_13	10(154)	6(85)	10(205)	12(229)	10(111)	17(135)	8(251)	0(274)	23(124)
a0_40_14	9(50)	6(188)	5(67)	11(212)	3(143)	17(79)	2(181)	1(231)	14(169)
a0_45_17	7(104)	10(172)	10(197)	4(224)	5(199)	10(226)	2(236)	5(248)	19(187)
a0_50_22	3(46)	4(84)	4(219)	12(229)	3(148)	3(158)	8(299)	9(234)	6(35)
a0_75_26	15(115)	3(222)	10(108)	5(130)	12(139)	13(160)	11(248)	3(259)	18(46)
a0_100_28	13(53)	6(120)	16(23)	15(196)	11(170)	26(134)	4(173)	3(120)	28(135)
a0_100_29	9(121)	13(214)	5(110)	10(172)	11(107)	18(170)	0(119)	7(238)	23(198)
Avg	*10(102)*	*7(159)*	*8(141)*	*11(181)*	*8(150)*	*15(137)*	*6(237)*	*4(239)*	*18(120)*

Table 1.3. *Number of global best solutions found, and number of improved solutions attained by each operator*

Despite the fact that some insertion operators (i.e. P2 and P3) do not contribute well to locating new best solutions, and they are infrequently put into service, the ALNS needs these operators as they are beneficial for possibly obtaining better solutions in the following iterations, and they are also necessary to avoid local optima. Therefore, P2 and P3 are assumed to get improved solutions. Consequently, it is firmly deduced that there is a positive contribution from the removal and insertion operators that help in acquiring high-quality solutions for the G-DARP.

Based on the literature, the performance of ALNS depends on the number of deleted users. Accordingly, the number of deleted users u is chosen randomly in the interval $[u_{min}= 0.175.n; u_{max}= 0.35.n]$.

We have adopted the following parameters based on the literature and our preliminary tests, as suggested by Ropke and Pisinger (2006) and Demir *et al.* (2012). To fine-tune the parameters (π_1, π_2, and π_3), the analysis in Table 1.4 was performed on a small data set, which was selected such that the number of requests ranges from small to large and with a different number of vehicles. For each instance, different score values are applied for each parameter π_1, π_2, and π_3 resulting in different combinations of "(π_1, π_2, and π_3)" as seen in the second line of Table 1.4. For instance, the combination (5, 10, 3) means that π_1 is equal to 5, π_2 is equal to 10, and π_3 is equal to 3. The average value of five runs for each combination (π_1, π_2, π_3) is given in Table 1.4. Since we have new components in our ALNS to diversify and intensify the solution, a non-improving solution (π_3) is more recommended than an improving solution (π_2). Thus, the adjustment parameters have been set as $\pi_1 \geq \pi_3 \geq \pi_2$ ($\pi_1 = 15, \pi_2 = 5$, and $\pi_3 = 10$).

Inst.	Effect of π_1, π_2 and π_3 on the solution quality						
	(5, 10, 3)	(3, 5, 1)	(15, 5, 10)	(5,1, 3)	(1, 5,3)	(3, 15, 5)	(1, 3, 5)
a0_20_1	270.68	272.81	271.99	271.06	271.26	271.92	**270.35**
a0_25_5	301.77	302.22	**294.14**	303.62	301.83	294.87	295.32
a0_30_8	**216.48**	222.37	219.94	223.25	217.77	219.15	217.77
a0_40_14	577.24	577.82	**576.42**	579.04	577.09	584.21	583.45
a0_40_16	738.78	737.01	738.61	**736.28**	737.58	742.22	740.49
a0_45_19	707.59	712.45	711.91	710.96	712.91	**707.09**	711.99
a0_50_23	790.92	**789.52**	792.04	790.72	790.77	789.90	791.70
a0_60_24	719.38	727.29	**719.32**	725.42	724.89	723.68	727.22
a0_75_26	895.16	896.59	895.12	**889.89**	895.82	891.90	893.37
Avg	*579.78*	*582.01*	*579.94*	*581.14*	*581.10*	*580.55*	*581.30*

Table 1.4. *A summary of parameter tuning*

1.5.3. *Computational analysis*

In this section, we present the detailed results obtained by our ALNS tested on generated instances of the G-DARP based on the benchmark instances of Masmoudi *et al.* (2018b) as well as the standard DARP instances of Masmoudi *et al.* (2017).

1.5.3.1. *Results on the DARP instances*

To evaluate the performance of our algorithms, we have used the large-sized benchmark DARP instances of Masmoudi *et al.* (2017) with different heterogeneity levels of users. Table 1.5 shows the results of our ALNS in comparison with the three EVO-VNS variants of Masmoudi *et al.* (2018b). The objective function is to minimize the total routing cost of the vehicles ($\sum_{k \in K} \sum_{(i,j) \in A} c_{ij} x_{ij}^k$). In this table, the column "BKS" presents the best-known solution provided by Masmoudi *et al.* (2018b). More specifically, the BKS value is the minimum routing cost obtained from the three Evolutionary VNS algorithms (EVO-VNS1, EVO-VNS2, and EVO-VNS3) proposed by Masmoudi *et al.* (2018b) on a given instance. The columns "Best%" presents the percentage of deviation of the best (average) solution from the best-known solution found by each algorithm, and the column "CPU" refers to the average CPU time in minutes. Each instance is computed five times using each algorithm as in Masmoudi *et al.* (2018b).

Inst.	BKS[a]	EVO-VNS1			EVO-VNS2			EVO-VNS3			ALNS		
		Best%	Avg%	CPU (min)	Best%	Avg%	CPU (min)	Best%	Avg%	CPU (min)	Best%	Avg%	CPU (min)
R1a	195.97	0.00	0.00	0.71	0.00	0.00	0.61	0.00	0.00	0.78	0.00	0.00	1.09
R2a	336.34	0.00	0.00	1.18	0.00	0.00	1.32	0.00	0.00	1.47	0.00	0.00	2.02
R3a	586.18	0.00	0.17	1.40	0.00	0.07	1.44	0.00	0.19	1.84	0.00	0.00	2.03
R4a	639.03	0.00	0.52	2.21	0.00	0.48	2.60	0.00	0.66	2.59	0.02	0.85	3.52
R5a	713.09	0.00	0.50	2.77	0.04	0.53	2.94	0.00	0.39	3.72	0.00	0.68	4.97
R6a	882.11	0.00	0.13	4.16	0.06	0.56	3.83	0.02	0.19	4.48	0.12	0.29	6.04
R7a	310.96	0.00	0.70	4.79	0.00	0.59	5.74	0.00	0.49	5.90	0.33	0.78	8.28
R8a	554.06	0.00	0.42	5.24	0.03	0.27	5.52	0.05	0.30	5.55	0.42	0.51	7.83
R9a	744.34	0.04	0.55	7.33	0.00	0.65	7.89	0.35	0.50	7.30	0.42	0.78	8.98
R10a	963.93	0.00	0.07	10.74	0.02	0.16	10.77	0.02	0.10	11.62	-0.58	0.13	15.83
R1b	190.39	0.00	0.00	0.80	0.00	0.00	0.91	0.00	0.00	1.11	0.00	0.00	1.52
R2b	312.92	0.00	0.00	1.63	0.00	0.23	1.75	0.00	0.00	1.94	0.00	0.00	2.56
R3b	551.95	0.00	0.22	2.06	0.00	0.24	2.29	0.03	0.23	3.91	0.00	0.00	4.57
R4b	605.29	0.00	0.53	2.95	0.05	0.20	5.46	0.08	0.55	3.41	0.00	0.00	4.54
R5b	640.50	0.00	0.25	4.42	0.00	0.25	5.70	0.00	0.23	4.65	0.09	0.59	6.57
R6b	832.79	0.00	0.37	5.51	0.00	0.24	6.50	0.02	0.24	7.18	0.25	0.65	9.30
R7b	276.17	0.00	0.16	1.21	0.00	0.25	0.81	0.00	0.29	1.21	0.00	0.51	1.63
R8b	529.96	0.00	0.35	4.24	0.00	0.25	4.41	0.00	0.32	5.49	0.13	0.63	7.24
R9b	698.13	0.00	0.32	6.54	0.08	0.39	6.28	0.11	0.46	6.91	-0.60	0.66	9.31
R10b	903.18	0.01	0.11	11.71	0.03	0.27	11.11	0.00	0.62	12.61	0.48	0.84	17.13
Avg	*573.36*	*0.00*	*0.27*	*4.08*	*0.02*	*0.28*	*4.39*	*0.03*	*0.29*	*4.68*	*0.05*	*0.40*	*6.25*

Table 1.5. *Comparison of our ALNS on the standard DARP instances of Masmoudi et al. (2017)*

The ALNS provides reasonable results compared to EVO-VNS1, EVO-VNS2, and EVO-VNS3 by obtaining nine best-known solutions (0.00% gap). For the average deviation of the average results from the best-known solutions, the ALNS is slightly inferior to EVO-VNS1, EVO-VNS2, and EVO-VNS3, with a gap equal to 0.40%, compared to 0.27%, 0.28%, and 0.29% for the EVO-VNS1, EVO-VNS2, and EVO-VNS3, respectively. For the average deviation of the best result over five runs, the gap is very small, whereas 0.05% is achieved by our ALNS, compared to the other three algorithms having 0.00%, 0.02%, and 0.03% gaps, respectively. We note that all the calculated gaps are relative to the best-known solutions found in the literature since optimal solutions of these large size instances are not yet known. In addition, two new best-known solutions are discovered by our ALNS for the instances R10a and R9b.

1.5.3.2. Results on the G-DARP instances

To evaluate the effectiveness of our ALNS to solve the G-DARP, we used the data set instances of Masmoudi *et al.* (2018b) that contain between two and three vehicles and 10–16 users. These instances are then solved using the commercial solver CPLEX 12.61, and the results are compared with those found by our ALNS. Table 1.6 presents the obtained results. The columns "Nb-Veh" and "Nb-Use" present the number of vehicles and the number of users, respectively, on each instance. The column "Nb-Ava-AFS" provides the number of AFSs available. Columns "Best" and "Avg" report the best and average solution values of our objective function, respectively. The columns "Fuel" and "CO_2e" present fuel consumption and carbon emissions, respectively. The columns "%" present the percentage of deviation from the optimal/lower bound result obtained by CPLEX while the column "CPU" refers to the average CPU time in minutes. In addition, for each instance, we report the number of AFSs visited in each solution in the column "NB-AFS".

From the detailed results of Table 1.6, we can see that CPLEX is only able to solve a few small size instances with two vehicles by optimality (8 instances out of 21). However, our ALNS can obtain all optimal solutions and outperform CPLEX in the other instances (as indicated in bold) with the shortest time.

Inst.	Nb-Veh	Nb-Use	Nb-Ava-AFS	CPLEX Fuel	CO2e	Best	Nb-AFS	CPU (min)	ALNS Fuel	CO2e	Best	%	Avg	%	CPU (min)	Nb-AFS
a0_10_1	2	10	4	153.53	402.25	214.94	0	45.64	153.53	402.24	214.94	0.00	214.94	0.00	1.46	0
a0_10_2	2	10	4	145.46	381.11	203.65	1	89.43	145.46	381.12	203.65	0.00	203.65	0.00	2.20	1
a0_12_3	2	12	5	163.76	429.05	229.26	1	161.69	163.76	429.04	229.26	0.00	229.26	0.00	1.48	1
a0_13_4	3	13	5	215.05	563.43	301.07	0	203.95	195.65	512.60	273.91	-9.02	273.91	-9.02	2.14	0
a0_14_5	3	14	5	230.00	602.61	322.01	0	240.00	211.20	553.34	295.68	-8.18	295.68	-8.18	1.66	0
a0_15_6	3	15	6	229.07	600.16	320.69	0	240.00	210.19	550.71	294.27	-8.24	294.27	-8.24	2.06	0
a0_16_7	3	16	6	224.67	588.65	314.54	1	240.00	185.42	485.80	259.59	-17.47	259.59	-17.47	2.87	1
a1_10_1	2	10	4	145.13	380.24	203.18	0	48.13	145.13	380.24	203.18	0.00	203.18	0.00	1.20	0
a1_10_2	2	10	4	150.98	395.56	211.37	0	88.09	150.98	395.56	211.37	0.00	211.37	0.00	2.21	0
a1_12_3	2	12	5	159.37	417.54	223.11	2	165.27	139.94	366.65	195.92	-12.19	195.92	-12.19	1.96	2
a1_13_4	3	13	5	231.35	606.15	323.89	0	201.67	212.68	557.22	297.75	-8.07	297.75	-8.07	1.70	0
a1_14_5	3	14	5	238.23	624.17	333.52	1	240.00	197.89	518.48	277.05	-16.93	277.05	-16.93	0.90	1
a1_15_6	3	15	6	219.58	575.3	307.41	0	240.00	184.66	483.82	258.53	-15.90	258.53	-15.90	2.24	0
a1_16_7	3	16	6	217.23	569.15	304.13	1	240.00	175.22	459.08	245.31	-19.34	245.31	-19.34	3.53	1
a2_10_1	2	10	4	165.64	433.97	231.89	0	44.07	165.64	433.97	231.89	0.00	231.89	0.00	1.14	0
a2_10_2	2	10	4	155.02	406.15	217.03	1	92.70	155.02	406.16	217.03	0.00	217.03	0.00	1.98	1
a2_12_3	2	12	5	155.57	407.58	217.79	2	159.75	155.56	407.58	217.79	0.00	217.79	0.00	2.09	2
a2_13_4	3	13	5	234.78	615.13	328.69	0	200.73	234.78	615.12	328.69	0.00	328.69	0.00	1.44	0
a2_14_5	3	14	5	230.12	602.91	322.17	0	228.06	208.79	547.02	292.30	-9.27	292.30	-9.27	1.53	0
a2_15_6	3	15	6	218.56	572.61	305.98	0	240.00	182.51	478.19	255.52	-16.49	255.52	-16.49	3.28	0
a2_16_7	3	16	6	214.26	561.37	299.97	1	240.00	170.60	446.97	238.84	-20.38	238.84	-20.38	4.89	1
Avg	-	-	-	*195.11*	*511.19*	*273.16*	-	*173.77*	*178.32*	*467.19*	*249.64*	*-7.69*	*249.64*	*-7.69*	*2.09*	-

Table 1.6. *Comparison of our ALNS with CPLEX on small size G-DARP instances*

To assess the effectiveness of using partial refueling strategy in our study, we compare our ALNS with different partial refueling values. In other words, partial refueling is allowed at a predefined constant tank level. To do so, we chose four different q values, for which partial refueling is performed at a constant level of the tank capacity with $q = 0.2$, $q = 0.3$, $q = 0.4$, and $q = 0.5$. In addition, we also implemented our ALNS using a full refueling strategy, for when the vehicle cannot visit the next user due to lack of fuel, in which case the tank is fully refueled. Table 1.7 shows the obtained results of using different partial refueling strategies by comparing them with a full refueling strategy. In this table, the column denoted by "PR" represents partial refueling, while the column "FR" presents full refueling. The experimental results are tested on medium and large size instances using our ALNS, and the best solution is reported on each partial refueling strategy.

From the detailed results of Table 1.7, we can see that using partial refueling instead of full refueling is more beneficial. The total routing cost is reduced by 0.70%, 0.86%, 0.41%, and 0.17% when the PR is allowed at the constant level on $q = 0.2$, $q = 0.3$, $q = 0.4$, and $q = 0.5$, respectively, compared to the FR. Moreover, we observe that when the PR is applied in $q = 0.2$ and $q = 0.3$, the solution contains a lesser number of visits to AFSs (as indicated in bold), while the number of visits to AFSs when $q = 0.2$ and $q = 0.3$ are the same as in the FR. Although, in some instances, the PR strategy gives a worse solution than the FR, in general, using the PR strategy has more potential in terms of the minimization of fuel and CO_2e emissions costs as well as visiting the AFSs.

In Table 1.8, we study the impact of using our diversification and intensification components (lines 13–17 in Algorithm 1.1) on the quality of the solution. For this purpose, we compare our ALNS to the standalone ALNS of Masmoudi *et al.* (2016) with respect to our G-DARP instances. The detailed results of this comparison are shown in Table 1.8. The columns "Best" and "Avg" outline the best and average solution values, respectively. The columns "Best%" and "Avg%" explain the percentage of deviation from the best solution value obtained by our ALNS algorithm (Best column) for a given instance. The column "CPU (min)" points to the average CPU time in minutes. Each instance is solved five times with each algorithm.

Inst.	FR		PR (q=0.2)			PR (q=0.3)			PR (q=0.4)			PR (q=0.5)		
	Nb-AFS	Best	Nb-AFS	Best	Best%	Nb-AFS	Best	Best%	Nb-AFS	Best	Best%	Nb-AFS	Best	Best%
a0_20_1	2	270.35	2	270.35	0.00	2	270.35	0.00	2	270.75	0.15	2	270.35	0.00
a0_20_2	2	295.30	2	296.59	0.44	2	296.59	0.44	2	296.59	0.44	2	295.80	0.17
a0_20_3	2	307.54	2	308.69	0.37	2	306.28	-0.41	2	310.41	0.93	2	311.50	1.29
a0_25_4	2	275.07	2	275.91	0.31	2	274.00	-0.39	2	276.87	0.65	2	275.89	0.30
a0_25_5	2	294.14	2	294.14	0.00	2	294.14	0.00	2	294.14	0.00	2	297.55	1.16
a0_25_6	3	435.94	3	432.95	-0.69	3	430.44	-1.26	3	433.02	-0.67	3	444.61	1.99
a0_25_7	3	458.72	3	461.28	0.56	3	448.92	-2.14	3	466.32	1.66	3	461.50	0.61
a0_30_8	0	216.48	0	214.48	-0.92	0	213.10	-1.56	0	215.75	-0.34	0	216.30	-0.08
a0_30_9	0	225.82	0	223.27	-1.13	0	220.28	-2.45	0	225.54	-0.12	0	223.99	-0.81
a0_30_10	3	404.66	3	394.15	-2.60	3	403.98	-0.17	3	390.04	-3.61	3	403.77	-0.22
a0_35_11	2	265.79	2	266.34	0.21	2	267.34	0.58	2	267.34	0.58	2	267.29	0.56
a0_35_12	3	458.71	3	445.81	-2.81	3	439.96	-4.09	3	448.02	-2.33	3	452.50	-1.35
a0_35_13	3	407.17	3	399.35	-1.92	3	396.87	-2.53	3	401.60	-1.37	3	403.83	-0.82
a0_40_14	4	576.42	4	561.88	-2.52	4	558.59	-3.09	4	562.06	-2.49	4	573.41	-0.52
a0_40_15	4	523.50	4	511.00	-2.39	4	524.85	0.26	4	508.04	-2.95	4	528.13	0.88
a0_40_16	5	736.28	4	716.95	-2.63	4	714.71	-2.93	5	734.84	-0.20	5	739.59	0.45
a0_45_17	4	573.28	4	566.66	-1.15	4	560.14	-2.29	4	567.40	-1.03	4	572.02	-0.22
a0_45_18	4	525.95	4	516.26	-1.84	4	516.98	-1.71	4	516.00	-1.89	4	525.45	-0.10
a0_45_19	5	707.09	4	684.63	-3.18	4	677.13	-4.24	5	710.11	0.43	5	708.62	0.22
a0_50_20	5	687.79	5	678.20	-1.39	5	671.30	-2.40	5	684.66	-0.46	5	684.40	-0.49
a0_50_21	5	677.10	5	665.00	-1.79	5	680.47	0.50	5	660.05	-2.52	5	675.44	-0.25
a0_50_22	5	772.82	5	754.88	-2.32	5	751.43	-2.77	5	756.06	-2.17	5	760.92	-1.54
a0_50_23	6	789.52	6	770.82	-2.37	6	760.66	-3.66	6	771.64	-2.26	6	778.14	-1.44
a0_60_24	5	719.32	5	714.66	-0.65	5	707.01	-1.71	5	715.64	-0.51	5	713.43	-0.82
a0_60_25	5	747.45	5	740.12	-0.98	5	732.81	-1.96	5	745.72	-0.23	5	741.36	-0.81
a0_75_26	6	889.89	5	865.60	-2.73	5	860.14	-3.34	5	870.66	-2.16	6	870.24	-2.21
a0_75_27	4	566.96	4	556.25	-1.89	4	558.18	-1.55	4	567.69	0.13	4	570.58	0.64
a0_100_28	4	575.02	3	545.96	-5.05	3	538.05	-6.43	3	560.62	-2.50	3	547.45	-4.79
a0_100_29	5	729.17	4	666.90	-8.54	4	662.51	-9.14	4	688.95	-5.52	4	694.93	-4.70
Avg	-	521.15	-	510.31	-1.71	-	508.18	-2.08	-	514.36	-1.05	-	517.55	-0.45

Table 1.7. ALNS with different partial refueling strategies

Inst.	Our ALNS				ALNS of Masmoudi et al.(2016)				
	Best	Avg	Avg %	CPU (min)	Best	Best %	Avg	Avg %	CPU (min)
a0_20_1	270.35	270.35	0.00	0.96	270.35	0.00	270.35	0.00	0.96
a0_20_2	295.30	295.30	0.00	1.01	295.30	0.00	295.30	0.00	1.01
a0_20_3	307.54	307.54	0.00	0.00	307.54	0.00	307.54	0.00	1.11
a0_25_4	275.07	275.07	0.00	0.00	275.07	0.00	275.07	0.00	1.19
a0_25_5	294.14	294.14	0.00	0.00	294.14	0.00	294.14	0.00	1.36
a0_25_6	435.94	435.94	0.00	0.00	435.94	0.00	435.94	0.00	1.12
a0_25_7	458.72	458.72	0.00	1.98	458.72	0.00	458.72	0.00	1.99
a0_30_8	216.48	216.48	0.00	0.00	216.48	0.00	216.48	0.00	1.76
a0_30_9	225.82	225.82	0.00	1.46	225.82	0.00	225.82	0.00	1.46
a0_30_10	404.66	404.66	0.00	0.00	404.66	0.00	404.66	0.00	1.60
a0_35_11	265.79	265.79	0.00	0.00	266.35	0.21	266.80	0.38	2.04
a0_35_12	458.71	458.71	0.00	0.00	458.71	0.00	459.83	0.24	1.51
a0_35_13	407.17	407.56	0.10	0.00	408.16	0.24	408.71	0.38	1.31
a0_40_14	576.42	576.42	0.00	0.00	576.42	0.00	577.79	0.24	2.51
a0_40_15	523.50	523.81	0.06	0.00	524.93	0.27	525.22	0.33	2.36
a0_40_16	736.28	742.43	0.84	0.00	737.95	0.23	743.89	1.03	2.51
a0_45_17	573.28	573.28	0.00	0.00	574.32	0.18	574.23	0.17	5.95
a0_45_18	525.95	525.95	0.00	0.00	527.17	0.23	527.38	0.27	3.95
a0_45_19	707.09	708.48	0.20	5.05	709.12	0.29	709.75	0.38	5.33
a0_50_20	687.79	687.79	0.00	0.00	689.45	0.24	691.68	0.57	4.23
a0_50_21	677.10	680.45	0.49	5.03	678.16	0.16	684.32	1.07	5.34
a0_50_22	772.82	773.75	0.12	7.03	774.44	0.21	776.46	0.47	7.66
a0_50_23	789.52	793.46	0.50	7.79	792.88	0.43	797.59	1.02	8.48
a0_60_24	719.32	722.88	0.49	7.16	723.47	0.58	724.09	0.66	7.86
a0_60_25	747.45	750.17	0.36	8.05	750.18	0.37	753.57	0.82	9.16
a0_75_26	889.89	900.59	1.20	8.46	892.92	0.34	904.78	1.67	9.64
a0_75_27	566.96	571.64	0.83	0.00	569.35	0.42	574.91	1.40	8.18
a0_100_28	575.02	584.92	1.72	10.75	578.02	0.52	587.11	2.10	14.06
a0_100_29	729.17	737.94	1.20	10.53	731.94	0.38	741.21	1.65	14.05
A0	*521.15*	*523.10*	*0.28*	*2.59*	*522.34*	*0.18*	*524.60*	*0.51*	*4.47*

Table 1.8. *Comparison of our ALNS with the ALNS of Masmoudi et al. (2016) with respect to G-DARP instances*

From the detailed results of Table 1.8, it is clearly shown that our ALNS provides better results in terms of solution quality and computational times than the ALNS of Masmoudi *et al.* (2016). The maximum gap (Avg %) over five runs for the instances is equal to 0.28% for our ALNS, compared to 0.51% for the ALNS of Masmoudi *et al.* (2016). On the other hand, a positive average gap of the best result over five runs is obtained by the ALNS of Masmoudi *et al.* (2016) with an average deviation equal to 0.18%. In terms of average processing times, our algorithm is better than the ALNS of Masmoudi *et al.* (2016) with an average equal to 2.59 min compared to 4.47 min for the ALNS of Masmoudi *et al.* (2016). The results articulate that the diversification and intensification mechanisms applied in our algorithm have a considerable contribution in reducing computational times and improving the solution quality.

1.6. Conclusion

In this chapter, we presented a new extension of the Dial-a-Ride Problem (DARP), in which a fleet of Alternative Fuel Vehicles (AFVs) is considered. Due to the limited driving range, the AFVs may visit some Alternative Fuel Stations (AFSs) to be refueled with a partial refueling quantity during its journey to serve all users' demands. The proposed variant is called the Green Dial-a-Ride Problem (G-DARP).

We proposed an efficient Adaptive Large Neighborhood Search (ALNS) algorithm for solving the G-DARP. The algorithm is supported by efficient local search operators to enhance the search and improve the quality of solutions, as well as a flexible acceptance function to more explore the search space. After thorough sensitivity analysis and parameter tuning, our algorithm is extensively tested on generated data sets based on Masmoudi *et al.* (2018b). The experimental results indicate that our algorithm obtains high-quality solutions within reasonable processing time and surpasses the commercial solver CPLEX. Moreover, the proposed algorithm is competitive and provides good quality solutions when compared with recent algorithms for the standard DARP with heterogeneous users. The results also indicate that using partial refueling in our study is better than full refueling.

Acknowledgments

Thanks are due to the editors and to the anonymous referees for their valuable comments and suggestions which helped to improve the quality of this chapter.

1.7. References

Adler, J. D. and Mirchandani, P. B. (2016). The vehicle scheduling problem for fleets with alternative-fuel vehicles. *Transportation Science*, 51(2), 441–456.

Amirgholy, M. and Gonzales, E. J. (2016). Demand responsive transit systems with time-dependent demand: user equilibrium, system optimum, and management strategy. *Transportation Research Part B: Methodological*, 92, 234–252.

Andelmin, J. and Bartolini, E. (2017). An exact algorithm for the green vehicle routing problem. *Transportation Science*, 51(4), 1288–1303.

Barth, M. and Boriboonsomsin, K. (2009). Energy and emissions impacts of a freeway-based dynamic eco-driving system. *Transportation Research Part D: Transport and Environment*, 14(6), 400–410.

Bektaş, T., Ehmke, J. F., Psaraftis, H. N., and Puchinger, J. (2019). The role of operational research in green freight transportation. *European Journal of Operational Research*, 274(3), 807–823.

Braekers, K., Caris, A., and Janssens, G. K. (2014). Exact and meta-heuristic approach for a general heterogeneous dial-a-ride problem with multiple depots. *Transportation Research Part B: Methodological*, 67, 166–186.

Braekers, K. and Kovacs, A. A. (2016). A multi-period dial-a-ride problem with driver consistency. *Transportation Research Part B: Methodological*, 94, 355–377.

Centers for Disease Control and Prevention (2012). Accessed October 24, 2016. Available at: https://www.cdc.gov.

Cordeau, J. F. and Laporte, G. (2003). A tabu search heuristic for the static multi-vehicle dial-a-ride problem. *Transportation Research Part B: Methodological*, 37(6), 579–594.

Demir, E. (2018). Value creation through green vehicle routing. In *Theory, Models, and Case Studies. Sustainable Freight Transport*, Zeimpekis, V., Aktas, E., Bourlakis, M., and Minis, I. (eds). Springer, Cham, 63–78.

Demir, E., Bektaş, T., and Laporte, G. (2012). An adaptive large neighborhood search heuristic for the pollution-routing problem. *European Journal of Operational Research*, 223(2), 346–359.

Demir, E., Burgholzer, W., Hrušovský, M., Arıkan, E., Jammernegg, W., and Van Woensel, T. (2016). A green intermodal service network design problem with travel time uncertainty. *Transportation Research Part B: Methodological*, 93, 789–807.

Demir, E., Huang, Y., Scholts, S., and Van Woensel, T. (2015). A selected review on the negative externalities of the freight transportation: modeling and pricing. *Transportation Research Part E: Logistics and Transportation Review*, 77, 95–114.

Desrochers, M. and Laporte, G. (1991). Improvements and extensions to the Miller-Tucker-Zemlin subtour elimination constraints. *Operations Research Letters*, 10(1), 27–36.

Erdoğan, S. and Miller-Hooks, E. (2012). A green vehicle routing problem. *Transportation Research Part E: Logistics and Transportation Review*, 48(1), 100–114.

European Environment Agency (2017). EU greenhouse gas emissions from transport increase for the second year in a row. *EEA*. Available at: https://www.eea.europa.eu/highlights/eu-greenhouse-gas-emissions-from-transport-increased.

European Parliament (2009). Regulation (EC) No 443/2009. Available at: https://eur-lex.europa.eu/legal-content/EN/ALL/?uri=CELEX:32009R0443.

Eurostat (2018). Greenhouse gas emission statistics – emission inventories. Statistics Explained. Available at: https://ec.europa.eu/eurostat/statistics-explained/pdfscache/1180.pdf.

Ho, S. C., Szeto, W. Y., Kuo, Y. H., Leung, J. M., Petering, M., and Tou, T. W. (2018). A survey of dial-a-ride problems: literature review and recent developments. *Transportation Research Part B: Methodological* 111, 395–421.

Hof, J., Schneider, M., and Goeke, D. (2017). Solving the battery swap station location-routing problem with capacitated electric vehicles using an AVNS algorithm for vehicle-routing problems with intermediate stops. *Transportation Research Part B: Methodological*, 97, 102–112.

Liao, C. S., Lu, S. H., and Shen, Z. J. M. (2016). The electric vehicle touring problem. *Transportation Research Part B: Methodological*, 86, 163–180.

Lim, A., Zhang, Z., and Qin, H. (2016). Pickup and delivery service with manpower planning in Hong Kong public hospitals. *Transportation Science*, 51(2), 688–705.

Lin, S. (1965). Computer solutions of the traveling salesman problem. *Bell System Technical Journal*, 44(10), 2245–2269.

Liu, M., Luo, Z., and Lim, A. (2015). A branch-and-cut algorithm for a realistic dial-a-ride problem. *Transportation Research Part B: Methodological*, 81, 267–288.

Masmoudi, M. A., Hosny, M., Braekers, K., and Dammak, A. (2016). Three effective metaheuristics to solve the multi-depot multi-trip heterogeneous dial-a-ride problem. *Transportation Research Part E: Logistics and Transportation Review*, 96, 60–80.

Masmoudi, M. A., Braekers, K., Masmoudi, M., and Dammak, A. (2017). A hybrid genetic algorithm for the heterogeneous dial-a-ride problem. *Computers & Operations Research*, 81, 1–13.

Masmoudi, M. A., Hosny, M., Demir, E., and Cheikhrouhou, N. (2018a). A study on the heterogeneous fleet of alternative fuel vehicles: reducing CO_2 emissions by means of biodiesel fuel. *Transportation Research Part D: Transport and Environment*, 63, 137–155.

Masmoudi, M. A., Hosny, M., Demir, E., Genikomsakis, K. N., and Cheikhrouhou, N. (2018b). The dial-a-ride problem with electric vehicles and battery swapping stations. *Transportation Research Part E: Logistics and Transportation Review*, 118, 392–420.

Molenbruch, Y., Braekers, K., and Caris, A. (2017). Typology and literature review for dial-a-ride problems. *Annals of Operations Research*, 259(1–2), 295–325.

Montoya, A., Guéret, C., Mendoza, J. E., and Villegas, J. G. (2017). The electric vehicle routing problem with nonlinear charging function. *Transportation Research Part B: Methodological*, 103, 87–110.

Nissan (2018). New Nissan NV400. Available at: https://media.nissan.eu/content/dam/ services/gb/brochure/fleet/ NV400%20Brochure.pdf.

Parragh, S. N. (2011). Introducing heterogeneous users and vehicles into models and algorithms for the dial-a-ride problem. *Transportation Research Part C: Emerging Technologies*, 19(5), 912–930.

Potvin, J. Y. and Rousseau, J. M. (1995). An exchange heuristic for routeing problems with time windows. *Journal of the Operational Research Society*, 46(12), 1433–1446.

Ropke, S. and Pisinger, D. (2006). An adaptive large neighborhood search heuristic for the pickup and delivery problem with time windows. *Transportation Science*, 40(4), 455–472.

Savelsbergh, M. W. (1992). The vehicle routing problem with time windows: minimizing route duration. *ORSA Journal on Computing*, 4(2), 146–154.

Schneider, M., Stenger, A., and Goeke, D. (2014). The electric vehicle-routing problem with time windows and recharging stations. *Transportation Science*, 48(4), 500–520.

Shaw, P. (1998). Using constraint programming and local search methods to solve vehicle routing problems. In *Principles and Practice of Constraint Programming*, Maher, M. and Puget, J. F. (eds). Springer, Berlin, Heidelberg, 417–431.

Tsokolis, D., Tsiakmakis, S., Dimaratos, A., Fontaras, G., Pistikopoulos, P., Ciuffo, B., and Samaras, Z. (2016). Fuel consumption and CO2 emissions of passenger cars over the New Worldwide Harmonized Test Protocol. *Applied Energy*, 179, 1152–1165.

US Department of Energy (DOE) (2018). Alternative fuels and advanced vehicles. Available at: https://www.afdc.energy.gov/fuels/.

Xiao, Y. and Konak, A. (2017). A genetic algorithm with exact dynamic programming for the green vehicle routing & scheduling problem. *Journal of Cleaner Production*, 167, 1450–1463.

2

Role of Green Technology Vehicles in Road Transportation Emissions – Case of the UK

This chapter highlights the role of green technologies and provides an insight into the ways in which they can help reduce carbon emissions. The chapter studies various options and features related to green technology (alternative fuel-powered vehicles [AFVs]) in terms of emissions in transportation and logistics. The chapter sheds light on AFVs providing information on the current UK market. It then goes into detail about their various types, including layout, design, and features. The chapter explains the comprehensive battery specification information: how various power auxiliaries affect energy consumption, the charging implications for the batteries and the costs involved. It also highlights specific features of the AFVs such as regenerative braking and CO_2 emissions; multiple avenues are explored when it comes to AFV emissions.

2.1. Introduction

Green logistics has attracted increased attention from researchers recently due to the growing public environmental awareness, as well as the legislations by numerous governments around the world. Road transport is a major factor in climate change and accounts for a large proportion of the total greenhouse emissions, including carbon dioxide (CO_2). With the increase in traffic and congestion levels, greener vehicles (more environmentally friendly) combined with efficient transport routing strategies will be of great importance. Transport organizations are increasing their awareness of the potential impacts, and their activities and services – both internally and externally – as they grow and develop. For example, the UK government has set its targets high and aims to reach its goal, from the Climate

Chapter written by Niaz WASSAN, Angus FURNEAUX and Said SALHI.

Change Act (2008), of reducing the UK's greenhouse gas (GHG) emissions by at least 80% by the year 2050 when compared with 1990's levels. This policy requires a drastic reduction in emissions as the road transport industry is one of the main contributors to these negative impacts. We believe this aspect ought not to be ignored where attention should be focused.

Climate change is happening as shown by the evidence across several key indicators, including the major four as noted in the following (2018 Progress Report to Parliament Committee on Climate Change).

– **Atmospheric CO_2 (Carbon Dioxide) concentrations** continue to rise, now exceeding 400 parts per million.

– **Global average surface temperature** has increased further, with 2017 being in the top three warmest years on record. Recent years have exceeded 1°C above pre-industrial levels.

– **Arctic Sea Ice** is still in decline, September sea ice extent has declined on average 13% each decade since 1979.

– **Global sea level** has been on the rise since the 1990s.

According to the International Energy Agency's figures [International Energy Agency (2017)], global emissions are still on the rise, though emissions produced by the developed countries were in fact reduced by 8% in 2015 when compared to 2000. However, developing countries doubled their emissions over that same period. This can be attributed to several factors, including a very strong growth in per capita economic output (+90%) combined with population growth (+23%). The CO_2 intensity of the energy mix also increased (+12%), mainly due to higher coal consumption in larger countries (International Energy Agency 2017).

Among the developed countries, the UK reduced emissions in 2017 by 3% compared to the previous year, with the power sector being most successful in reducing its emissions in electricity production: a 75% reduction in 2018 from 2012. However, while other sectors including buildings and industry also saw a reduction in emissions, transport consumed an increase of 1% in 2017 over the previous year. Since 2014, transport sector has been the largest emitting sector in the UK economy accounting for a staggering 27% of UK greenhouse gases produced in 2017. Cars, vans and heavy goods vehicles (HGVs) account for the largest percentage of this transport sector. Policies must be introduced in order to meet the UK government's target of 100% of new car sales to be ULEVs (Ultra Low Emission Vehicles) by the year 2040 (ULEV in the UK 2015). AFVs can reduce direct transport emissions drastically and, when combined with greener electricity generation, could provide a solution to the UK's growing transport emission crisis. However, it is worth noting that their high battery cost and limited range may constrain their effectiveness.

The aim of this chapter is to highlight the role of green technologies and provide insight into ways to help reduce carbon emissions. We aim to study various options and features related to green technology (AFVs) in terms of emissions in transportation and logistics.

In the following sections, we introduce AFVs, providing information on the current UK market and then go into detail about their various types, including layout, design, and features. We provide comprehensive battery specification information: how various power auxiliaries affect energy consumption, the charging implications for the batteries and the costs involved. We also highlight specific features of the AFVs such as regenerative braking and CO_2 emissions. Multiple avenues are explored when it comes to AFV emissions followed by our conclusion.

2.2. Alternative Fuel-Powered vehicles market

Among the alternative powered vehicles, the Ultra-low Emission Vehicles (ULEVs), such as Battery Electric Vehicles (BEVs), Plug-In Hybrid Electric Vehicles (PHEVs) and Extended Range Electric Vehicles (EREVs) are becoming increasingly important to cut down greenhouse gas emissions and air pollution in the transport sector. The ULEV uptake in the UK is prominent; recent advancement in battery technology means that these electric vehicles are now becoming increasingly viable for general use. AFVs have increased rapidly in popularity in recent years within the UK. Looking solely at electric vehicle sales, they have increased from 3,500 in 2013 to more than 150,000 by May 2018 (Electric Car Market Statistics 2018). Figure 2.1 shows the recent electric vehicle uptake in the UK on a six-point rolling average.

This particular rolling average is important, as it removes the peaks created by the new vehicle registrations that happen in March and September, and the troughs before these months as people wait for the new vehicle registration and dealers purchase a large number of newly registered vehicles in bulk. These peaks and troughs due to the new vehicle registrations are well-known within the motor trade industry. The increase in popularity is evident in the large increase in the sales of EVs, the most popular type of EV currently available is the EREV Hybrid Petrol Vehicle, with monthly sales almost doubling in the last 2 years. Plug-in hybrids also prove to be popular in the UK market with the BEVs trailing behind. The last quarter of 2018 saw zero Hybrid diesel vehicle registrations. This could be due to a number of factors including the increase in diesel tax, more stringent emission tests, and the lack of hybrid diesel–electric vehicles being manufactured. The EV market now has 8% share of the UK New Vehicle market, an increase of 7% from July 2013.

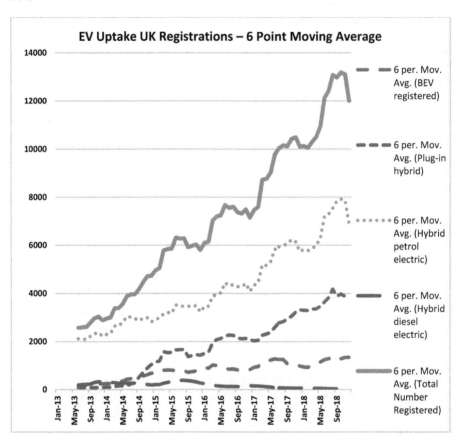

Figure 2.1. *EV uptake in the UK over the last 5 years (Data acquired from the Society of Motor Manufacturers and Traders). For a color version of this figure, see www.iste.co.uk/besbes/transport.zip*

2.3. Electric vehicles – options and features

Electric vehicles vary according to a number of different parameters. Table 2.1 shows the different variations of AFVs available with their drivetrain configurations, electric range and the grams of CO_2 per km, for example, of that particular type of vehicle.

Type	Drivetrain configuration	Range (km)	gCO$_2$/km (WLTP*)
PHEV (Plug-in Hybrid Electric Vehicle)	ICE (Internal combustion engine) and chargeable electric engine powering wheels	48–64 electric	46 (Mitsubishi Outlander PHEV)
E-REV (Extended-Range Electric Vehicle)	All electric with ICE generator support for the battery	112–350 electric	0 (Battery only)/162 (BMW i3 Empty Battery)
BEV (Battery Electric Vehicle)	All electric	128–400 electric	0
HEV (Hybrid Electric Vehicle)	ICE with additional support of electric engine, internally charged	8–32 electric	98 (Suzuki Ignis 1.2 SZ5)
FCEV (Fuel Cell Electric Vehicle)	Fuel cell providing power to electric engine and battery for energy storage	480–640 electric (with hydrogen fuel)	0

* Worldwide Harmonized Light Vehicle Test Procedure

Table 2.1. *Electric vehicle types*

Three different plug-in vehicles exist today which consumers can choose between to satisfy their needs: the plug-in hybrid electric vehicle (PHEV), the extended-range electric vehicle (E-REV), and the battery–electric vehicle (BEV). The basic design premise is shown in Figure 2.2.

The plug-in hybrid electric vehicles (PHEVs) contain a conventional combustion engine alongside an electric engine. The two can work together or independently, often each engine powering a separate axle. This type of vehicle can provide a reduction in both transportation costs and greenhouse gas emissions when compared to a comparable conventional vehicle, as when in full electric mode, PHEV's create zero direct emissions. The PHEVs have the capability of an electric vehicle such as charging from a regular power outlet with the added benefit of a gasoline-powered engine for long-distance trips. The electrical engine can operate in two different modes: Charge Depleting (CD) mode or Charge Sustaining (CS) mode (Arslan *et al.* 2015). The CD mode is when the vehicle uses the electric motor to generate the necessary power using the batteries as a power supply. Once the battery is depleted, the PHEV will then switch to the CS mode. In this mode, the vehicle uses the combustion engine to generate the required power; however, in this mode, the combustion engine also generates enough energy to recharge the vehicles battery supply while driving. Typically, the battery will never reach zero charge in order to prolong battery life. PHEVs can be refueled at regular fuel stations similar to conventional cars and can be charged at designated charging points or at regular power outlets similar to the BEVs. Some examples of a PHEV include the Mitsubishi Outlander PHEV, Chevrolet Volt, BMW-i8, Toyota Prius, Volvo V70 PHEV, Honda Accord Plug-in Hybrid, and Porsche Panamera S E-Hybrid.

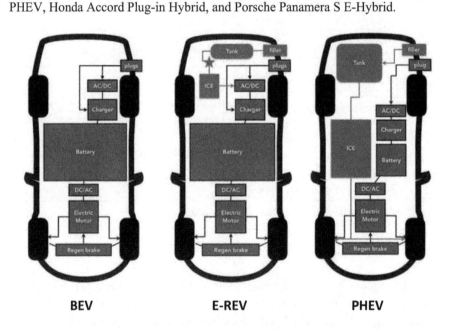

BEV   E-REV   PHEV

Figure 2.2. *Conventional layouts for the typical electric vehicles in the current market (Onewedge 2018). For a color version of this figure, see www.iste.co.uk/besbes/transport.zip*

Extended-range electric vehicles or E-REVs have a plug-in battery pack and an electric motor, as well as a combustion engine like the PHEVs. However, the difference is that, in the E-REVs, the electric motor always drives the wheels, with the internal combustion engine acting as a generator to supply power to the battery when it is depleted. As such, small combustion engines with low fuel consumption can be used as they are solely used to generate electricity for the E-REVs motors; as a result, these vehicles are capable of long-ranges between refueling. There are multiple generations of combustions engines designed to operate the generator for the electric motor. The first generations were designed with combustion engines used by normal convention vehicles. Generation 2 is where new engines were designed to develop a fairly constant load suited to the generator for the electric motor (Sumper and Baggini 2012). The most recent development includes microturbines and fuel cells which provide a constant load, and are most suited to the electric generators needs where a constant load is favored. Microturbines present a real opportunity for many domestic and commercial users. Several buses have recently been developed adopting this extended-range vehicle with microturbines and can see large improvements. For example, Capstone has developed this turbine technology and is currently the market leader in the area (Capstone Turbines Technology 2017). An example of an E-REV is the BMW i3 REX.

Battery Electric Vehicles or BEVs are traditional electric vehicles. They have been around since the mid-19th century, providing a preferred method of transport over the traditional combustion engines at the time. A BEV relies entirely on electricity for fuel and, as a consequence, direct emissions are zero. Typically their range is around 100–200 miles. They are wholly-driven by an electric motor which receives its power from a chargeable Lithium ion (Li-ion) battery. Electric motors are very simple when compared to the traditional combustion engine and can achieve very high efficiencies of around 95% (AEA 2008; JEC 2011). They can provide very high torque compared to others and can avoid the need for gearboxes and torque converters. The UK's top-selling BEV is the Nissan Leaf with 20,000 units sold as of July 2017 (Nissan News 2017).

One of the biggest drawbacks of the BEV technology is the range limitation (Graham-Rowe *et al.* 2012); however, recent technological advances have nullified this problem. Wireless inductive charging is being introduced, thus reducing charging times for users. However, if this technology can be introduced on the roads, then it opens up an opportunity called dynamic charging, which is covered in more detail in section 2.3.2 of this chapter. BEVs are completely emission-free (except brake and tire wear) and perceived as more silent in operation. They are also becoming increasingly viable for organizations and businesses. CEP and pharmaceutics services typically deliver in regionally limited areas, with their average daily distance ranging below 140 km (Afroditi *et al.* 2014). Now, other businesses, such as FedEx and taxi companies, are also incorporating electric vehicles into their fleets, even though one major drawback is their cost-effectiveness when compared to conventional vehicles/trucks. Davis and Figliozzi (2013) conducted a study in the U.S. using three types of electric delivery trucks in order to examine their competitiveness to conventional trucks under varying scenarios. The study showed that electric trucks can be competitive in case the cost savings from the reduced operational cost are enough to overcome the significantly high purchase costs. However, the authors did not include in their study an important factor – namely, the charging cost infrastructure that will be needed to be installed in order to facilitate the extra demand on the charging network.

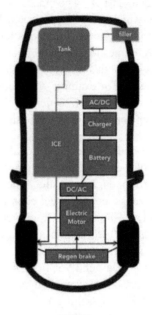

HEV

Figure 2.3. *Conventional layouts for Hybrids Vehicles (Onewedge 2018). For a color version of this figure, see www.iste.co.uk/besbes/transport.zip*

The parallel hybrid car (or conventional hybrid HEV), has an internal combustion engine as well as an electric motor, that are both connected to the wheels, proveding to be a good compromise for the range anxieties that arise from BEVs. In the conventional hybrid case, the electric battery is charged up using the internal combustion engine and regenerative braking; however, either the engine or both can be powering the wheels at one specific time. This can then be used for short-range electric driving before the internal combustion engine takes over. Optimizing time spent using this electric energy is a crucial way to improve efficiency in conventional hybrids. These vehicles benefit from regenerative braking, as well as weight savings over the BEVs which can play a large role in energy consumption. Due to the configuration and the fact that both engines can power the wheels, they can be equipped with smaller engines, thus increasing efficiency. Typically, HEVs have smaller battery packs, ranging from 5 kWh to 10 kWh, due to the fact that they need to be charged and discharged quickly and frequently. However, HEVs can also be complex, due to their nature of two systems constantly trying to cooperate and work together to provide the desired torque value.

The fuel cell electric vehicle or the FCEV is a popular topic among researchers at the moment, due to its potential benefits. They are predominantly powered by hydrogen with the only by-product of water vapor and warm air. Their basic layout can be shown in Figure 2.4. Similar to traditional combustion vehicles, they can be refilled in less than 10 minutes with a driving range of around 300 miles. They work in a similar way to that of the BEVs by using electricity to power an electric motor produced by a hydrogen fuel cell. A fuel cell is a device that directly takes stored chemical energy into electrical energy. The chemical energy that is stored between the fuels, such as hydrogen, methane and gasoline, is taken through two electrochemical reactions where it is converted directly into electricity. The major components of the fuel cell are the electrolyte, which also acts as a separator that keeps the reactants from mixing together. Next, the electrodes. These are catalysts made of graphite where the electrochemical reactions occur. These are contained within a bipolar plate (also known as a separator) that allows the current to be collected and voltage to be built from the cell. The most efficient fuel is hydrogen due to its ease of forming ions. The gas is highly combustible and has high energy content. However, hydrogen in its pure form is not readily available like conventional fossil fuels. Typically, their efficiencies are in the 60%–64% range (AEA 2008). There are cells which consume gasoline and convert them into hydrogen-rich streams to run fuel cells; however, the process is very complex and hence designers and technicians are less attracted. Due to hydrogen's low density, the design of the onboard hydrogen storage systems is becoming a design challenge. The volume of the fuel cell is relatively large compared to the internal volume of a combustion engine, thus making its fitment inside a vehicle to be difficult, through technology for smaller packing of the fuel cell or more efficient packing. At room temperature and pressure, the equivalent energy contained in a petrol tank would require a hydrogen tank around 800 times the volume. In order to combat this, the hydrogen is pressurized up to 7,000 times than that of atmospheric pressure. At these pressures, cryogenic systems have to be incorporated in order to effectively cool and liquefy the hydrogen; metal-hydrides are also used. These metal alloys absorb the hydrogen under high pressures.

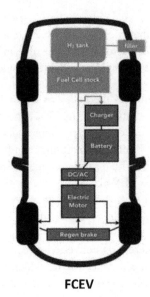

FCEV

Figure 2.4. *Layout of the Fuel-Cell Electric Vehicle (Onewedge 2018). For a color version of this figure, see www.iste.co.uk/besbes/transport.zip*

2.3.1. *Battery relevance*

The batteries found in BEVs vary massively, according to the role that they need to fulfill and the environment in which they are used, and play a vital role in a BEV. Energy density is a key factor when considering battery types, as higher energy density allows more energy to be stored in a smaller battery, ultimately improving efficiencies. Battery energy densities are constantly improving, allowing longer ranges within electrically-powered vehicles. The most popular UK EV, the Nissan Leaf, uses Lithium-ion (Li-ion) manganese batteries, providing moderate to high energy density with relatively low internal resistance. The longer range and more expensive Tesla uses Li-ion cobalt batteries which take slightly longer time to charge, but typically – a higher energy density. The manganese-based Li-ion batteries chosen for the Nissan Leaf and other EVs have excellent lab results. Manufacturers also choose their batteries based on cost; some batteries are more suited for keeping the battery at high voltage *and* elevated temperatures than others. In some cases, as the CE tests reveal, these two conditions can cause more damage than cycling (Battery University 2016). Table 2.2 provides the reader with a comprehensive overview of the various types of batteries used by manufacturers today.

From Table 2.2, it can be seen not only how these energy densities vary from different battery types, but also a vast number of alternative factors that all have a key role in the decision on which to select for its purpose. Information such as that in Table 2.2 can be imported into transport systems for meeting the optimum conditions for various vehicles when modeling to ensure correct charging/running procedures. Just as engine maintenance is important for a combustion engine, battery health is of great importance for Li-ion batteries. Although maintenance is not required, they do have a limited lifecycle of around 500–1,000 charges before degradation can appear. The four suspected factors responsible for the capacity loss and the eventual end-of-life of the Li-ion battery are as follows.

– Mechanical degradation of electrodes or loss of stack pressure in pouch-type cells. Careful cell design and correct electrolyte additives minimize this cause.

– Growth of solid electrolyte interface (SEI) on the anode. A barrier forms that obstructs the interaction with graphite, resulting in an increase of internal resistance. SEI is seen as a cause for capacity loss in most graphite-based Li-ion when keeping the charge voltage below 3.92 V/cell. Electrolyte additives reduce some of the effects.

– Formation of electrolyte oxidation at the cathode that may lead to a sudden capacity loss. Keeping the cells at a voltage above 4.10 V/cell and at an elevated temperature promotes this phenomenon.

– Lithium-plating on the surface of the anode caused by high charging rates. (Elevated capacity loss at higher C-rates might be caused by this.)

Along with these factors of capacity loss, thermal management plays a key role in BEVs. As shown in Table 2.2 on the next page, batteries have a certain operating window when charging and discharging. Temperature has a large impact on the performance of EV batteries and should not be overlooked. At cold temperatures, battery performance is lower due to poor ion movement; viscosity changes result in slow electrochemistry (see Figure 2.5). Resistance, therefore, increases with temperature affecting the relative capacity. This has a substantial effect on the range and the acceleration when compared to conventional vehicles. Low temperature affects the charging, allowing for a possible increase in dendrite creation, and also has a profound effect when the heaters are used due to the smaller EV range the increase in energy.

Specifications	Lead acid	NiCd	NiMH	Li-ion		
				Cobalt	Manganese	Phosphate
Specific energy density(Wh/kg)	30–50	45–80	60–120	150–190	100–135	90–120
Internal resistance (mΩ)	<100	100–200	200–300	150–300	25–75	25–50
	12 V pack	6 V pack	6 V pack	7.2 V	per cell	per cell
Life cycle (80% discharge)	200–300	1,000	300–500	500–1,000	500–1,000	1,000–2,000
Fast-charge time	8–16 h	1 h typical	2–4 h	2–4 h	1 h or less	1 h or less
Overcharge tolerance	High	Moderate	Low	Low. Cannot tolerate trickle charge		
Self-discharge/month (room temp)	5%	20%	30%	<10%		
Cell voltage (nominal)	2 V	1.2 V	1.2 V	3.6 V	3.8 V	3.3 V
Charge cut-off voltage(V/cell)	2.4	Full charge detection		4.2		3.6
	Float 2.25	By voltage signature				
Discharge cut-off voltage (V/cell, 1 C)	1.75	1		2.50–3.00		2.8
Peak load current	5°C	20°C	5°C	>3°C	>30°C	>30°C
Best result	0.2°C	1°C	0.5°C	<1°C	<10°C	<10°C
Charge temperature	–20°C to 50°C	0°C–45°C		0°C–45°C		
	–4°to 122°F	32–113°F		32–113°F		
Discharge temperature	–20°C to 50°C	–20°C to 65°C		–20°C to 60°C		
	–4 to 122°F	–4 to 149°F		–4 to 140°F		
Maintenance requirement	3–6 months	30–60 days	60–90 days	Not required		
	(topping charge)	(discharge)	(discharge)			

Safety requirements	Thermally stable	Thermally stable, fuse protection common	Protection circuit mandatory		
In use since	Late 1800s	1950	1990	1991	1996	1999
Toxicity	Very high	Very high	Low	Low		

Table 2.2. *Battery specifications (Battery University 2018)*

output results in a higher energy loss compared to a conventional vehicle. For example, in cold weather conditions, the effect of the heater can nearly double the energy consumption and cut the range in half when using specific driving cycles. Table 2.3 provides the reader with the net power needed for common vehicle functions. With an already limited range, additional auxiliary functions can limit the range of BEVs further. As a result, they can have a seriously reduced range in cold/hot weathers when additional auxiliary functions such as cabin heaters or A/C are used.

Accessory	Range impacts	Comments
Air conditioning	Up to 30%	Highly dependent on cabin temperature, ambient temperature and air volume
Heating	Up to 35%	Highly dependent on cabin temperature and ambient temperature
Power steering	Up to 5%	Necessity
Power brakes	Up to 5%	Necessity
Defroster	Up to 5%	Depending on the use
Other – lights, radio, phone, power-assisted seats, windows, locks, etc.	Up to 5%	Depending on the use

Table 2.3. *Impact of equipment on EV Performance (EV Auxiliary Systems Impact 2018)*

It is therefore important that these factors need to be taken into account when planning electric vehicle routes, as they can affect the range by a large amount. Powertrain efficiencies of BEVs are higher compared to the engine-powered counterparts, making the accessory loads more significant for some driving styles.

One crucial aspect that needs highlighting is the hot climate environment. At hot temperatures, the battery can become in danger of degradation and, at extremely high temperatures, can cause serious harm with thermal runaway – a process in which a rise in battery temperature triggers reactions and additional heat, eventually leading to the battery exploding. Although manufacturers introduced strict thermal management practices within their production of their vehicles, EVs batteries still rise significantly during the charging process. The effect is more profound when fast charging; in order to minimize degradation, battery operating temperature should be kept between 15°C and 35°C. This can be monitored on all BEVs vehicles and often BEVs limit their charging speeds according to the battery temperature. Figure 2.5 shows a graph demonstrating the effect of thermal management on battery life in a reader-friendly format.

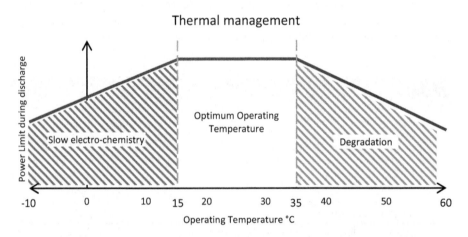

Figure 2.5. *Thermal management for Li-ion batteries in an EV. (This graph was created based on data found here http://www.nrel.gov/docs/fy13osti/58145.pdf.) For a color version of this figure, see www.iste.co.uk/besbes/transport.zip*

2.3.2. *Charging implications*

One main influencing factor on the temperature of the battery is charging. The speed at which a vehicle is charged is directly related to its temperature. Manufacturers that use large batteries often employ battery cooling techniques to allow the batteries to still charge at a fast rate without thermal management issues. Charging can also be negatively affected due to microscopic fibers of lithium, called "dendrites," growing on the cathodes. Dendrite growth is progressively worse with the increase in the reacting surface area. The reaction process is accelerated by almost a factor of 10 in worse case scenarios at −20°. Future developments in the design of batteries show that we could be heading toward the use of ultracapacitors as well. Ultracapacitors can store significantly more charge than regular capacitors due to the effective material used in their production; they can also be charged more than 1 million times, meaning they could provide a viable solution to electric vehicle distance anxiety. Combining the two can protect from surges in the fuel cells proving excellent power and energy density (NASA 2010).

Charging Types – There are three main EV charger types that are currently in use:

– Slow: these slow charging units provide up to 3 kW and are best suited for overnight charges, as a full charge on a typical vehicle can take anywhere between 6 and 8 hours.

– Fast: these chargers provide between 7 and 22 kW of power which offers charging times between 3 and 4 hours.

– Rapid: these charging units are the most powerful and provide 45–50 kW, capable of providing vehicles with an 80% charge in as little as 15–30 min. These charging points come in two different variants, alternating current (AC) and direct current (DC).

The number of charging points has been steadily increasing in the UK, with just over 9,000 points as of September 2015 and over 19,000 as of January 2019 (Zap-Map 2019), with many more planned to be installed by the UK government as the electric vehicle market increases. Slow chargers use (in most of the cases) a standard single phase 13 A three-pin plug, the very first charging points installed were of this type; however, they are now being replaced by Fast and Rapid charge points. Almost every vehicle can be slow charged with each vehicle provided with a standard three-pin plug at the charging point outlet and a Type-1 (J1772) or seven-pin Type 2 (Mennekes) connector for the vehicle inlet. Fast chargers reduce the rate of the slow charger times significantly; this is accomplished by doubling the available Amperes to 32 A or 7 kW for a single phase. This type of charger is the most commonly installed with over 5,500 installed in the UK as of September 2015. For larger commercial vehicles, such as trucks and buses, fast three-phase charging is available and capable of delivering 22 kW in total.

Rapid chargers, while growing in popularity, are relatively new. They come equipped with a tethered cable with a non-removable connector coupled with an inlet socket. The AC variants are the least popular since only a few UK EV models are designed to accept them. Rapid AC chargers are rated at 63 A, 43 kW (three-phase) using high-power AC supply and the Type 2 (Mennekes) connector. The DC rapid charge variant provides high-power DC supply at 125 A, 50 kW. These DC rapid chargers are fitted with either a JEVS (CHAdeMO) or a nine-pin

CCS (combo) connector. Around 1,500 rapid chargers are currently installed in the UK (as of early 2016). As mentioned previously, due to the high amperage of this form of charging, the internal battery temperature increases dramatically; with frequent rapid charging/discharging, this has more bearing. When charged at a fast rate, dendrites appear from the surface of the lithium electrode and spread across the electrolyte until they reach the other electrode. An electrical current passing through these dendrites can possibly short-circuit the battery, causing it to rapidly overheat and in some instances catch fire. Efforts to solve this fairly new problem by inhibiting dendrite growth have been met with limited success (Li-ion roots).

Nissan is one of the leaders in electric vehicles and as two electric vehicles in the global market. One being the Nissan Leaf designed for public use, with the 2016 model providing an EPA-estimated 107 mile range (but a large 155-mile range according to the new European driving style), with the 2019 model anticipated to have an EPA range of over 225 miles. The other being the e-NV200, a short wheel-based commercial van, aimed at businesses with a similar range of 106 miles with 4.2 m^3 of loading space and a loading bay of 2.04 m. Both vehicles use the same charging modes and require similar charging times: 8 hours on the slow 3-kW charger, 4 hours on the fast 7-kW chargers, and capable of an 80% charge in 30 minutes using the rapid charge. These rapid chargers mean that these electric vans can be viable solutions to logistic firms wanting to reduce their overall carbon footprint. The cost of charging cannot be written off, however, and as the infrastructure improves and more companies offer charging facilities, price variations in charging will occur. The current market leader for electric charging stations is Ecotricity, with the most comprehensive charging network in Europe (Ecotricity 2016). The price for a 30-minute rapid charge (43 kW AC up to 50 kW DC) is around £6, providing up to 80% charge, depending on battery capacity. However, for home/business use on personal electricity, the Society of Motor Manufacturers and Traders (SMMT) says that the typical cost of electricity to charge an EV is approximately 3 p/mile compared with the petrol/diesel costs of around 16 p/mile. This value was calculated when recharging times were considered to be at night when energy is largely subsidized (Schönewolf 2011). As mentioned before, the batteries themselves can suffer from degradation from overcharging. Bashash et al. (2011) provide an optimal charge pattern plan for plug-in hybrid vehicles; however, the premise can be carried across BEVs also. This paper focuses on the total cost of electricity and fuel, and the total battery degradation over a 24 hour period. Among the researchers, the common definition for the battery's end-of-life is around 70%–80% of its original energy. However, researchers have found that this value can be significantly less in real-life situations, since most people do not drive more than 40 miles per day (Saxena et al. 2015). The authors suggest using an alternative metric of defining battery retirement when it no longer meets the daily travel needs of a driver. Botsford and Szczepanek (2009) investigate the issues facing widespread use of electric vehicles. The study shows an example of how limiting only slow charging can be and how rapid chargers could help with the adoption of EVs.

During charging, BEVs do not necessarily need to be fully charged before leaving the charging station. Goeke and Schneider (2014) use a full maximum charging system at a constant rate, in their electric vehicle routing problem with time windows and mixed fleet. The mixed fleet contains both combustion and electric vehicles. Keskin and Catay (2016) relax the full recharge restriction and allow partial recharging, which is more practical in the real world due to the shorter recharging duration. The results highlight that partial recharging may significantly improve routing decisions. Specifically, they modeled charging time as a function of the State of Charge (SOC) of the battery. Table 2.3 shows the results of running common EV functions. The results were based on the popular Nissan Leaf BEV. For full Leaf information, the reader is directed to Nissan Leaf Specs (2016).

Dynamic charging could allow electric vehicles to charge while they are driving. A localized electromagnetic field is created between the charging pad on the electric vehicle and the corresponding charging pad in the road and a current induced charging the battery. Although still in its infancy, the technology exists and would have worthy benefits in applications such as traffic queues and traffic lights. The use of Li-ion batteries will significantly minimize the emissions; however, there is a limited amount of lithium and the future of the BEVs could be unknown. Online electric vehicles (OLEVs) draw their power from electric coils that are underground wirelessly (Suh 2011). Su *et al.* (2015) look at how the infrastructure supports wireless inductive charging for OLEVs in Korea, analyzing the benefits of the dynamic charging with an economic model of the battery size and the required charging infrastructure. With dynamic charging, EVs can charge more often and thus smaller batteries can be used in operation (Lukic and Pantic 2013). Using real-life data, the authors found that although a larger initial cost for installation was needed for dynamic charging, more cost-saving can be accomplished by extending the battery life. Future steps within the electric vehicle routing problem could identify these dynamic chargers using a stochastic charging model. Another novel idea that is highly popular among the researchers is the possibility of battery swapping, where depleted batteries from electric vehicles can be exchanged for recharged ones on long trips (Brown *et al.* 2010; Yang and Sun 2015; Zheng *et al.* 2013). The success depends upon the infrastructure of the swapping stations and the ease of service.

2.3.3. *Relevance of regenerative braking technology*

EVs mostly employ regenerative braking technology. This allows the vehicles to convert kinetic energy into electrical energy, which can then be stored in the battery when slowing or traveling down a slope. The electric motor functions as a generator, supplying the battery with the electrical energy generated. Regenerative braking also brings with it additional benefits such as reduced brake wear and the ability to use one pedal when driving (also known as an e-pedal). Single pedal driving is a relatively new concept, although it allows regenerative braking to be used to its full potential. When the user fully releases the pedal, the vehicle is in the maximum regeneration mode. This acts just as normal combustion engine brakes would and stops the car with considerable force. When the user wishes to come to a gradual stop, the pedal is released partially and a percentage of regenerative braking force is used instead.

2.3.4. *Emissions*

For determining the emissions generated from a vehicle, a three-scope approach can be used. This is a widely accepted approach, which is used here, to identify and categorize emission-releasing activities into three groups known as scopes. Each activity is listed as either Scope 1, Scope 2, or Scope 3; More information on how the scopes are used, as well as all other aspects of reporting, can be found in the Greenhouse Gas Protocol Corporate Standard (GOV.UK).

– *Scope 1 (direct emissions):* Emissions from activities owned or controlled by an organization. Examples of Scope 1 emissions include emissions from combustion in owned or controlled boilers, furnaces, and vehicles; emissions from chemical production in owned or controlled process equipment.

– *Scope 2 (energy indirect):* Emissions released into the atmosphere associated with the consumption of purchased electricity, heat, steam, and cooling. These are indirect emissions that are a consequence of an organization's energy use, but which occur at sources they do not own or control.

– *Scope 3 (other indirect):* Emissions that are a consequence of your actions, which occur at sources that you do not own or control and which are not classed as Scope 2 emissions. Examples of Scope 3 emissions are business travel by means not owned or controlled by your organization, waste disposal which is not owned or controlled, or purchased materials or fuels. Deciding if emissions from a vehicle, office, or factory that you use is Scope 1 or Scope 3 may depend on how you define your operational boundaries. Scope 3 emissions can be from activities either upstream or downstream from an organization.

The generated emissions for scope 1 of various types of conventional vehicle can be found in Figure 2.6. Passenger cars conversion factors are related to the market segments specifically defined by SMMT (Society of Motor Manufacturers and Traders). The conversion factors are based on information generated from the department for transport, who regularly analyses the mix of cars on the road using number plate recognition. The CO_2 emissions generated from these AFVs are significantly less than their diesel and petrol counterparts – 44% and 46%, respectively.

AFVs play a key role in the quest to reduce emissions. Traditional petroleum-based powered vehicles produce many emissions mainly at Scope 1. The emissions generated by these vehicles and their effects on humans are explained in detail within section 2.4 alongside the UK emissions. Scope 1 emissions from these petroleum-based vehicles are harmful not only to the environment, but also to the people. Direct tailpipe emissions can lead to air pollution; NO_2 and PM exceedances in cities are becoming increasingly common. Congested traffic poses a real threat to air quality and it is well-known that road transport in the urban area is a major source of air pollution across the world. However, in Europe, all the vehicles have to comply with the EU emission standards. The emissions are tested using the legislated standard driving cycles. Unfortunately, these often do not represent real-world driving emissions. This is because, compared to the legislated driving cycle, real-world driving uses different engine power configurations, differing speeds, different acceleration rates, varying traffic congestion, continuously changing road gradients, different cold start conditions, and various numbers of stop/start events all occurring with varying weather conditions; the outcome will inevitably result in different emissions. The true emissions generated by these petroleum-based vehicles is actually very different than the emissions calculated on these driving cycle tests. It is therefore important that we must address air pollution in these urban areas. BEVs generate zero emissions and therefore make great candidates for heavily urban areas where traffic congestion is a major issue, and range is also less important due to reduced driving distances in cities, increased congestion and reduced speed limits. Although BEVs generate little to no emissions, indirect emissions must also be considered. The electric vehicle emissions are classified as mainly Scope 2 and are directly related to the fuel mix that is used to create the electricity. As mentioned previously, the UK's Power Sector has reduced its emissions drastically and this is directly proportional to the emissions generated by BEVs. The emissions do, however, also depend on other factors, such as the type of day, where different combinations/mixes of power generation are used. With the previously mentioned recent technological advancements, such as autonomous vehicles, dynamic charging, and reduced charging times, it opens us a wider range of emission-reducing possibilities. With faster charging, the vehicles are suitable for long-range drivers, thus allowing minimal stopping times and appealing EV driving to a wider audience. With the introduction of dynamic charging, streets in cities that are normally filled with idling vehicles can now be replaced by electric vehicles that can be wirelessly charged during motion, thus leading to a significant reduction in urban air pollution. Autonomous electric vehicles help optimize the charging times and can charge themselves when the national grid is at its least demand, meaning just green energy.

CO_2 g/km (sales weighted average)		2000	2007	2016	2017	2017 v 2016	2017 v 2000
	Total market	181.0	164.9	120.1	121.0	0.8%	-33.1%
	Registrations ('000s)	2,222	2,404	2,693	2,541	-5.7%	14.4%
BY FUEL TYPE	Diesel	167.7	164.3	120.1	122.0	1.6%	-27.3%
	Registrations ('000s)	313	967	1,285	1,066	-17.1%	240.3%
	Petrol	183.2	165.7	123.7	125	1.1%	-31.8%
	Registrations ('000s)	1,908	1,420	1,319	1,355	2.7%	-29.0%
	AFV	127.3	127.0	66.8	87.5	3.0%	-47.0%
	Registrations ('000s)	0	17	89	120	34.8%	33454%
BY SALES TYPE (STARTS 2001)	Private	176.4	165.8	122.3	122.7	0.3%	-30.4%
	Registrations ('000s)	1,212	1,046	1,206	1,124	-6.8%	-7.2%
	Fleet	175.4	164.0	118.3	119.8	1.3%	-31.7%
	Registrations ('000s)	1,031	1,195	1,381	1,319	-4.5%	27.9%
	Business	195.0	165.9	119.0	118.8	-0.2%	-39.1%
	Registrations ('000s)	214	163	108	99	-7.8%	-54.5%
BY SEGMENT	Mini	153.8	128.5	105.5	105.9	0.4%	-31.2%
	Registrations ('000s)	52	22	77	69	-10.1%	31.9%
	Supermini	152.9	141.8	111.1	110.7	-0.4%	-27.6%
	Registrations ('000s)	689	771	873	748	-14.3%	8.7%
	Lower Medium	175.3	158.6	114.8	115.8	0.9%	-34.0%
	Registrations ('000s)	662	722	735	728	-0.9%	10.1%
	Upper Medium	192.4	169.1	119.0	120.5	1.3%	-37.4%
	Registrations ('000s)	477	386	257	243	-5.4%	-49.1%
	Executive	235.6	192.6	120.8	121.6	0.7%	-48.4%
	Registrations ('000s)	105	104	128	123	-3.6%	17.8%
	Luxury	292.3	273.8	182.4	178.9	-1.9%	-38.8%
	Registrations ('000s)	11	13	11	9	-12.5%	-19.4%
	Sports	220.5	226.0	161.4	155.0	-4.0%	-29.7%
	Registrations ('000s)	67	86	50	48	-4.5%	-29.2%
	Dual Purpose	259.4	228.3	141.4	141.3	-0.1%	-45.5%
	Registrations ('000s)	99	176	438	460	5.1%	364.1%
	MPV	211.0	179.7	128.7	132.0	2.6%	-37.4%
	Registrations ('000s)	60	143	125	112	-10.7%	86.6%

Figure 2.6. *Average new car CO_2 emissions and registrations (New Car CO_2 Report 2018)*

production is needed to meet demands. This, in turn, allows BEVs to charge at zero Scope 2 pollution; this aspect is covered in more detail in the following chapter.

2.4. UK transport emissions and the impact of BEVs

All vehicles generate emissions whether directly or indirectly. With an increasing number of vehicles being registered each year within Britain advancements in engine technology and emission reduction hardware are critical. The UK government have their sights firmly on reducing transport pollution within Britain, focusing on urban areas such as London [Ultra Low Emission Zone (ULEZ) 2018]. The UK government has brought in a ban on all new petrol and diesel cars from the year 2040, which has recently been brought forward to 2030 by UK mayors (Sadiq 2018). Along with a £255 million fund to help councils tackle emissions, it is clear to see the emphasis the leading officials are placing on improving the air quality around our streets. British vehicles and LGVs and HGVs amassed a combined 60.9 billion miles in 2014, an increase of 5.5% and 2.0%, respectively (Great 2014). Using the average fuel consumption data from the Department for Statistics (LGV – 13.6 mpg, HGV – 7.9 mpg), this mileage equates to 5.32 billion gallons of fuel. This amounts to 64.8 million tons of CO_2. This is a huge amount of potential pollution that is being created. The use of alternative methods of transport could reduce this amount with electric vehicles being a viable way forward.

With most goods vehicles currently in the market being diesel, in this section, we will focus on these combustion engine types, rather than petroleum-fueled combustion engines. We then go on to discuss future engines with electric vehicles and ultra-low emissions vehicles. Diesel vehicles are very common in medium-to-heavy goods vehicles, and also popular among the public due to their longer driving range, higher engine efficiency, low running costs, and durability when compared with their petrol counterparts. However, they have recently seen a big drop off in sales. March 2018 saw a 37% reduction with the previous year (New Vehicle Registrations 2018). Recent emissions scandals, whereby companies such as Volkswagen (VW) were found to be using emission cheating devices built into the engine control unit, have caused a lot of doubts around the actual emissions generated by these diesel engines (Autocar 2015; Mathiesen and Neslen 2015). The vehicle could sense when it was under test conditions and employ all of its available emissions reduction systems to reduce the emissions to below the required limit. When under normal driving conditions on the road, some of these systems were not working as effectively; this provided an enhanced driving experience with better performance, but increased the emissions. Running without the device, the vehicles were found to be producing around 40 times the allowed amount of nitrogen oxide in the US. The result of the scandal was dramatic: VW Group was issued a fine around £4.7 billion, with the possibility of a maximum fine of £13.7 billion; however, this figure does not include the cost of repairing the vehicles. As a result, the company's shares dropped by 30% in the short period following the scandal. The increased emissions dramatically affect the environment with the vehicles in the US creating 10,392–41,571 tons of toxic gas into the air each year, rather than the expected 1,039 tons of NO_x (Mathiesen and Neslen 2015). Recently, however, it has been found that other manufacturers including Mercedes have also been found guilty of having emission defeat devices fitted and are now recalling more than 770,000 vehicles (BBC News 2018). There are seven main Greenhouse Gases (GHGs) that contribute to climate change, as covered by the Kyoto Protocol: carbon dioxide (CO_2), methane (CH4), nitrous oxide (N_2O), hydrofluorocarbons (HFCs), perfluorocarbons (PFCs), sulfur hexafluoride (SF6), and nitrogen trifluoride (NF3). Different activities emit different gases. GHG emissions from transport have been fluctuating over the last two decades, although remained fairly stagnant over the last 4 years. The government aims to reduce CO_2 levels by 80% by the year 2050 (ULEV in the UK 2015). Other than an increase in technology and advances in transport, the government adopts various policies to try and reduce the overall impact. Some research carried out by the government includes looking at various scenarios and how they will affect the GHG emissions within the transport sector. Figure 2.7 shows how these policies will affect emissions.

It can be seen that if only baseline policies were met, the estimated emission increases. The baseline reference is based on central estimates of economic growth and fossil fuel prices, and indicates further actions must be taken to reduce CO_2 emission. As can be seen from the graph, fuel price has a vital role in the reduction of emissions. With a low fuel price, consumers are more likely to use their traditional combustion engine vehicle, thus resulting in increased pollution. On the other hand, a high fuel price can be the main factor in reducing emissions, this will drive people to AFVs and alternative means of transport. These alternative fuel vehicles must still be monitored carefully as they are not emission-free.

When diesel combusts, it emits many different pollutants of which several are very harmful. During the combustion process, fuel is injected at very high pressures, this is then put under immense compression during the combustion stroke of the engine, generating the required heat to cause the diesel fuel to ignite. In an ideal environment with exceptionally high combustion efficiencies, the by-product of the combustion would be only CO_2 and H_2O (Prasad and Bella 2010). However, factors such as combustion temperature, air-fuel ratio, and turbulence in the combustion chamber reduce the efficiency and a number of harmful products are generated such as CO, PM, NO_x, SO_x, and HC.

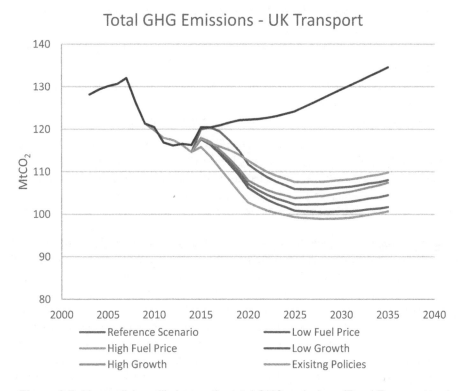

Figure 2.7. *How policies will change the total GHG emissions (Road Transport and Environment 2016). For a color version of this figure, see www.iste.co.uk/besbes/transport.zip*

– Carbon Monoxide (CO) – produced by internal combustion engines and can lead to carbon monoxide poisoning, causing serious health issues and in severe cases death. (NHS 2019).

– Particulate matter (PM) – consistently associated with respiratory and cardiovascular illness and increased mortality. Diesel engine exhaust has been classified as carcinogenic to humans by the World Health Organization. Secondary PM contributes to the acidification of ecosystems.

– Nitrogen Oxides (NOx) – are harmful pollutants generated from diesel engines, which not only have detrimental effects on the environment but also cause most health problems. They can cause inflammation of the airways, and long-term exposure may affect lung function and respiratory symptoms. High levels can also have an adverse effect on vegetation. NOx contributes to acidification and/or eutrophication of habitats and to the formation of secondary particles and ground-level ozone, both of which are associated with ill-health effects. Actions are needed to reduce this health issue for both the workers and the general population (Sydborn *et al.* 2001).

– Sulfur Oxides (SOx) – causes constriction of the airways of the lung. Involved in the formation of PM. This contributes to the acidification of terrestrial and aquatic ecosystems, damaging habitats, and leading to biodiversity loss.

– Hydrocarbons (HC) – these are chemical compounds found on Earth and are the reason fossil fuels combust – extremely important in modern-day society. Diesel fuel contains larger hydrocarbon molecules with more carbon atoms than petroleum, and as such has a higher fuel density. Issues arise when incomplete combustion takes place, releasing emissions pollution into the atmosphere.

Diesel engines produce the highest level of these gases from their exhausts and have been shown to be linked to carcinogenetic effects which can lead to cancer of the lungs (Diesel Engine Exhaust Carcinogenic 2012). The study conducted by the IARC was mainly composed of workers exposed to diesel exhaust gas fumes. However, in the past carcinogens that have been shown to have high risk to heavily exposed groups were also found to be present to the general public. It has been estimated that 20%–70% of PM is attributed to the combustion-derived particles from traffic (Gong *et al.* 2005; Reis *et al.* 2018; Rückerl *et al.* 2007). Diesel emissions are linked to causing inflammation and tissue damage, and with chronic exposure harmful physiological changes can occur within multiple organ systems (Reis *et al.* 2018).

With the British transport industry currently making up 27% of all UK GHG emissions, it is of the utmost importance that we aim to reduce this negative effect. This could be achieved by identifying new technology and methods to improve air pollution levels. In 2017, diesel vehicles provided a 42% market share of new cars; on average, these diesel vehicles produce 122 CO_2 g/km. By contrast, AFVs provide a smaller 5% market share emitting on average of just 67.5 CO_2 g/km. These figures are measured at the tailpipe to evaluate in-use emissions performance. BEVs produce zero tailpipe emissions, and an increase in BEV sales will provide a crucial reduction in direct CO_2 emissions and can have a beneficial impact on the dangerous emissions emitted by combustion engines for the public. However, BEVs are not completely emission-free, and they can still produce emissions indirectly. Accurately understanding the emissions generated by charging, the batteries can provide a further reduction in these indirect emissions.

Limited research has been carried out to calculate the emissions actually generated from ULEVs. Well-to-wheel emission is generally used where the emissions are calculated from how the fuel is produced and the way in which the vehicle is operated. In this study, the center of the focus is on BEVs; however, the information can easily be carried over to PHEVs as well. For more detailed information on the emissions of PHEVs, the reader is directed to (Jung and Li 2018).

When compared with internal combustion engines (ICEs), EVs have many advantages including (Fiori *et al.* 2016):

– Greater energy efficiency through the use of onboard electric devices.

– Regenerative braking, reducing driving emissions.

– The possibility of obtaining greener fuel sources.

– Zero tailpipe emissions.

– Less noise pollution.

As already described in section 3.3, regenerative braking allows EVs to recover energy that is normally lost in the braking phase and convert it back into stored electrical energy. This is the opposite to the case of the traditional ICE vehicle where the energy generated from braking is lost as thermal losses. Several empirical studies have shown that EVs consume less energy while driving in urban areas and are able to recover energy while braking (De Gennaro *et al.* 2014; Rambaldi *et al.* 2011). Traditionally, the electric vehicle is thought of as an emission-free vehicle, due to zero tailpipe emissions while on the move. However, the electricity that is needed to power the engine creates emissions on production/generation.

The amount of emissions is generally down to the fuel mix from the country of origin. The following research has taken data from the government fuel disclosure mix 2015 and 2017. The Department for Environment, Food and Rural Affairs (DEFRA) quotes the figure as 0.527 kg/kWh of electricity generated. This figure is used by businesses to provide a carbon emission estimation, a requirement for Public Limited Companies (PLCs) The indigenous fuel mix for the year 2015 and 2017 is shown in Figure 2.8.

The shift away from coal as an energy source can be seen, reducing coal power generation share by 3% from 2015 to 2017. Bioenergy and waste as an energy source on the other hand has increased its power germination share by 2% from 2015 to 2017. This shift toward a greener electricity fuel mix provides a direct reduction in BEV emissions. However, due to the nature of electric vehicles, the emissions they create are entirely dependent on the fuel mix in the country where they are being used. In the combustion process of the different fuels of each fossil, fuels emit different amounts of CO_2.

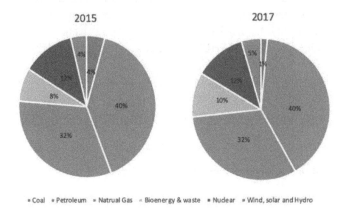

Figure 2.8. *The Indigenous Fuel Mix for the UK in 2015 and 2017 (Energy Trends 2019). For a color version of this figure, see www.iste.co.uk/besbes/transport.zip*

The Fuel Mix for the period April 01, 2014, to March 31, 2015, can be seen in Table 2.4, which includes the transmission loss factor of 1.12. Please note that this is the overall energy source including energy produced from other countries, hence obtaining varying values when compared to the indigenous mix as shown in Figure 2.8.

Using the information shown in Table 2.4, one can calculate the average weight (kg) of CO_2 per kWh. This equates to 0.527 $kgCO_2/kWh$ at the time of data recording. This value represents an average emission factor of the electricity generated in the UK.

Energy source	Residual (%)	UK (%)	CO_2 (g/kWh)
Coal	38.7	26.7	910
Natural Gas	36.2	29.7	380
Nuclear	14.2	22.2	0 (0.007 g/kWh)
Renewables	4.6	19.3	0
Other Fuels	6.3	2.1	600

*high-level radioactive wastes

Table 2.4. *The fuel mix of the UK with the estimated CO_2 produced for each energy source (UK GOV 2017).*

All conversion factors presented here are in units of CO_2. CO_2e is the universal unit of measurement to indicate global warming potential (GWP) of Green Houses Gases (GHGs), expressed in terms of the GWP of one unit of carbon dioxide. The residual percentage is nothing more than a grid emission factor. The residual mix incorporates the allocation of renewable energy by those who have purchased electricity tracking certificates such as guarantees of origins (GOs). As it can be seen from Table 2.5 on the next page, the emissions generated via coal and other fuels produce significantly more CO_2 emissions per kWh than other sources of energy. However this is often the cheapest form and as such is favorable in terms of cost. However, long-term effects can bring serious detrimental environmental impacts. Other sources of fuel include pumped storage, as well as alternative sources of electricity generated abroad and distributed to the UK. Although nuclear energy does not produce CO_2 emissions as a direct product, there is the production of radioactive material. This is a major problem with nuclear energy and there is yet to be a viable solution to this waste problem. The UK government has introduced new planning regimes for its power generation recently. These include the installation of new nuclear reactors, large wind farms, reservoirs and railways (World Nuclear 2018). However, as this study is focused on the current fuel mix, the aforementioned issues are beyond the scope of this work. The fuel mix varies dramatically over the course of a day. Peak and off-peak grid times involve a different combination of power sources, resulting in varying emissions and evidently different prices.

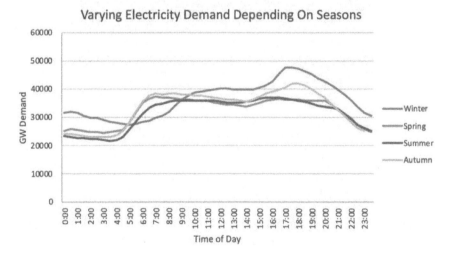

Figure 2.9. *Varying energy demand throughout the day dependent on seasons. For a color version of this figure, see www.iste.co.uk/besbes/transport.zip*

Figure 2.9 demonstrates how much these peak loads change over the course of the day. The values are calculated from Gridwatch (2019) using past history for the year 2015. Each data series represents the average Wednesday electricity demand during the middle of each season. Wednesday was chosen as it is halfway through the normal working week and provided a good estimate on the demands when routing commercial vehicles during working hours. The peak hours can be seen to be around 16:00 to 19:00, with more being generated in winter. This is due to people arriving back from work and using appliances within their homes and the need for heating in winter. As electricity demands change throughout the day, so does the energy source used to create electricity. A more detailed breakdown can be found at the Renewable Energy Foundation (REF 2019), where the changes to the fuel mix during peak and low grid times can be seen. By examining the past data, predictive models can be created to forecast the amount of emissions generated at certain times of the day, while generating accurate predictive emissions models for EV charging. Using this information on varying power demand as shown in Figure 2.9 and linking to the UK fuel mix in Table 2.5 and emissions of those power sources, an accurate emission evaluation can be achieved. We have implemented a simple breakdown of the results in Table 2.5 and provided the emission cost for charging an EV with a 30 kWh capacity at different times of a day.

Season	Time of day to recharge	Emissions generated $kgCO_2$ for 30 kWh
Winter	7:00	11.04
Summer	7:00	7.52
Winter	12:00	11.44
Summer	12:00	7.46
Winter	17:00	11.84
Summer	17:00	7.44
Winter	00:00	8.92
Summer	00:00	7.04

Table 2.5. *Emissions generated to charge a 30 kWh EV during different times throughout the day*

One can clearly see the benefits of scheduled charging when looking at the emissions generated at different periods throughout the day for the UK. The two days selected were January 30, 2019, for the winter comparison and August 1, 2019, for the summer. During winter months, energy consumption is much higher as can be seen in Figure 2.9; this has a direct effect on emission when charging EVs. In the case presented earlier, the difference of charging your 30 kWh EV at 17:00 and 00:00 in winter is a staggering 2.5 kg. When looking at summer fluctuations, the differences are noticeably less, and the benefits drop to 0.5 kg when charging at night. This case as mentioned is for the UK where renewable energy sources make up around 20% of the fuel mix. As this percentage is increased and electricity becomes greener, the importance of charging times increases.

2.5. Cost implications

The cost of the various AFVs varies according to their type. Costs are a large influence when considering what vehicle to purchase and can often put consumers off EVs. While important to the general consumer, fleet owners are heavily influenced by vehicle prices as it is their main cost alongside fuel. In the UK, the government is providing incentives for EVs in a bid to make them more financially viable.

– PHEV – As the PHEV combines both conventional combustions engines with electric motors, the cost is substantially more compared to its counterpart. The most popular PHEV in the UK is the Mitsubishi Outlander PHEV (Mitsubishi 2016) with an average retail price of £37,000 after grants. A similar spec Mitsubishi Outlander conventional combustion engine is around £30,000 (Mitsubishi 2016). The increase in cost is mainly down to the battery, the additional research and design, and the electronics needed in the production of the vehicle. The battery alone costs in the region of £230 per kWh (Nykvist and Nilsson 2015) and while PHEV's batteries tend to be smaller than BEV, the costs still add up as the capacity in the Outlander PHEV is 12 kWh. Servicing costs are typically higher as well, as specialist tools are needed.

– E-REV – E-REVs are typically less common than PHEVs or BEVs. Several manufacturers add in-range extenders as an additional option on standard BEVs such as in the BMW i3 which costs an additional £2,900 to the base models £34,070 price tag (Car Buyer 2018). Current prices are difficult to find accurately, due to the current lack of available models.

– BEV – BEVs are increasing in popularity. This is a result of a rise in eco-consciousness and also due to the reduction in cost, thanks to lower battery production costs. Nykvist and Nilsson found that battery prices in 2015 were already below the target for 2017 (Nykvist and Nilsson 2015). A typical BEV (Nissan Leaf 30 kWh 2016) costs in the region of £25,000, whereas a comparable spec combustion vehicle Nissan Pulsar 2016 is around £19,000. These costs are potentially offset in the future due to the running costs compared between the two types over a certain number of miles and the government grant provided for the EV (Nissan UK 2016).

– HEV – HEVs have been around for a while now and as such their value is considerably less. They were introduced before the mainstream BEVs and since the increase in range allowance PHEVs are becoming increasingly uncommon. Batteries are guaranteed for 8 years and operate at 30%–80% SOC to reduce stress and large voltage changes. However, they provide a high-cost low-density solution, nearly, all today use nickel-metal hydride batteries (Battery University 2016; *Zhou et al.* 2013).

– FCEV – FCEVs are relatively new technology and as a result, their cost is typically very high. They are not readily available in most markets with the majority used currently in testing.

Many countries are offering incentives for electric vehicles in a bid to make them more appealing to the consumers. Jin *et al.* (2014) suggest that these incentives are important factors when trying to promote electric car sales. Outside the UK, countries such as China employs tax incentives when purchasing an EV. Exemption from acquisition and excise taxes can range from £4500 to £7500. In European countries, other examples of cost incentives such as in Norway include BEVs being exempt from VAT (Mock and Yang 2014). The UK government provides up to £4,500 for cars and this increases up to £8,000 for commercial vehicles (UK GOV 2016). The costs of batteries are a major reason why in general electric vehicles are more expensive than their traditional internal combustion engine counterparts. Battery prices have recently hit their lowest cost for the last 9 years, and it is expected that as technology increases, these costs will continue to drop. In 2013, the International Energy Agency (IEA) estimated that, by the year 2020, battery prices will fall low enough so that electric vehicle match conventional vehicles with a cost of £220/kWh of capacity. However, the current cost has already met this target with a current price of just £200/kWh a fall of 73% since 2007 when the price was £760/kWh (International Energy Agency 2019; US Department of Energy 2016). This information provides encouraging signs on the possibility of manufacturer batteries at low prices enabling EVs to be readily available to consumers at good prices.

2.6. Conclusion

The chapter sheds light on various options and features of the green technology-based vehicles in terms of emissions related to the transport industry. It is perceived that the range of AFVs is very diverse, carrying with them both advantages and disadvantages. As technology flourished consequently these characteristics may change, incorporating them within transport systems can not only provide better accuracy when developing transport routing strategies, but they can also provide companies and policy-makers with alternatives that can have a positive impact on the environment. In our view, they have a key role to play in the UK's transport network and combined with a robust infrastructure can make a positive impact toward reducing the emissions. The incorporation of a structured EV network is key when looking toward a greener future; examples demonstrated in this chapter highlight the importance of charging times and the recent advancements in technology. Combining the two can help reduce air pollution and help fight climate change. The study in this chapter is also meant to trigger further research on fleet management, modeling investigating features and options that are not incorporated in the previously developed relevant models.

2.7. References

AEA. (2008). Assessment with respect to long term CO_2 emission targets for passenger cars and vans [Online]. https://ec.europa.eu/clima/sites/clima/files/transport/vehicles/docs/2009_co2_car_vans_en.pdf. Accessed January 23, 2019.

Afroditi, A., Boile, M., Theofanis, S., Sdoukopoulos, E., and Margaritis, D. (2014). Electric vehicle routing problem with industry constraints: trends and insights for future research. *Transportation Research Procedia*, 3, 452–459.

Arslan, O., Yıldız, B., and Karasan, O. E. (2015). Minimum cost path problem for plug-in hybrid electric vehicles. *Transportation Research Part E: Logistics and Transportation Review*, 80, 123–141.

Autocar. (2015). Report [Online]. https://www.autocar.co.uk/car-news/industry/vw-emissions-scandal-nine-vw-vehicles-have-false-co2-ratings. Accessed June 24, 2018.

Bashash, S., Moura, S. J., Forman, J. C., and Fathy, H. K. (2011). Plug-in hybrid electric vehicle charge pattern optimization for energy cost and battery longevity. *Journal of Power Sources*, 196, 541–549.

Battery University. (2016). Hybrid electric vehicles and the battery [Online]. http://batteryuniversity.com/learn/article/hybrid_electric_vehicles_and_the_battery. Accessed November 5, 2016.

Battery University. (2018). Battery specifications [Online]. https://batteryuniversity.com/learn/article/secondary_batteries. Accessed January 30, 2019.

BBC News. (2018). Mercedes defeat devices. Report [Online]. https://www.bbc.co.uk/news/business-44444361. Accessed June 18, 2018.

Botsford, C. and Szczepanek, A. (2009). Fast charging vs. slow charging: pros and cons for the new age of electric vehicles. *Proceedings of 24th International Battery Hybrid Fuel Cell Electric Vehicle Symposium,* Stavanger, Norway.

Brown, S., Pyke, D., and Steenhof, P. (2010). Electric vehicles: the role and importance of standards in an emerging market. *Energy Policy,* 38(7), 3797–3806.

Capstone Turbines Technology. (2017). Capstone turbines [Online]. http://www.capsto neturbine.com. Accessed March 12, 2017.

Car Buyer. (2018). Car Buyer News [Online]. https://www.carbuyer.co.uk/news/160068/ bmw-i3-updated-with-new-batteries-and-options.

Climate Change Act. (2008). UK Government Legislation [Online]. https://www.legislation. gov.uk/ukpga/2008/27/contents. Accessed January 30, 2019.

Davis, B. and Figliozzi, M. (2013). A methodology to evaluate the competitiveness of electric delivery trucks. *Transportation Research Part E: Logistics and Transportation Review,* 49(1), 8–23.

De Gennaro, M., Paffumi, E., Martini, G., and Scholz, H. (2014). A pilot study to address the travel behaviour and the usability of electric vehicles in two Italian provinces. *Case Studies on Transport Policy,* 2(3), 116–141.

Diesel Engine Exhaust Carcinogenic. (2012). International Agency for Research on Cancer. Report [Online]. https://www.iarc.fr/wp-content/uploads/2018/07/pr213_E.pdf. Accessed January 31, 2019.

Ecotricity. (2016). Ecotricity Charging Stations [Online]. https://www.ecotricity.co.uk/for-the-road. Accessed January 15, 2017.

Electric Car Market Statistics. (2018). Plug in hybrid guide [Online]. https://www. nextgreencar.com/plugin-hybrid-cars/buying-guide/. Accessed January 15, 2019.

Energy Trends. (2019). UK Government. Report [Online]. https://www.gov.uk/government/ statistics/total-energy-section-1-energy-trends. Accessed January 31, 2019.

EV Auxiliary Systems Impact. (2018). EV Auxiliary Systems Impact. Report, Idaho National Laboratory, Clean Energy & Transportation [Online]. https://avt.inl.gov/sites/default/ files/pdf/fsev/auxiliary.pdf. Accessed March 10, 2019.

Fiori, C, Ahn, K., and Rakha, H. (2016). Power-based electric vehicle energy consumption model: model development and validation. *Applied Energy,* 168, 257–268.

Goeke, D. and Schneider, M. (2014). Routing a mixed fleet of electric and conventional vehicles. Technical Report, Darmstadt Technical University, Department of Business Administration, Economics and Law, Institute for Business Studies (BWL).

Gong, H., Linn, W., Clark, K., Anderson, K., Geller, M., and Sioutas, C. (2005). Respiratory responses to exposures with fine particulates and nitrogen dioxide in the elderly with and without COPD. *Inhalation Toxicology,* 17(3) 123–132.

Graham-Rowe, E., Gardner, B., Abraham, C., Skippon, S., Dittmar, H., Hutchins, R., and Stannard, J. (2012). Mainstream consumers driving plug-in battery-electric and plug-in hybrid electric cars: a quantitative analysis of responses and evaluations. *Transportation Research Part A: Policy and Practice*, 46(1), 140–153.

Great, B. (2014). Road traffic estimates. Report, UK Government [Online]. https://www.gov.uk/government/statistics/road-traffic-estimates-in-great-britain-2014. Accessed June 4, 2016.

Gridwatch. (2019). G.B. National Grid Status [Online]. https://www.gridwatch.templar.co.uk. Accessed March 6, 2017.

International Energy Agency. (2017). CO_2 emissions from fuel combustion [Online]. https://www.iea.org/publications/freepublications/publication/CO2EmissionsfromFuelCombustionHighlights2017.pdf. Accessed January 30, 2019.

International Energy Agency. (2019). Energy storage [Online]. https://www.iea.org/tcep/energyintegration/energystorage/. Accessed January 30, 2019.

JEC. (2011). Well-to-wheels, Appendix 2, WTW GHG Emissions of Externally Chargeable Electric Vehicles. Report, JEC (Joint Research Centre – EUCAR – CONCAWE Collaboration) [Online]. http://iet.jrc.ec.europa.eu/about-jec/sites/iet.jrc.ec.europa.eu.aboutjec/files/documents/wtw3_wtw_appendix2_eurformat.pdf. Accessed October 20, 2018.

Jin, L., Searle, S., and Lutsey, N. (2014). Evaluation of state-level US electric vehicle incentives. Report, The International Council on Clean Transportation.

Jung, H. and Li, C. (2018). Emissions from plug-in hybrid electric vehicle (PHEV) during real world driving under various conditions. Report, University of California, Riverside, Centre for Environmental Research and Technology.

Khan, S. (2018). Strategy for the future of London's transport. Report. UK Government [Online]. https://www.london.gov.uk/press-releases/mayoral/strategy-for-the-future-of-londons-transport. Accessed November 16, 2018.

Keskin, M. and Çatay, B. (2016). Partial recharge strategies for the electric vehicle routing problem with time windows. *Transportation Research Part C: Emerging Technologies*, 65, 111–127.

Lukic, S. and Pantic, Z. (2013). Cutting the cord: static and dynamic inductive wireless charging of electric vehicles. *IEEE Electrification Magazine*, 1(1), 57–64.

Mathiesen, K. and Neslen, A. (2015). VW scandal caused nearly 1m tonnes of extra pollution, analysis shows [Online]. https://www.theguardian.com/business/2015/sep/22/vw-scandal-caused-nearly-1m-tonnes-of-extra-pollution-analysis-shows. Accessed August 15, 2016.

Mitsubishi. (2016). Mitsubishi UK. Report [Online]. https://www.mitsubishi-cars.co.uk/new-cars/outlander/phev/. Accessed July 17, 2017.

Mock, P. and Yang, Z. (2014). Driving electrification. A global comparison of fiscal incentive policy for electric vehicles. Report, International Council on Clean Transportation.

NASA. (2010). Ultracapacitors technology [Online]. https://technology.nasa.gov/patent/ MFS-TOPS-76. Accessed December 21, 2018.

New Car CO_2 Report. (2018). Society of Motor Manufacturers and Traders. Report [Online]. https://www.smmt.co.uk/wp-content/uploads/sites/2/SMMT-New-Car-Co2-Report-2018-artwork.pdf. Accessed January 31, 2019.

New Vehicle Registrations. (2018). Society of motor manufacturers and traders [Online]. https://www.smmt.co.uk/category/news/registrations/. Accessed January 15, 2019.

NHS. (2019). Carbon monoxide poisoning. Report [Online]. https://www.nhs.uk/conditions/ carbon-monoxide-poisoning/. Accessed January 31, 2019.

Nissan Leaf Specs. (2016). Argonne National Laboratory [Online]. http://www.anl.gov/ energy-systems/group/downloadable-dynamometer-database/electric-vehicles/2012-nissan-leaf. Accessed July 9, 2016.

Nissan News. (2017). Nissan [Online]. https://uk.nissannews.com/en-GB/releases/release-426191418. Accessed November 30, 2019.

Nissan UK. (2016). New vehicle pricings [Online]. https://www.nissan.co.uk. Accessed October 30, 2016.

Nykvist, B. and Nilsson, M. (2015). The EV paradox – a multilevel study of why Stockholm is not a leader in electric vehicles. *Environmental Innovation and Societal Transitions*, 14, 26–44.

Onewedge. (2018). An EV taxonomy [Online]. https://onewedge.com/2018/02/19/an-ev-taxonomy/. Accessed January 30, 2019.

Prasad, R. and Bella, V. R. (2010). A review on diesel soot emission, its effect and control. *Bulletin of Chemical Reaction Engineering & Catalysis*, 5(2), 69–86.

2018 Progress Report to Parliament Committee on Climate Change. (2018). Reducing UK emissions – 2018 progress report to Parliament. Report, Committee on Climate Change [Online]. https://www.theccc.org.uk/comingup/ccc-report-2018-progress-report-parliament. Accessed February 3, 2019.

Rambaldi, L., Bocci, E., and Orecchini, F. (2011). Preliminary experimental evaluation of a four wheel motors, batteries plus ultracapacitors and series hybrid powertrain. *Applied Energy*, 88(2), 442–448.

Renewable Energy Foundation (REF) (2019). [Online]. https://www.ref.org.uk/energy-data. Accessed March 20, 2019.

Reis, H., Reis, C., Sharip, A., Reis, W., Zhao, Y., Sinclair, R., and Beeson, L. (2018). Diesel exhaust exposure, its multi-system effects, and the effect of new technology diesel exhaust. *Environment International*, 114, 252–265.

Road Transport and Environment. (2016). UK Government. Report [Online]. https://www.gov.uk/transport/road-transport-and-the-environment. Accessed February 16, 2017.

Rückerl, R., Greven, S., Ljungman, P., Aalto, P., Antoniades, C., Bellander, T., Berglind, N., Chrysohoou, C., Forastiere, F., Jacquemin, B., von Klot, S., Koenig, W., Küchenhoff, H., Lanki, T., Pekkanen, J., Perucci, C. A., Schneider, A., Sunyer, J., and Peters, A. (2007). Air pollution and inflammation (interleukin-6, C-reactive protein, fibrinogen) in myocardial infarction survivors. *Environmental Health Perspectives*, 115(7), 1072–1080.

Saxena, S., Le Floch, C., MacDonald, J., and Moura, S. (2015). Quantifying EV battery end-of-life through analysis of travel needs with vehicle powertrain models. *Journal of Power Sources*, 282, 265–276.

Schönewolf, W. (2011, October 25). E-City-Logistik. *Status-Seminar Elektromobilität BerlinBrandenburg*, Berlin.

Su, Y. C., Beom, W. G., Seog, Y. J., and Chun, T. R. (2015). Advances in wireless power transfer systems for roadway-powered electric vehicles. *IEEE Journal of Emerging and Selected Topics in Power Electronics*, 3(1), 18–36.

Suh, I. S. (2011). Intelligent wireless EV fast charging with SMFIR technology. *Journal of Integrated Design and Process Science*, 15(3), 3–12.

Sumper, A. and Baggini, A. (2012). *Electrical Energy Efficiency: Technologies and Applications*. ISTE Ltd, London and Wiley, New York.

Sydborn, A., Blomberg, A., Parnia, S., Stenfors, N., Sandstrom, T., and Dahien, S.-E. (2001). Health effects of diesel exhaust emissions. *European Respiratory Journal*, 17, 733–746.

Ultra Low Emission Zone (ULEZ). (2018). Report. Transport for London [Online]. https://tfl.gov.uk/modes/driving/ultra-low-emission-zone. Accessed December 4, 2018.

ULEV in the UK. (2015). UK Government [Online]. https://assets.publishing.service.gov.uk/government/uploads/system/uploads/attachment_data/file/464763/uptake-of-ulev-uk.pdf. Accessed January 10, 2019.

UK GOV. (2016). Government provisional emission statistics. Report, UK Government [Online]. https://www.gov.uk/government/publications/2010-to-2015government-policy-greenhouse-gas-emissions/2010-to-2015-government-policygreenhouse-gas-emissions. Accessed December 2, 2016.

UK GOV. (2017). Fuel mix disclosure tables. Report, UK Government [Online]. https://www.gov.uk/government/collections/fuel-mix-disclosure-data-tables. Accessed February 5, 2019.

US Department of Energy. (2016). Cost and price metrics for automotive lithium-ion batteries. Report, US Department of Energy [Online]. https://www.energy.gov/sites/prod/files/2017/02/f34/67089%20EERE%20LIB%20cost%20vs%20price%20metrics%20r9.pdf. Accessed May 24, 2017.

World Nuclear. (2018). Nuclear power in the UK [Online]. http://www.world-nuclear.org/information-library/country-profiles/countries-t-z/united-kingdom.aspx. Accessed January 20, 2019.

Yang, J. and Sun, H. (2015). Battery swap station location-routing problem with capacitated electric vehicles. *Computers & Operations Research*, 55, 217–232.

Zap-Map. (2019). Charging location statistics [Online]. https://www.zap-map.com/statistics/ #region. Accessed January 10, 2019.

Zheng, Y., Dong, Z. Y., Xu, Y., Meng, K., Zhao, J. H., and Qiu, J. (2013). Electric vehicle battery charging/swap stations in distribution systems: comparison study and optimal planning. *IEEE Transactions on Power Systems*, 29(1), 221–229.

Zhou, X., Young, K., West, J., Regalado, J., and Cherisol, K. (2013). Degradation mechanisms of high-energy bipolar nickel metal hydride battery with AB5 and A2B7 alloys. *Journal of Alloys and Compounds*, 580, S373–S377.

3

Transport Pooling: Moving Toward Green Distribution

Supply chain pooling is a powerful strategy used to improve the profits and performance of the supply chain. From this perspective, the pooling of shipments has been highlighted and recently studied in several publications. In this context, this chapter attempts to, first, present a general framework for logistical sharing and collaboration and, second, to present a review of the literature in order to follow how these concepts are applied. Subsequently, in the case of distribution in urban and interurban environments, a conceptual framework modeling transport pooling is presented through various scenarios. Finally, we end with an analysis of the proposed scenarios in terms of minimizing the distances traveled and greenhouse gas (GHG) emissions. Consequently, this work allows those people who make use of pooling to choose the most appropriate scenario while pooling resources in order to reduce GHG emissions.

3.1. Introduction

Some logistics activities contribute to congestion, pollution, and wasting of resources. These activities can affect delivery efficiency, mobility, the environment, and human health. This explains the need to develop other strategies in order to create new and more efficient logistics systems such as collaborative logistics. In this case, the shared supply chain is proving to be a useful choice for producers and logistics service providers to improve their economic and environmental performances.

In addition to the traditional objectives of efficiency and control of the supply chain, there are now challenges in terms of CSR (corporate social responsibility) and sustainable development (Chay *et al.* 2013). To achieve these objectives,

---

Chapter written by Alaeddine ZOUARI.

entrepreneurs must move toward new inter-organizational configurations, such as logistics pooling, in order to optimize their pooled material resources (warehouses and means of transport) through the appropriate selection of a scenario that minimizes transport and storage costs in addition to the volume of GHG emissions. In order to consolidate the successful pooling of transport, interested parties should share and exchange data and information to facilitate the implementation of this concept (Lundqvist 2018).

In order to improve economic performance while maintaining social and environmental objectives, different forms and approaches to logistics pooling have been studied in several publications, such as collaborative urban transportation (Cleophas *et al.* 2019), collaborative transportation management (Okdinawati *et al.* 2015), collaborative transport planning (Wang and Kopfer 2014), collaborative transport between terminals (Gharehgozli *et al.* 2017), pooled transport for children with disabilities (Tellez *et al.* 2016), pooling of last-mile delivery (Liakos and Delis 2015), collaborative air traffic flow management (Murça 2018), and collaborative intermodal transport (Liu *et al.* 2019).

Transport pooling allows partners to benefit from several advantages that lead to green and sustainable transport, integrating sustainable development objectives (Moutaoukil *et al.* 2013). At the economic level, we can mention the following: the lowering of logistical costs, carbon taxes, and fuel costs (Guajardo and Rönnqvist 2016; Wang *et al.* 2017). At the ecological level, it is worth mentioning the following: the simultaneous lowering of GHG emissions, noise, the exploitation of natural resources (energy), the encouragement of recycling, and waste processing (Alvarez *et al.* 2018; Niu and Li 2019; Ntziachristos *et al.* 2016; Senkel *et al.* 2013). At the societal level, we can consider the following: the expectations of various stakeholders, establishing a culture of sharing (Wang *et al.* 2018), minimizing stress for drivers – less congestion (Gonzalez-Feliu and Battaia 2017; Hensher 2018) – and saving time (Ghaderi *et al.* 2016; Moutaoukil *et al.* 2015).

In this context, a literature review will be presented to highlight the techniques of collaboration, pooling, and resource sharing, in addition to their benefits for goods-producing companies. Furthermore, a suggestion of seven scenarios for pooling between a set of three companies is discussed. This is done in the urban and interurban distribution phases in order to optimize resources and minimize the distances traveled. As a result, we achieve reductions in transportation costs, congestion, and GHG emissions. In addition, the study continues through the analysis of the presented scenarios in order to choose the optimal path by showing the challenges and opportunities of this pooling.

3.2. Concepts of collaborative logistics

3.2.1. *Definitions and issues*

The definition of collaborative logistics is difficult to define, given that it differs from one case to another. According to Cao and Zhang (2010), supply chain collaboration refers to the ability of two or more autonomous companies to work effectively together, plan, and execute supply chain operations in order to achieve common objectives. In addition, Moutaoukil *et al.* (2012) added that pooling is mainly about bringing together efforts to achieve a mutual objective. Thus, independent companies work together to reduce their operating costs and increase their revenues. On the other hand, Moharana *et al.* (2012) have stipulated that collaboration is a common interactive process that translates into joint decisions and activities, and their joint implementation can be considered as a team effort.

Rakotonarivo *et al.* (2009) identified four main stages of collaboration: transactional, informational, decision-making, and strategic. In addition, Rajaaa and Ibnoulkatib (2019) have identified four urban logistics issues:

– functional issues: planning cities to meet traffic needs;

– economic issues: increasing the size of the market;

– urban issues: movement of goods in the city and location of these platforms;

– environmental issues: corporate social responsibility in terms of environmental protection.

However, Chanut and Paché (2013) added that societal issues are also important for preserving the living conditions of future generations, preventing them from being faced with a hostile, polluted, and vehicle-saturated environment. In this social perspective of the sustainability of urban distribution, Wang *et al.* (2018) proposed a prototype platform for the integration of collaborative and social urban distribution, the objective of which is flexible coordination between the operators described in the crowdsourcing and sharing economy. They stipulate that this open integrated platform gives participants (customers, vendors, suppliers, logistics service providers, and the general public) several advantages. In general, collaboration can be applied in terms of the design (Gonzalez-Feliu *et al.* 2013), planning and execution of work (Tornberg and Odhage 2018), decisions (Perboli *et al.* 2016), research and development (Bustinza *et al.* 2019), risk management (Chen *et al.* 2013), and so on. It reduces the cost of transport and storage, in addition to allowing significant economic gains. Collaboration thus allows companies to be agile and resilient (Camarinha-Matos 2014).

3.2.2. *Forms of logistical collaboration*

Companies are currently seeking to create synergies with other organizations and create value chains through horizontal and/or vertical collaboration with logistics partners.

3.2.2.1. *Horizontal collaboration*

In logistics, horizontal collaboration consists of a collaboration between operators at the same level (between suppliers, manufacturers, distributors, etc.) in a supply network. Vanovermeire *et al.* (2013) declared that horizontal collaboration can be defined as the grouping of transport companies which operate at the same level of the supply chain, and which have similar or complementary transport needs. It is also a collaboration between a group of stakeholders from different supply chains, acting at the same levels and with similar needs (Gonzalez-Feliu *et al.* 2013).

According to McKinnon and Edwards (2010), horizontal collaboration overcomes financial and commercial barriers and benefits society by reducing the number of vehicles and, therefore, CO_2 emissions and congestion. It also reduces prices due to bulk purchasing, reduces supply risks, reduces administrative costs due to centralized purchasing activities, and also reduces inventory, transport, and logistics costs and facilities. All these benefits are achieved through a rationalization of the use of equipment and better sharing of human labor and information (Bahinipati *et al.* 2009).

3.2.2.2. *Vertical collaboration*

Vertical collaboration occurs between partners operating in different levels of the logistics network, where the benefits of collaboration include lower supply costs due to the synchronization effect through information sharing (Moutaoukil *et al.* 2012). In this regard, Fernandez *et al.* (2016) have stated that vertical collaboration is proposed when shippers and customers collaborate on their objectives. This concept is used to develop long-term relationships, as well as loyalty and commitment. Sharing information and technology in the vertical supply relationship is a crucial factor in supply chain efficiency.

Successful models can cross these two areas of collaboration (Figure 3.1). Cases of vertical collaboration mainly focus on the exchange of information between entities and involve members of the same value chain (industrial and distributor). However, most cases of horizontal collaboration focus on the pooling of resources or structures with the aim of expanding flows, which involves companies that can provide complementary goods or services, whether they are competing or not (among several manufacturers).

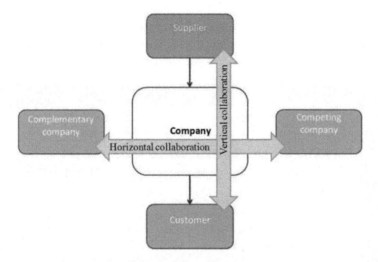

Figure 3.1. *Types of logistical collaboration (Destouches and Gaide 2011).*
For a color version of this figure, see www.iste.co.uk/besbes/transport.zip

However, in practice, logistics pooling presents certain obstacles that discourage logistics service providers from applying it. Abbad (2014) and Abbad *et al.* (2016) have identified the obstacles to horizontal pooling, which relate to storage activities, transport activities, and the specifics of the context studied:

– The obstacles to the pooling of goods storage: nature of products, location of operators, sharing of information, logistics services, and so on.

– The obstacles to the pooling of transportation of goods: compatibility of goods, proximity of delivery of goods, and so on.

– Cultural barriers related to certain practices.

However, several positive effects of a shared management of supplies, which are related to these obstacles, have been identified from three perspectives in a global manner or for distributors and manufacturers alone:

– Global: reduction of transport costs, reduction of GHG emissions, standardization of processes and organizations, and so on.

– Distributors: increase in delivery frequency, increase in service rate, and decrease in required stock levels.

– Industrial: pooling of logistical costs and better management of the marketing of new products, seasonal products, and promotions.

In the same perspective, Chanut *et al.* (2010) presented several aspects of motivations and obstacles that are related to vertical and horizontal pooling: see Table 3.1.

	Motivations	Obstacles
Vertical sharing	– Competitive advantage – Source of power – Ownership and stock management – Number of suppliers/references	– Network size – Financial constraints – Efficient upstream logistics organization by supplier
Horizontal sharing	– Competitive advantage – Optimization of logistics platforms – Capital connections – Regulatory constraints – Societal pressure and collective objectives	– Reluctance to share data between competing companies – Reactions from independent distributors

Table 3.1. *Motivations and obstacles of logistics pooling, inspired by Chanut* et al. *(2010)*

3.3. Pooling of physical flows between organizations

Logistics pooling corresponds to co-design between partners (suppliers, customers, transporters, etc.) with the common objective of a logistics network of pooled resources (warehouses, platforms, means of transport, etc.), in order to share these networks with the data needed for management. By seeking a common objective and with the proximity of facilities, pooling is adapted for supply chains that operate in the same sectors (Pan *et al.* 2013). This co-design results in a shared network logistics where the different entities jointly share and manage their skills, structures (distribution warehouses, offices, etc.), and resources (handling equipment, transport vehicles, information systems, etc.). This is why Ballot and Fontane (2008) have considered pooling as a form of horizontal collaboration.

There are several types of pooling, including, for example, the pooling of resources. Thus, resource pooling is the cooperation and beneficiation between the different partners in a supply chain. It is possible to talk about the resources developed by the shared partners, the disposition of work tools, resources, collaboration tools, and so on (Hadj Taieb *et al.* 2014). The pooling of physical flows can be mentioned here. Indeed, the pooling of resources allows the sharing of resources and methods in terms of improving quality and reducing costs. It guarantees a better functioning of the management of different operations. In order to assess this pooling, two criteria can be used. The first is the economic criterion (costs of transport, transfer platform, storage, etc.) and the second is the environmental criterion (greenhouse gas emissions, congestion, noise, pollution, etc.) (Zouari and Cherif 2018).

3.4. Literature review

3.4.1. *Choice of articles*

The concepts of pooling and logistical collaboration in distribution are still poorly developed in the literature. In this context, we have focused on 28 studies that have looked at these two concepts and are being published in the period of 2010–2019. The works mentioned in Table 3.2 are selected after an analysis of about 100 articles published in the *ScienceDirect* and *Google Scholar* databases in the period mentioned above. For the choice of the articles treated, the filtering is done according to the title; in other words, the articles are structured around collaborative distribution. The study of these articles consists of identifying the knowledge bases and methods of analysis that have led to the validation of certain benefits and opportunities (one or more at a time) that have been obtained through the pooling of the distribution of goods, related to the pillars of sustainable development.

Authors	Methods	Opportunities
Cao and Zhang (2010)	- Hypothesis - CFA; SEM	- Improving financial performance
Pan (2010)	- Scenarios and hypotheses - Linear programming	- Minimization of CO_2 emissions - Minimization of logistics costs
Chan and Zhang (2011)	- Scenarios - Simulation	- Improving transporter flexibility - Reduction of total cost
Gonzalez-Feliu (2011)	- Scenarios - Simulation - Semi-greedy algorithm	- Reduction in road occupancy rates - Reduction of total cost - Reduction of travel times - Reduction of GHG emissions and noise

Authors	Methods	Opportunities
Qiu and Huang (2011)	- Mathematical models - Simulation - Analysis of variance	- Reduction of the total cost of the supply chain
Ghaderi *et al.* (2012)	- Questionnaire - Hypotheses - Analysis of variance	- Reduction of transport costs
Gonzalez-Feliu and Salanova (2012)	- Scenarios - Simulation - FRETURB model - TMS model	- Reduction of transport costs - Reduction of road occupancy rates - Reduction of GHG emissions - Risk reduction
Thompson and Hassall (2012)	- Scenarios - Simulation - Calculation	- Reduction of costs - Reduced distances traveled - Reduction in the number of vehicles
Chen *et al.* (2013)	- Questionnaire and hypotheses - CFA, SEM	- Reduction of SC risks - Improvement of operational performance
Gonzalez-Feliu *et al.* (2013)	- Scenarios and simulation - Fast heuristic algorithm - Non-hierarchical clustering method - Semi-greedy algorithm	- Reduction of costs - Reduction of travel times - Reduction of distances traveled
Moutaoukil *et al.* (2013)	- Scenarios	- Minimization of costs - Minimization of CO_2 emissions - Minimization of accident risks
Pan *et al.* (2013)	- Linear programming	- Reduction of GHG emissions
Senkel *et al.* (2013)	- Analysis of 10 industrial cases	- Reduction of costs - Increase in the filling rate - Reduction of GHG emissions - Customer satisfaction

Authors	Methods	Opportunities
Vanovermeire *et al.* (2013)	- Scenarios - Shapley value	- Reduction of transport costs
Abbad (2014)	- Professional press review	- Reduction of storage and transport costs - Reduction of GHG emissions - Superior responsiveness - Better customer service
Danloup *et al.* (2015)	- Scenarios - Simulation - Linear programming	- Reduction of transport costs - Reduction of GHG emissions
Muñoz-Villamizar *et al.* (2015)	- Scenarios - Linear programming	- Reduction of transport costs - Reduction of road occupancy - Reduction of CO_2 emissions
Perez-Bernabeu *et al.* 2015)	- Scenarios - Algorithm - Java application	- Reduction of distribution cost - Reduction of GHG emissions - Reduction of delivery times
Perboli *et al.* (2016)	- ERP "Odoo" - Optimization algorithm	- Reduction of CO_2 emissions
Sanchez *et al.* (2016)	- Metaheuristic clustering - Shapley value	- Reduction of carbon footprint - Improving economic gains
Gonzalez-Feliu and Battaia (2017)	- Scenarios - Simulation - Mathematical models	- Reduction of total cost - Reduction of road occupancy
Wang *et al.* (2017)	- Clustering - Dynamic programming - Heuristic algorithm - Shapley value	- Reduction of total cost
Silbermayr *et al.* (2017)	- Scenarios - Optimization - Mathematical models	- Environmental performance - Economic performance

Authors	Methods	Opportunities
Abbassi *et al.* (2018)	- Scenarios - Metaheuristic (annealing algorithm)	- Reduction of total cost - Reduction of time - Reduction of the number of trips
Alvarez *et al.* (2018)	- Questionnaire - Statistical analysis	- Pollution - Congestion
Zissis *et al.* (2018)	- Simulation - Mathematical models	- Reduction of time - Reduction of carbon emissions
Wang *et al.* (2019)	- Scenarios - Multi-objective optimization of Pareto	- Reduction of carbon emissions - Reduction of costs - Reduction of time
Junior *et al.* (2019)	- Scenarios - Multi-agent simulation	- Reduction of costs - Responsiveness to dynamic events

Table 3.2. *Summary of research work on logistics pooling*

3.4.2. *Analysis and discussion of the results*

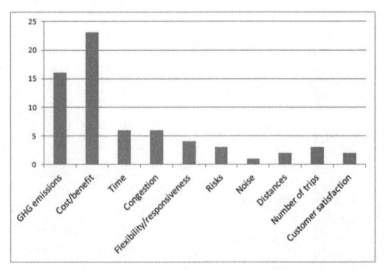

Figure 3.2. *Opportunities for transport pooling*

Logistics pooling is one of the strategies used to improve competitiveness and bring benefits to all stakeholders. Based on the results of the articles studied, we can see the rarity of articles dealing with purely vertical collaboration on one side, and on the other, we can see that the majority of articles refer either to horizontal collaboration or to integrated horizontal and vertical collaborations. Figure 3.2 shows the opportunities for transport pooling.

The pooling of transport has a positive effect on:

– Economic performance: through cost reduction, financial gains by 82%, logistics time reduction by 21%, and improved flexibility and responsiveness of transporters by 14%.

– Environmental performance: through the reduction of GHG emissions by 57%, road congestion and occupation by 21%, and noise.

– Social and societal responsibility: through the reduction of risks by 11%, the number of trips by 11%, the improvement of customer satisfaction by 7%, and the reduction of distances traveled by 7%.

It should be noted that the majority of articles mainly focus on economic gain and/or GHG reduction, but with less intensity on the social and societal sides. However, among these opportunities, several have a strong interaction and can have effects on all three aspects of sustainability:

– GHG emissions can be related to economic performance (CO_2 tax, fuel costs, etc.). Similarly, reducing it is part of social responsibility (smog, health of residents, etc.).

– Congestion increases GHG emissions, noise, time loss, fuel consumption, driver stress, customer dissatisfaction in the event of delays, accident risks, and so on.

– Reducing distances and the number of trips leads to a reduction in fuel consumption, GHG emissions, and costs, saved time, better use of resources (less depreciation of trucks), better working conditions for drivers, and so on.

It can, therefore, be deduced that pooling and logistical collaboration make it possible to:

– reduce logistics costs;

– reduce GHG emissions;

– reduce logistics times;

– reduce congestion;

– improve the flexibility and responsiveness of transporters;

– reduce risks;

– optimize the use of resources (number of trucks, distances traveled, loading, etc.).

At present, manufacturers are aware of the importance of optimizing their supply chain. This optimization is based on an economic approach, which is manifested through the integration of economic, environmental, and social concerns, which in turn are in line with the objectives of sustainable development. Thus, the environmental and societal degradation that goes hand in hand with economic development calls for serious action by all stakeholders, including regulators such as government, industry operators, and consumers.

In this context, the literature review shows that the majority of authors used scenarios as the initial source of knowledge for their analysis, with a rate of 57%. However, other sources are also used, such as hypotheses, questionnaires, and empirical data. In order to analyze the initial knowledge, the authors used a variety of tools and methods (both accurate or approximate). This majority opted for simulation in order to validate their basic proposal, with a rate of 35%. Figure 3.3 shows the methods based on mathematical models such as statistical analysis, linear programming, and heuristics/metaheuristics with a rate of 18% each. Similarly, Shapley optimization and values were also used with a rate of about 11% each.

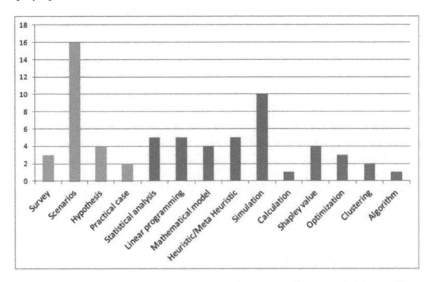

Figure 3.3. *Analysis tools and methods used. For a color version of this figure, see www.iste.co.uk/besbes/transport.zip*

In most of the articles on how to deal with problems, the most notable approach is to first propose scenarios and validate them, and then to use a single analytical method such as simulation (Chan and Zhang 2011; Junior *et al.* 2019; Thompson and Hassall 2012), linear programming (Muñoz-Villamizar *et al.* 2015; Pan 2010), metaheuristics (Abbassi *et al.* 2018), the Shapley value (Vanovermeire *et al.* 2013), optimization (Wang *et al.* 2019), and the algorithm (Perez-Bernabeu *et al.* 2015); or two methods, such as the mathematical model/simulation (Gonzalez-Feliu and Battaia 2017; Gonzalez-Feliu and Salanova 2012), metaheuristics/simulation (Gonzalez-Feliu 2011), linear programming/simulation (Danloup *et al.* 2015), and mathematical model/optimization (Silbermayr *et al.* 2017). On the other hand, Gonzalez-Feliu *et al.* (2013) used three methods to analyze the scenarios they proposed: namely, metaheuristics, clustering, and the Shapley value. In addition, some other authors adopted questionnaires and/or hypotheses and validated them with statistical analysis (Alvarez *et al.* 2018; Cao and Zhang 2010; Chen *et al.* 2013; Ghaderi *et al.* 2012).

3.5. Proposal of pooling scenarios for the urban distribution of goods

Pooling in the distribution phase consists of bringing together means of transport, warehouses, distribution centers, and, of course, information. Before focusing on pooling scenarios, we will emphasize on a scenario where companies do not use this technique: see Figure 3.4.

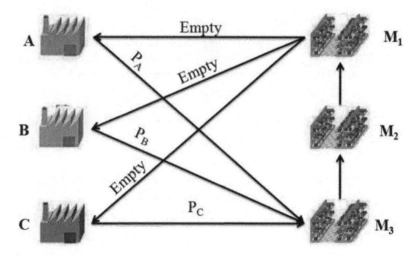

Figure 3.4. *Scenario 0 without urban pooling. For a color version of this figure, see www.iste.co.uk/besbes/transport.zip*

The scenarios are based on the following assumptions:

– The trucks used have a maximum load of 3 and 9 tons.

– The demand is equal to the supply. The three manufacturers each supply 1 ton of their product to each of the three customers.

– The trajectories are recorded for the round trip (loaded truck)/(empty truck).

In scenario 0 (Figure 3.4), each manufacturer distributes 3 tons of its product with its own 3-ton truck. They make a trip to deliver a ton of product to each customer.

In scenario 1 (Figure 3.5), each manufacturer uses its own vehicle to transport the products to the transfer hub, where the three manufacturers exchange their products so that each truck is loaded with one ton of each type of product. A forklift truck ensures the transfer of products between the three trucks in seven operations, as shown in Figure 3.6. Each truck delivers its load to one of the three customers and returns to the owner company, either through the hub (S1) or through the shortest route (S1a).

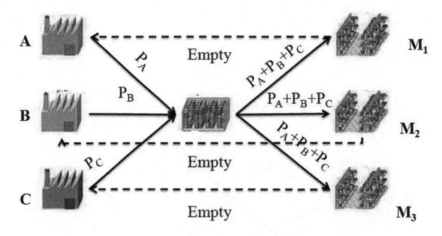

Figure 3.5. *Scenario 1 of urban pooling. For a color version of this figure, see www.iste.co.uk/besbes/transport.zip*

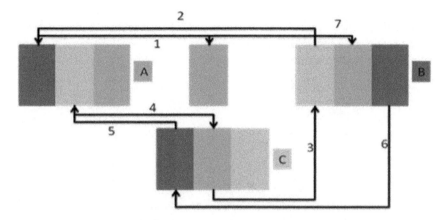

Figure 3.6. *Exchange of products in the warehouse. For a color version of this figure, see www.iste.co.uk/besbes/transport.zip*

In scenario 2 (Figure 3.7), as in scenario 1, each manufacturer uses its own 3-ton truck to transport its product to the warehouse. Subsequently, the distribution of different types of products is done in the form of a tour. The tour can either be done with a single rented 9-ton truck (S2a) or with three trucks, after having exchanged products with each other (S2).

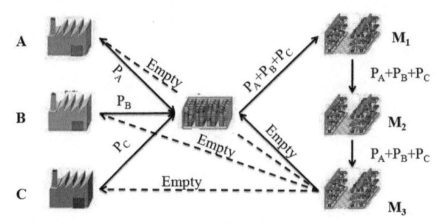

Figure 3.7. *Scenario 2 of urban pooling. For a color version of this figure, see www.iste.co.uk/besbes/transport.zip*

Scenario 3 (Figure 3.8) relates to the pooling of information and physical flows. Transport to the warehouse is done with a single vehicle, in the form of a tour. The warehouse then supplies each of the customers using a different vehicle. Therefore, in order to supply the hub with 3 tons of each product, either a 3-ton truck is used in three tours (S3) or a 9-ton truck is used in a single tour (S3a).

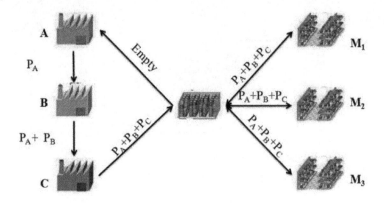

Figure 3.8. *Scenario 3 of urban pooling. For a color version of this figure, see www.iste.co.uk/besbes/transport.zip*

In scenario 4 (S4), as shown in Figure 3.9, company B is used as a consolidation center: all products are gathered in this center. A forklift performs the transfer (Figure 3.10), loading the three trucks with 1 ton of each product. Each truck loaded with the three types of product serves a different customer and returns empty to the owner company.

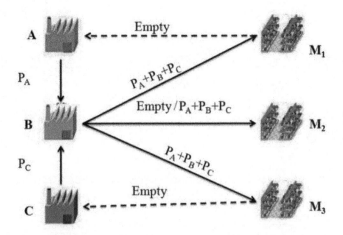

Figure 3.9. *Scenario 4 of urban pooling. For a color version of this figure, see www.iste.co.uk/besbes/transport.zip*

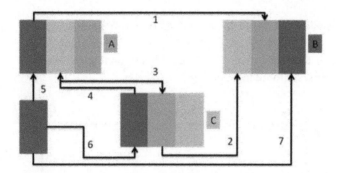

Figure 3.10. *Transfer of products to B. For a color version of this figure,*
see www.iste.co.uk/besbes/transport.zip

As in scenario 4, Company B is used as a consolidation center for scenario 5: see Figure 3.11.

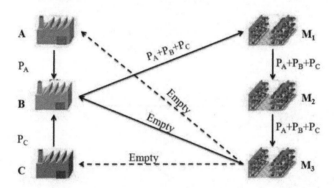

Figure 3.11. *Scenario 5 of urban pooling. For a color version of this figure,*
see www.iste.co.uk/besbes/transport.zip

In this case, the first part is similar to scenario 4, but the distribution of the different products to customers' stores is done in the form of tours, either using three 3-ton trucks, one from each company, (S5) or a 9-ton truck from company B (S5a). In the first case, the loading/unloading is similar to scenario 4, whereas in the second case, the forklift unloads the two trucks from A and C into the 9-ton truck and completes the load with 3 tons of product B.

Scenario 6 (Figure 3.12) involves making tours between manufacturers and customers. A 3-ton truck is supplied with one-third of its capacity each time it passes through a manufacturer. This truck continues its tour to the customers in order to deliver one-third of its load of A, B, and C products to each customer. In this case, either three tours are made with a single 3-ton truck or three 3-ton trucks (S6) are used. The tour can also be done with a 9-ton truck (S6a). Like in scenario 3, this scenario uses information pooling.

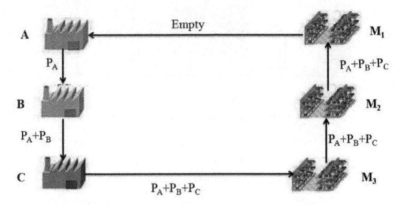

Figure 3.12. *Scenario 6 of urban pooling. For a color version of this figure, see www.iste.co.uk/besbes/transport.zip*

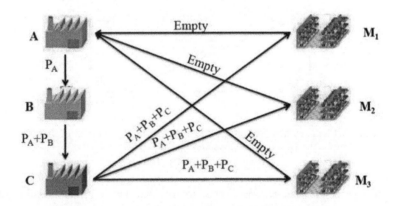

Figure 3.13. *Scenario 7 of urban pooling. For a color version of this figure, see www.iste.co.uk/besbes/transport.zip*

In scenario 7 (S7), as shown in Figure 3.13, the three 3-ton trucks leave from company A to C while passing through company B. At each company, they supply themselves with one-third of their loads with a type of product. Each truck then supplies a customer and returns to company A.

3.6. Comparison of scenarios

Now that these scenarios have been discussed, we can choose the best one based on the distance traveled by the vehiclês. The shorter the distance, the lower the cost of transportation and GHG emissions. In addition, the lower the number of trucks used, the lower the congestion and the higher the truck operating rate will be.

3.6.1. *Distances traveled*

Figure 3.14 shows the distances between different organizations.

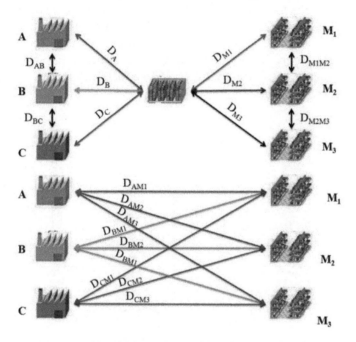

Figure 3.14. *Distances between different organizations. For a color version of this figure, see www.iste.co.uk/besbes/transport.zip*

For the rest of the study, we can consider the following assumptions:

– The companies and the warehouse use trucks with a capacity of 3 or 9 tons.

– Each manufacturer, A, B, and C, supplies 3 tons of its product (P_A, P_B, and P_C).

– Each customer, M_1, M_2, and M_3, receives 1 ton of each product type.

– D_i (i = A, B, C) is the distance between company i and the hub.

– D_{Mj} (j = 1, 2, 3) is the distance between the hub and customer M_j.

– D_{AB} is the distance between manufacturer A and manufacturer B.

– D_{BC} is the distance between manufacturer B and manufacturer C.

– D_{M1M2} is the distance between client M_1 and client M_2.

– D_{M2M3} is the distance between client M_2 and client M_3.

– D_{iMj} is the distance between company i and customer M_j.

To calculate the travel distances of the different scenarios, a Microsoft Excel spreadsheet is used, as shown in Figure 3.15. We simply enter the distances between organizations (Table 3.3) in order to get all the travel distances for the different scenarios, based on the shortest route, which can be determined by Google Maps. The results showed that each scenario could be the shortest route based on the distances between organizations.

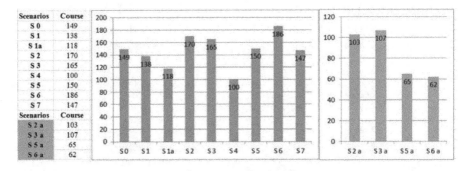

Figure 3.15. *Travel distances of the scenarios. For a color version of this figure, see www.iste.co.uk/besbes/transport.zip*

D_A	D_B	D_C	D_{M1}	D_{M2}	D_{M3}	D_{AB}	D_{BC}	D_{M1M2}	D_{M2M3}	D_{AM1}	D_{AM3}	D_{BM1}	D_{BM3}	D_{CM1}	D_{CM3}	D_{BM2}	D_{CM2}	D_{AM2}
10	12	8	15	10	14	7	4	8	6	18	20	15	14	21	19	12	16	20

Table 3.3. *Distances between organizations*

It is worth mentioning that in Figure 3.15, scenario S2 has the shortest route (96 km) when using 3-ton trucks. In addition, it should be noted that with 9-ton trucks, all scenarios (S2a, S3a, S5a, and S6a) are slower than that with 3-ton, and hence, scenario S6a is the shortest route.

3.6.2. *Greenhouse gas emissions*

To calculate the CO_2 equivalent $(EqCO_2)$ of exhaust emissions from trucks (CH4, Cox, etc.), the following formula is used:

$$EqCO_2 = Fem. Conso \qquad [3.1]$$

where *Fem* is the mean $EqCO_2$ emission factor for a diesel engine (kg/L) and *Conso* is the mean fuel consumption (L).

To calculate consumption (Conso), a recognized modeling that meets the standard BP X 30-323 (2015) is used, as shown by equation [3.2][1].

$$Conso = \frac{x}{100} \times \left[\left(\frac{2}{3} + \frac{1}{3} \left(\frac{Actual\ Load}{Useful\ Load} \right) \right) + empty\ return\ rate\ \times \frac{2}{3} \right] \times$$
$$Distance \qquad [3.2]$$

where (x) is the consumption of the full truck expressed in L/100 km, 2/3 of the consumption is related to the empty weight, and 1/3 of the consumption is related to the loaded weight.

The consumption (x) of a 3-ton truck is 15 L/100 km and that of the 9-ton truck is 25 L/100 km.

The *Fem* amounts to 2.662 $EqCO_2$/L of fuel (diesel)[2].

As for the calculation of the travel distances of the different scenarios, a Microsoft Excel spreadsheet is used to calculate the $EqCO_2$ for each scenario, keeping the same inter-organizational distances, as shown in Figure 3.16. The results show that scenario S4 is the least expensive despite the fact that it is neither the shortest nor the least polluting scenario.

---

1 EcoTransIT: Environmental Methodology and Data – May 2003.
2 *Comité Professionnel Du Pétrole* (CPDP), Newsletter no. 9501 from December 08, 2004.

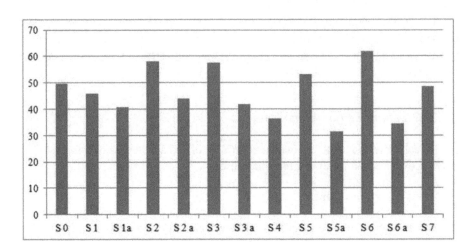

Figure 3.16. *EqCO$_2$ for the different scenarios*

3.6.3. *Distribution cost*

The distribution cost (*Ct Dist*) is determined on the basis of the transport cost and the handling cost (loading and unloading), as shown by equation [3.3]:

$$Ct\ Dist = Ct\ Tr + Ct\ Ch \tag{3.3}$$

The transport cost (*Ct Tr*) is calculated according to the distance of the journey traveled and the unit cost of the means of transport (3-ton or 9-ton truck, rented or not), as shown by equation [3.4].

$$Ct\ Tr = (journey\ C3T \times Ctu\ C3T) + (journey\ C9T \times Ctu\ C9T) + (journey\ Dist\ C3T \times Ctu\ Dist\ C3T) \tag{3.4}$$

where *journey C3T* is the course traveled by a 3-ton truck (km), *journey C9T* is the course traveled by a 9-ton truck (km), *journey Dist C3T* is the course traveled by a 3-ton truck from the distributor, *Ctu C3T* is the unit cost of transport by a 3-ton truck (DT/km), *Ctu C9T* is the unit cost of transport by a 9-ton truck (DT/km), and *Ctu Dist C3T* is the unit cost of transport by a 3-ton truck from the distributor (DT/km).

The cost of loading and unloading is a based on the amount that is loaded/unloaded and the relative time for loading and unloading a ton of product, in addition to the hourly cost of the handling equipment. The loading time (t Ch) is calculated by the following formula [3.5]:

$$t\ Ch = Nb\ Ch - D \times Charge\ C \times time\ Ch/T \qquad [3.5]$$

where Charge C is the number of tons loaded/unloaded, Nb Ch is the number of times that Charge C has been repeated, and time Ch/T is the loading time for 1 ton of product.

The loading cost (Ct Ch) is the product of the loading time and the hourly cost of the handling equipment (equation [3.6]).

$$Ct\ Ch = t\ Ch \times Ct\ Ch - D/h \qquad [3.6]$$

The equations are processed by an Excel sheet for the different scenarios, and the results are shown in Figure 3.17.

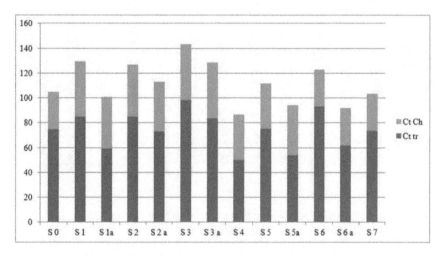

Figure 3.17. *Distribution costs for the different scenarios. For a color version of this figure, see www.iste.co.uk/besbes/transport.zip*

3.6.4. *Delivery time*

The delivery time (t Liv) is the sum of the transport times (ttr) and the loading time (t Ch), as shown by equation [3.7].

$$tLiv = \sum ttr + tCh \qquad [3.7]$$

where (t Ch) is the total loading/unloading time, as shown by equation [3.5], and $\sum ttr$ is the sum of transport times (ttr) without counting the returns, as shown by equation [3.8].

$$ttr = journey \times Vmoy \hfill [3.8]$$

where *journey* is the maximum distance of a 3-ton and/or 9-ton truck from the manufacturer to the customer without counting the return, and *Vmoy* is the mean speed (day or night) of a 3-ton and/or 9-ton truck.

On the Excel sheet, the equations are processed for the different scenarios. The results, which are presented in Figure 3.18, show that for the same inter-organizational distance setup as in the previous section, scenario S7 has the shortest delivery time with a duration of 4.28 h.

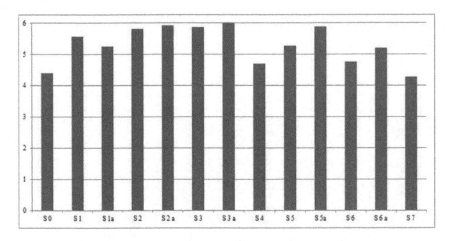

Figure 3.18. *Delivery times for the different scenarios*

3.6.5. *Best scenario*

With different Excel sheets, we have built a spreadsheet to calculate the values of different variables for all scenarios ($EqCO_2$), distribution cost, and delivery time). However, the variables have different units, which makes it quite difficult to choose the optimal scenario. In order to overcome this problem, we have opted to calculate ratios relating to each criterion. The ratio (Rat) is calculated using the relationship between the value found and the maximum value of the studied variable (in other words, for ($EqCO_2, Rat\ Eq\ COe = EQ\ CO2i\ /\ Max\ (EQ\ CO_21,.EQ\ CO_2n)$ and $i = 1$ to n). To this extent, the optimal scenario will be the one that has the minimum sum of the ratios of different variables, given that all variables are looking to be minimized. The results of the Excel sheet (as shown in Figure 3.19), which make it possible to calculate the ratios of various criteria and help choose the optimal scenario, show that scenario S4 is the best choice.

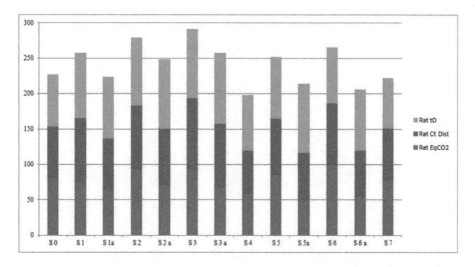

Figure 3.19. *Comparison of the different scenarios. For a color version of this figure, see www.iste.co.uk/besbes/transport.zip*

3.7. Proposal for a shared long-distance distribution model

The scenarios for pooling urban distribution, which have already been mentioned, have shown the role of pooling in reducing congestion and GHG emissions. The combination of urban and interurban distributions can generate more significant improvements. Therefore, the model we are going to propose is four cities. In each city, there are manufacturers and a consolidation warehouse that manages urban and/or interurban distribution to customers.

In scenario 1 (Figure 3.20), manufacturers in the same city transport their shipments to a warehouse that will then deliver individual orders for each customer in the city. In addition, the warehouse transports collective orders from customers in other cities through the relative warehouses. When returning, the trucks bring back collective orders from customers in the warehouse of departure from the first warehouse destination.

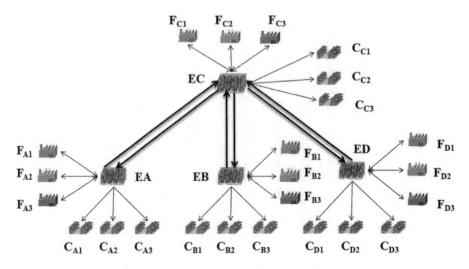

Figure 3.20. *Scenario 1. For a color version of this figure,
see www.iste.co.uk/besbes/transport.zip*

For example, manufacturers in City A (F_{Ai}) transport their products to the *EA* warehouse, which distributes them to customers C_{Ai} and F_{Aj}, and to the *EC* warehouse which in turn distributes them to customers in the city (C_{Ci} and F_{Ci}) and to other corresponding *EB* and *ED* warehouses. When returning to the *EC* warehouse, the trucks transport the goods to the *EA* warehouse. Therefore, each customer/manufacturer in each city receives all products from all manufacturers located in their city or elsewhere.

In scenario 2 (Figure 3.21), F_{Ai} manufacturers transport their products to the *EA* warehouse for distribution to C_{Ai} customers and to the *EB* warehouse, which in turn distributes them to C_{Bi} customers and the *EC* warehouse. Upon return, trucks from the *EA* warehouse will be loaded with products from the *EB* warehouse network (F_{Bi} manufacturers and the *EC* warehouse can receive products from F_{Ci} and F_{Di} manufacturers) to be delivered to customers in the *EA* warehouse. Therefore, customers in City A can receive products from all manufacturers (F_{Ai}, F_{Bi}, F_{Ci}, and F_{Di}), and in addition to this, F_{Ai} manufacturers receive their supplies that have been manufactured in other cities.

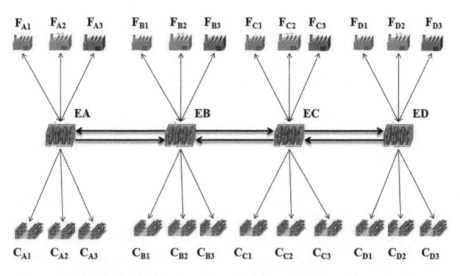

Figure 3.21. *Scenario 2. For a color version of this figure,*
see www.iste.co.uk/besbes/transport.zip

The combination of the two scenarios allows us to implement our model presented in Figure 3.22.

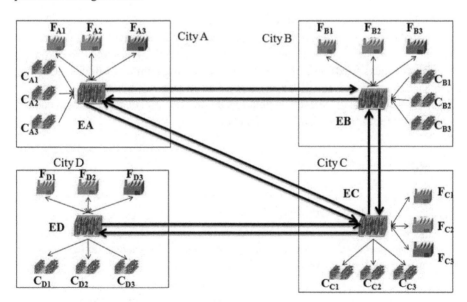

Figure 3.22. *Urban and interurban pooling models. For a color version of*
this figure, see www.iste.co.uk/besbes/transport.zip

This model can generate benefits for all stakeholders. The most significant advantage is that vehicles do not make empty returns, which leads to improved service efficiency, reduced GHG emissions, reduced road occupancy rates, better resource optimization (inventory, trucks, etc.), and reduced logistics costs.

In addition, this model clearly shows the role that pooling has in reducing GHG emissions – by reducing the number of vehicles used – and also in reducing congestion, given that pooling warehouses only allow small vehicles to be used in the city center.

3.8. Conclusion

The scenarios which we have suggested make it possible to identify some opportunities for transport pooling, such as the reduction of congestion and GHG emissions, while also considering the economic and social opportunities and gains. The comparison between the pooling scenarios and the scenario in which pooling is absent makes it possible to clearly show the improvements made by pooling transport in terms of distribution. The spreadsheet allows employees to choose the optimal scenario by considering different sustainability variables that lead to more efficient guidelines.

In conclusion, this is a multi-criteria decision support study using the following criteria: the cost of transportation (based on distance traveled), GHG emissions (based on distance traveled and truck characteristics), congestion (based on the number of trucks used), use of resources (based on the number of trucks used), and delivery time (based on distance, number of trucks used, and congestion). In addition, we plan discrete event simulations in order to consider the random concept of transport times in any distribution function.

3.9. References

Abbad, H. (2014). La gestion mutualisée des approvisionnements : mythe ou réalités ? *Logistique & Management*, 22(2), 41–50.

Abbad, H., Durand, B., and Senkel M.-P. (2016). La mutualisation physique et informationnelle en logistique. In *Organisation, Information et Performance*, Meyssonnier, F. and Rowe, F. (eds). Editions PUR, Rennes.

Abbassi, A., Kharraja, S., Alaoui, A.E., and Parra, D. (2018). Comparative study of mutualisation scenarios for distribution of non-medical products. *3rd SCA International Conference on Smart City Applications*, Tetouan, Morocco.

AFNOR. (2015). Principes généraux pour l'affichage environnemental des produits de grande consommation – Partie 0 : principes généraux et cadre méthodologique. Report, no. BP BP X 30-323, Agence De l'Environnement et de la Maitrise de l'Energie (ADEME), Angers, France.

Alvarez, P., Serrano-Hernandez, A., Faulin, J., and Juan, A.A. (2018). Using modelling techniques to analyze urban freight distribution. A case study in Pamplona (Spain). *Transportation Research Procedia*, 33, 67–74.

Bahinipati, B.K., Kanda, A., and Deshmukh, S.G. (2009). Horizontal collaboration in semiconductor manufacturing industry supply chain: an evaluation of collaboration intensity index. *Computers & Industrial Engineering*, 57(3), 880–895.

Ballot, E. and Fontane, F. (2008). Reducing transportation CO2 emissions through pooling of supply networks: perspectives from a case study in French retail chains. *Production Planning & Control: the Management of Operations*, 21(6), 640–650.

Bustinza, O.F., Gomes, E., Vendrell-Herrero, F., and Baines, T. (2019). Product–service innovation and performance: the role of collaborative partnerships and R&D intensity. *R&D Management*, 49(1), 33–45.

Camarinha-Matos, L.M. (2014). Collaborative networks: a mechanism for enterprise agility and resilience. In *Enterprise Interoperability VI: Interoperability for Agility, Resilience and Plasticity of Collaborations, Proceedings of the I-ESA Conferences*, Mertins, K., Benaben, F., Poler, R., and Bourrières, J.-P. (eds). Springer International Publishing, Cham.

Cao, M. and Zhang, Q. (2010). Supply chain collaboration: impact on collaborative advantage and firm performance. *Journal of Operations Management*, 29(3), 163–180.

Chan, F.T.S. and Zhang, T. (2011). The impact of Collaborative Transportation Management on supply chain performance: a simulation approach. *Expert Systems With Applications*, 38(3), 2319–2329.

Chanut, O. and Paché, G. (2013). La culture de mutualisation du PSL peut-elle favoriser l'émergence d'une logistique urbaine durable ? *RIMHE: Revue Interdisciplinaire Management, Homme Entreprise*, 3, 94–110.

Chanut, O., Capo, C., and Bonet, D. (2010). La mutualisation des moyens logistiques ne concerne-t-elle que les grandes entreprises ? Le point des pratiques dans les systèmes verticaux contractuels. *8èmes RIRL Rencontres Internationales de la Recherche en Logistique*, Bordeaux, France, September–October.

Chay, Y., Chanut, O., Michon, V., and Roques, T. (2013). La mutualisation logistique pour des Supply Chains durables. In *La logistique: une approche innovante des organisations*, Fabbe-Costes, N. and Pache, G. (eds). Presse Universitaire de Provence, Aix-en-Provence.

Chen, J., Sohal, A.S., and Prajogo, D.-I. (2013). Supply chain operational risk mitigation: a collaborative approach. *International Journal of Production Research*, 51(7), 2186–2199.

Cleophas, C., Cottrill, C., Ehmke, J.F., and Tierney, K. (2019). Collaborative urban transportation: recent advances in theory and practice. *European Journal of Operational Research*, 273(3), 801–816.

Danloup, N., Mirzabeiki, V., Allaoui, H., Goncalves, G., Julien, D., and Mena, C. (2015). Reducing transportation greenhouse gas emissions with collaborative distribution: a case study. *Management Research Review*, 38(10), 1049–1067.

Destouches, G. and Gaide, F. (2011). Pratiques de logistique collaborative: quelles opportunités pour les PME/ETI ? Report, Pôle interministériel de prospective et d'anticipation des mutations économiques (PIPAME).

Fernandez, E., Fontana, D., and Speranza, M.G. (2016). The Collaboration Uncapacitated Arc Routing Problem. *Computers and Operation Research*, 67, 120–167.

Ghaderi, H., Darestani, S.A., Leman, Z., and Ismail, M. (2012). Horizontal collaboration in logistics: a feasible task for group purchasing. *International Journal of Procurement Management*, 5(1), 43–54.

Ghaderi, H., Dullaert, W., and Amstel, W.P.V. (2016). Reducing lead-times and lead-time variance in cooperative distribution networks. *International Journal of Shipping and Transport Logistics*, 8(1), 51–65.

Gharehgozli, A.H., De Koster, R., and Jansen, R. (2017). Collaborative solutions for inter terminal transport. *International Journal of Production Research*, 55(21), 6527–6546.

Gonzalez-Feliu, J. (2011). Costs and benefits of logistics pooling for urban freight distribution: scenario simulation and assessment for strategic decision support. *Seminario CREI*, Rome, Italy.

Gonzalez-Feliu, J. and Battaia, G. (2017). La mutualisation des livraisons urbaines : quels impacts sur les coûts et la congestion ? *Logistique & Management*, 25(2), 107–118.

Gonzalez-Feliu, J. and Salanova, J. (2012). Defining and evaluating collaborative urban freight distribution systems. *Procedia – Social and Behavioral Science*, 39, 172–183.

Gonzalez-Feliu, J., Morana, J., Grau, J.-M.S., and Ma, T.-Y. (2013). Design and scenario assessment for collaborative logistics and freight transport systems. *International Journal of Transport Economics/Rivista internazionale di economia dei trasporti*, 4(2), 207–240.

Guajardo, M. and Rönnqvist, M. (2016). A review on cost allocation methods in collaborative transportation. *International Transactions in Operational Research*, 23(3), 371–392.

Hadj Taieb, N., Mellouli, R., and Affes, H. (2014). Impact of means and resources pooling on supply-chain management: case of large distribution. *3rd IEEE ICALT'14, International Conference on Advanced Logistics and Transport*, Hammamet, Tunisia.

Hensher, D.A. (2018). Tackling road congestion – what might it look like in the future under a collaborative and connected mobility model. *Transport Policy*, 66, A1–A8.

Junior, D.P.A., Novaes, A.G.N., and Luna, M.M.M. (2019). An agent-based approach to evaluate collaborative strategies in milk-run OEM operations. *Computers & Industrial Engineering*, 129, 545–555.

Liakos, P. and Delis, A. (2015). An interactive freight-pooling service for efficient last-mile delivery. *16th IEEE International Conference on Mobile Data Management*, Pittsburgh, USA.

Liu, D., Deng, Z., Sun, Q., Wang, Y., and Wang, Y. (2019). Design and freight corridor-fleet size choice in collaborative intermodal transportation network considering economies of scale. *Sustainability*, 11(4), 990–1008.

Lundqvist, B. (2018). Data collaboration, pooling and hoarding under competition law. Faculty of Law, Stockholm University Research Paper.

McKinnon, A. and Edwards, J. (2010). Opportunities for improving vehicle utilization. In *Green Logistics: Improving the Environmental Sustainability of Logistics*, McKinnon, A., Cullinane, S., Browne, M., and Whiteing, A. (eds). Kogan Page Publisher, London.

Moharana, H.S., Murty, J.S., Senapati, S.K., and Khuntia, K. (2012). Coordination, collaboration and integration for supply chain management. *International Journal of Interscience Management Review*, 2(2), 46–50.

Moutaoukil, A., Derrouiche, R., and Neubert, G. (2012). Pooling supply chain: literature review of collaborative strategies. *13th Working Conference on Virtual Enterprises*, Bournemouth, UK.

Moutaoukil, A., Derrouiche, R., and Neubert, G. (2013). Modélisation d'une stratégie de mutualisation logistique en intégrant les objectifs de Développement Durable pour des PME agroalimentaires. *13e CIGI'13 Congrès International de Génie Industriel*, La Rochelle, France.

Moutaoukil, A., Neubert, G., and Derrouiche, R. (2015). Urban freight distribution: the impact of delivery time on sustainability. *IFAC-PapersOnLine*, 48(3), 2368–2373.

Muñoz-Villamizar, A., Montoya-Torres, J.R., and Vega-Mejía, C.A. (2015). Non-collaborative versus collaborative last-mile delivery in urban systems with stochastic demands. *Procedia CIRP*, 30, 263–268.

Murça, M.C.R. (2018). Collaborative air traffic flow management: incorporating airline preferences in rerouting decisions. *Journal of Air Transport Management*, 71, 97–107.

Niu, F. and Li, J. (2019). An activity-based integrated land-use transport model for urban spatial distribution simulation. *Environment and Planning B: Urban Analytics and City Science*, 46(1), 165–178.

Ntziachristos, L., Papadimitriou, G., Ligterink, N., and Hausberger, S. (2016). Implications of diesel emissions control failures to emission factors and road transport NOx evolution. *Atmospheric Environment*, 141, 542–551.

Okdinawati, L., Simatupang, T.M., and Sunitiyoso, Y. (2015). Modelling collaborative transportation management: current state and opportunities for future research. *Journal of Operations and Supply Chain Management*, 8(2), 96–119.

Pan, S. (2010). Contribution à la définition et à l'évaluation de la mutualisation de chaînes logistiques pour réduire les émissions de CO2 du transport : application au cas de la grande distribution. PhD thesis, École Nationale Supérieure des Mines, Paris.

Pan, S., Ballot, E., and Fontane, F. (2013). The reduction of greenhouse gas emissions from freight transport by pooling supply chains. *International Journal Production Economics*, 143(1), 86–94.

Perboli, G., Rosano, M., and Gobbato, L. (2016). Decision support system for collaborative freight transportation management: a tool for mixing traditional and green logistics. *6th ILS International Conference on Information Systems, Logistics and Supply Chain*, Bordeaux, France.

Perez-Bernabeu, E., Juan, A.A., Faulin, J., and Barrios, B.B. (2015). Horizontal cooperation in road transportation: a case illustrating savings in distances and greenhouse gas emissions. *International Transactions in Operational Research*, 22(3), 585–606.

Qiu, X. and Huang, G.Q. (2011). On storage capacity pooling through the supply hub in industrial park (SHIP): the impact of demand uncertainty. *IEEM'2011 IEEE International Conference on Industrial Engineering and Engineering Management*, Singapore.

Rajaa, M. and Ibnoulkatib, G. (2019). La logistique urbaine: identification des concepts clés (revue de littérature). *European Scientific Journal*, 15(2), 57–71.

Rakotonarivo, D., Gonzalez-Feliu, J., Aoufi, A., and Morana, J. (2009). La mutualisation. Report, LUMD: Logistique Urbaine Mutualisée Durable, Université Lyon 2. Available: https://halshs.archives-ouvertes.fr/halshs-01056188.

Sanchez, M., Pradenas, L., Deschamps, J.-C., and Parada, V. (2016). Reducing the carbon footprint in a vehicle routing problem by pooling resources from different companies. *NETNOMICS: Economic Research and Electronic Networking*, 17(1), 29–45.

Senkel, M.-P., Durand, B., and Hoa Vo, T.L. (2013). La mutualisation logistique : entre théories et pratiques. *Logistique & Management*, 21(1), 19–30.

Silbermayr, L., Jammernegg, W., and Kischka, P. (2017). Inventory pooling with environmental constraints using copulas. *European Journal of Operational Research*, 263(2), 479–492.

Tellez, O., Vercraene, S., Lehuede, F., Peton, O., and Monteiro, T. (2016). Optimisation du transport mutualisé d'enfants en situation de handicap avec véhicules reconfigurables. *ROADEF'2016 17e congrès de la société Française de Recherche Opérationnelle et d'Aide à la Décision*, Compiègne, France, February.

Thompson, R.G. and Hassall, K.P. (2012). A collaborative urban distribution network. *Procedia – Social and Behavioral Sciences*, 39, 230–240.

Tornberg, P. and Odhage, J. (2018). Making transport planning more collaborative? The case of Strategic Choice of Measures in Swedish transport planning. *Transportation Research Part A: Policy and Practice*, 118, 416–429.

Vanovermeire, C., Sörensen, K., Van Breedam, A., Vannieuwenhuyse, B., and Verstrepen, S. (2013). Horizontal logistics collaboration: decreasing costs through flexibility and an adequate cost allocation strategy. *International Journal of Logistics: Research and Applications*, 17(4), 339–355.

Wang, X. and Kopfer, H. (2014). Collaborative transportation planning of less-than-truckload freight. *OR Spectrum*, 36(2), 357–380.

Wang, Y., Ma, X., Li, Z., Liu, Y., Xu, M., and Wang, Y. (2017). Profit distribution in collaborative multiple centers vehicle routing problem. *Journal of Cleaner Production*, 144, 203–219.

Wang, X.-X., Liu, X.-Y., and Li, Z.-Q. (2018). A social collaborative urban distribution integration platform. *Journal of Interdisciplinary Mathematics*, 21(5), 1109–1113.

Wang, J., Lim, M.K., Tseng, M.-L., and Yang, Y. (2019). Promoting low carbon agenda in the urban logistics network distribution system. *Journal of Cleaner Production*, 211, 146–160.

Zissis, D., Aktas, E., and Bourlakis, M. (2018). Collaboration in urban distribution of online grocery orders. *The International Journal of Logistics Management*, 29(4), 1196–1214.

Zouari, A. and Cherif, M. (2018). La mutualisation des transports : cas de la distribution urbaine – Partie 1 revue de littérature. *CESCA'2018, 1er Colloque International sur l'E-Supply Chain*, Agadir, Morocco.

4

A Ruin and Recreate Solution Method for a Lexicographic Vehicle Routing Problem Integrating Park-and-Loop and Car Sharing

The vehicle routing problem (VRP) aims at finding optimal vehicle routes that visit a set of jobs in a given region. In the classical VRP formulation, each employee moves from a job to another by driving her/his assigned car. In the proposed generalization of the VRP, workers are allowed to walk or use a light transportation mode, and car sharing is additionally enabled, as a heavy resource can transport more than one worker. These new features are likely to reduce both the driving distance and the heavy-vehicle fleet, which are the two main objective functions optimized in the VRP literature, where, in general, minimizing the number of used vehicles is the primary objective. Such gains on the distance traveled by heavy transportation resources, as well as on the number of heavy vehicles used, have a direct and positive influence on the environmental impact of the undertaken transportation activities.

4.1. Introduction

The *Vehicle Routing Problem* (VRP) aims at finding optimal vehicle routes that visit a set of jobs in a given region. Depending on the situation, a job can be a service provided on-site, a delivery of goods, or a collection of components. For each job, we know its duration as well as its time window during which it must be performed. When building the routes of the workers for performing the on-site services, the systematic use of cars (which is the main hypothesis in the VRP literature) can be inefficient when only light equipment is carried and when

---

Chapter written by Olivier GALLAY and Nicolas ZUFFEREY.

distances between some jobs could allow lighter transportation modes (e.g. walking or electric kick scooters). The use of such greener transportation options opens the door for decreasing the environmental footprint that is associated with urban logistics, particularly regarding the emission of greenhouse gases.

Using only independently light transportation modes, as in the VRP with heterogeneous fleet (Baldacci *et al.* 2008), might not be always appropriate because of the restricted range of such transportation modes (i.e. the upper bound on the possible distance to travel). In such contexts, synchronizing heavy (e.g. cars, vans, and trucks) and light (e.g. workers on foot and electric kick scooters) transportation modes is a promising answer. We focus on situations involving, jointly, light and heavy transportation modes to serve jobs, where both transportation resources can move independently and where the light resources can be embedded in the heavy ones for some parts of their routes. In the classical VRP formulation, each employee moves from a job to another by driving her/his assigned car. In the proposed generalization of the VRP (denoted here as problem (P)), workers are allowed to walk or use a light transportation mode, and car sharing is additionally enabled, as a heavy resource can transport more than one worker. These new features are likely to reduce both the driving distance and the heavy-vehicle fleet, which are the two main objective functions optimized in the VRP literature (Koc *et al.* 2016), where, in general, minimizing the number of used vehicles is the primary objective. Such gains on the distance traveled by heavy transportation resources, as well as on the number of heavy vehicles used, have a direct and positive influence on the environmental impact of the undertaken transportation activities.

The present research axis (i.e. the problem (P)) has been motivated by the network of a European energy provider (denoted here as *EEP*: it cannot be named because of a non-disclosure agreement) in which the employees have to visit clients in order to perform various tasks (e.g. upgrade consumer settings and evaluate consumption). *EEP* has noticed that their employees often leave their cars to achieve clustered jobs on foot even if their planning mentions to drive to their next location. Obviously, this situation is enhanced in an urban context, where distances between jobs are short and hence allow for walking. Furthermore, when parking spots turn out to be scarce and traffic is dense, walking is a way to reduce the high uncertainty affecting travel times by car.

Strongly relying on Coindreau *et al.* (2017a, 2017b, 2018) and Gallay and Zuffrey (2018), we describe in this chapter how car sharing and independent loops (traveled by foot or electric kick scooter) allow for more sustainable transportation activities. To accurately measure the relevance of park-and-loop and car sharing, we investigate two intermediate vehicle routing formulations leading to problem (P) and denoted here as (A) and (B) (as initially proposed by Coindreau *et al.* (2017b)). (A) corresponds to the classical VRP situation where each worker has to use her/his single assigned car to move from one job to the other. (B) is a relaxation of (A) where park-and-loop is allowed. More precisely, a worker can also move from one job to another either by walking or using an electric kick scooter. (P) is hence the car-sharing extension of (B), as multiple workers can be transported in the same vehicle. As these problems are NP-hard, exact methods are not appropriate for solving real-case instances and they will not be investigated here (e.g. preliminary experiments have shown that mixed-integer linear programming formulations are limited to instances up to 15 jobs for problem (P)). A local-search metaheuristic based on the *ruin and recreate* principle is proposed to generate efficient solutions to these problems. The algorithm starts with an initial solution (generated by a greedy heuristic) and tries to improve it iteratively. Two phases are employed at each iteration: (1) remove jobs from some routes of the solution *ruin* phase and (2) reinsert sequentially the removed jobs in the *recreate* phase.

This chapter is organized as follows. In section 4.2, we give a brief overview of the related literature. We formally describe the considered problem (P) in section 4.3. In section 4.4, we explain the adopted lexicographic approach to handle the various considered objectives. The used solution methodology is described in section 4.5. The obtained results are detailed in section 4.6. Finally, conclusions and future research directions are given in section 4.7.

4.2. Literature review

A rather scarce literature addresses the problem of synchronizing light and heavy transportation resources in a routing context. Focusing on home health-care staff scheduling, a recent contribution considers the synchronization of driving and walking (Fikar and Hirsch 2015). The main discrepancy with the current modeling framework lies in the fact that nurses do not drive a car, and an independent transportation system ensures their transportation between jobs. In the work of Fikar and Hirsch (2015), it is shown that the vehicle fleet can be reduced by up to 90% if the external transporter picks up and drops off nurses (note that nurses are also allowed to walk from a location to another). The drawback of this fleet reduction is an augmentation of the total number of employed workers. Furthermore, the main focus in the work of Fikar and Hirsch (2015) aims at minimizing the number of vehicles without considering any trade-off with the overall driving distance. In (P), the benefits resulting from the vehicle fleet reduction, and its impact (sometimes positive!) on the total driving distance, are analyzed. In the context of light-goods delivery, where foot couriers can be coupled with vans, it is shown by Lin (2011) that both the van fleet and the average cost can be reduced when compared to the situation where vans are treated as independent transportation modes. This double gain is obtained despite the study only considering coordination during the van outbound and return legs. In the context of parcel delivery, coupling a light resource (a drone) with a single truck (i.e. the heavy resource) can lead to saving 20% on the truck use (Murray and Chu 2015).

The papers cited above successfully show the relevance of synchronizing heterogeneous vehicles having different characteristics. In (P), we consider the case where the employees can choose between moving by car, using an electric kick scooter, or simply walking. Moreover, carpooling is enabled. The potential gain offered by the synchronization of such different transportation modes is measured and discussed in the next sections.

When transporting the same worker along her/his path of jobs with different vehicles, it leads to a transportation problem of persons, which is referred to as the *Dial-A-Ride-Problem* (DARP) in the literature (Masson *et al.* 2014). However, problem (P) raises additional complexity compared to the DARP. First, all the routes that involve the same employee along her/his schedule are interdependent, which means that a delay in a route could be propagated to several other routes. In other words, a specific temporal precedence constraint (between pick-up and delivery pairs) is added to the DARP. Second, the list of pick-up and delivery locations is not provided as an input, but it is inherent to the optimization process. In the DARP context, the only dependencies of that type can be found in the *DARP with transfers*, for which the transportation requests can be divided into various sub-routes where the transport can be ensured by different vehicles. As the pick-up time at transfers depends on the previously associated drop-off time, dependencies will appear explicitly at transfer points. A need for synchronization also occurs in the *Vehicle Routing Problem with Trailers and Transshipment* (VRPTT) (Drexl 2012), where both autonomous (trucks) and non-autonomous (trailers) vehicles are synchronized in order to complete given routing requests. In (P), the employees driving their own car can be modeled as being autonomous, but the employees without an associated car cannot be considered as non-autonomous. Indeed, these workers are semi-autonomous, as they need to be transported when longer distances have to be traveled, whereas walking or employing an electric kick scooter allows them to move locally. Based on this important discrepancy, one can remark that the VRPTT literature does not help for tackling problem (P).

4.3. Considered problem

We study a new formulation that allows for the synchronization of cars (heavy resource) and workers (light resource), the latter being possibly equipped with electric kick scooters. First, the heavy resource is faster and it can move several employees, but its associated pollution impact and costs are larger. Second, the light resource is less expensive, but it is obviously limited by its range and its speed. Moreover, if the light resource is not embedded in the heavy resource, it can only serve jobs that are close to the depot. As a result, great detours would have to be performed by the heavy resources in order to serve distant jobs in the same route.

To overcome the individual drawbacks of each of these two transportation modes (i.e. heavy and light), a straightforward idea is to put electric kick scooters (and their associated workers) into cars (with their associated drivers). A promising approach is to develop an efficient coordination and synchronization of these two types of resources. More precisely, we open the door to carpooling, where each heavy resource can transport several light resources. There are two types of workers: the car drivers and the passengers. Heavy and light resources are allowed to couple and uncouple as often as needed. Drivers can not only serve jobs but can also walk as well or use an electric kick scooter to reach jobs. However, returning to her/his car is mandatory. Passengers can reach the next job either by walking or by using an electric kick scooter, and afterward, they can be picked up elsewhere than at the drop-off location. The studied problem can be seen as a multi-modal extension of the well-known VRP with time windows, where each driver must leave and come back to the depot within the working day.

Three sets are considered, namely, J, W, and K. J denotes the set of n jobs that have to be performed in n different locations. W is the worker set, and K is the heavy-vehicle set (identical), where each vehicle has a finite capacity of Q (i.e. not more than Q workers can be transported in each vehicle). Each vehicle and each worker starts and ends its working day at the central depot 0. As is the case for the VRP, we consider a complete graph $G = (V, A)$, where $V = J \cup \{0\}$ is the node set and $A = \{(i,j)|i,j \in V, i \neq j\}$ is the arc set. A processing time p_j and a time window $[e_j, l_j]$ are associated with each job $j \in J$. With each arc $(i,j) \in A$, two driving times are associated: $T_{i,j}^h$ for the heavy transportation resource and $T_{i,j}^l$ for the light one. Moreover, $d_{i,j}$ denotes the distance between nodes i and j. Idling is allowed, meaning that a worker can wait at a node before serving its associated job within its time window. Finally, the daily distance that can be traveled by each light transportation resource is upper-bounded.

When car sharing is allowed, the number $|K|$ of vehicles can be lower than the number $|W|$ of workers. Therefore, the workers have to be split into two categories: drivers and passengers. Drivers have to (1) perform their assigned jobs and (2) fulfill transportation requests of passengers. The driver and passenger employees can either use an electric kick scooter or walk to reach the next job, but the return path to the car is mandatory for the driver. When walking or using an electric kick scooter, a path between consecutive jobs is called a *loop*. In the case of the synchronization of heavy and light resources, the jobs can be partitioned into loops, and the loops have to be dispatched in the planning of the employees. A loop can be viewed as a delivery (respectively, pick-up) point where the loop starts (respectively, ends). Note that the pick-up and delivery points are the same for the driver. Therefore, from the transportation point of view, a loop can be agglomerated in two aggregated nodes (delivery and pick-up), the characteristics of which (total duration and aggregated time window) are computed with respect to the job sequence belonging to the loop. The heavy vehicles only visit these aggregated nodes, and the loop sequences appearing in all the worker's planning determine the set of all pick-ups and deliveries to be performed.

As mentioned previously, three formulations are considered, and they are denoted as (A), (B), and (P).

(A) VRP: each worker is a driver that can only move using her/his assigned car.

(B) $|K| = |W|$: each worker has her/his own assigned car, but a worker can also visit a set of jobs either by walking or using an electric kick scooter, as long as the range/autonomy (i.e. largest allowed distance) of the employed light transportation resource is not exceeded.

(C) $|K| < |W|$: we can have fewer cars than workers, and therefore, a vehicle can transport multiple workers (i.e. car sharing). Each worker can walk or use an electric kick scooter to reach a job, as long as the range of the employed light transportation resource is not exceeded.

An example of the benefit of formulation (P) is shown in Figure 4.1, where the workers are allowed to park their car and use a light transportation mode (walking or electric kick scooter) to reach a job whenever this is possible (*Park-and-Loop* (Gussmagg-Pfliegl *et al.* 2011)) and where car sharing is enabled. Each employee is associated with a color code: light gray is used for employee w_1, gray denotes w_2, a double line represents w_3, and black is finally employed for w_4. Plain (respectively, dashed) lines represent heavy (respectively, light) resources. w_1 and w_4 initially quit the depot in the same vehicle. w_4 is dropped off at job j_{30} and then s/he uses a light resource to move to job j_1, where s/he is picked up by employee w_1. Note that some drivers are traveling sub-routes with the use of a light resource (e.g. w_2 along the path $j_4 - j_8 - j_{37} - j_{19}$). All employees and cars start and end their working day in the middle of the grid at the central depot.

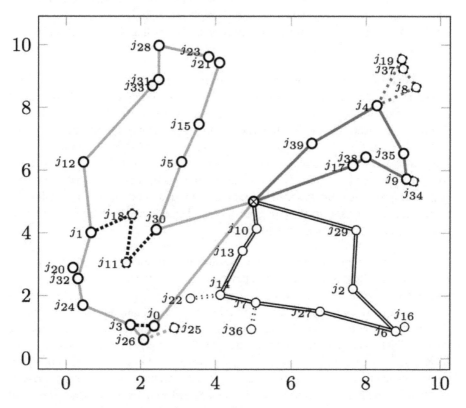

Figure 4.1. *Solution exhibiting coordination between light and heavy transportation modes*

4.4. Lexicographic approach

In problem (P), three different objectives have to be minimized: the number f_{work} of workers, the number f_{car} of cars, and the total driving distance f_{dist}. Such multi-objective problems often arise in various industrial contexts. Formally, it consists in optimizing $o > 1$ objectives that are generally in conflict. A common approach to solving such problems is to assign the same importance to each objective function and to optimize the values $(f_1, ..., f_o)$ of all objectives. This methodology is known as *Pareto Optimization* (PO), in which all *Pareto* optimal solutions are generated along the *efficient frontier*. The output of such a way of simultaneously optimizing all objectives leaves the decision makers with various trade-off solutions. The decision makers have then to choose and implement the most appropriate one for their company. From a practical perspective, this selection process among various trade-off solutions might be complicated. In fact, it often results in complex and conflicting discussions regarding how to quantify the importance of each objective.

In contrast, with *Lexicographic Optimization* (LO), the managerial-sensitive discussion takes place before performing any optimization process and thus without being in front of solutions. In other words, the decision makers have to initially determine a clear ranking of the (potentially conflicting) objectives (formally, $f_1 > f_2 > ... > f_o$). Consequently, a cumbersome and tricky multi-objective problem is transformed into a single-objective problem, consisting in minimizing a weighted function $f = \sum_i \alpha_i \cdot f_i$, where the coefficients α_i are discriminating enough (i.e. no improvement on f_{i+1} can compensate any deterioration of f_i). In addition, each f_i can have its specific unit (e.g. cost, time, distance, and pollution) and there is thus no need to translate each f_i into a cost.

LO has been applied successfully to various industrial contexts with the help of metaheuristics (Respen *et al.* 2017b; Thevenin *et al.* 2018; Zufferey 2002). From the perspective of *EEP*, the first priority in (P) is to minimize the number of employed workers. Second, attention is paid to favoring car sharing and hence to minimizing the number of used vehicles. Finally, the focus is on decreasing the total routing costs, which are directly proportional to the total driving distance. This lexicographic ranking $f_{work} > f_{car} > f_{dist}$ between the three considered objectives is implemented in the following way: for each instance, every time a feasible solution is found, a new instance is generated by reducing either $|W|$ (the number of workers) or $|K|$ (the number of cars) by one unit, and the driving distance is minimized for this given amount of resources.

4.5. Solution method

Exact methods (e.g. branch and bound, dynamic programming) are able to guarantee the optimality of the provided solutions. However, for most real-life optimization problems, such methods need too much time to find optimal solutions because the involved problems are NP-hard (Garey and Johnson 1979). For these challenging problems, it is preferable to quickly find a satisfying solution, which is the goal of a heuristic solution method. Formally, a *heuristic* can be viewed as an optimization procedure that generates, in a reasonable amount of time, a satisfying solution, which is not necessarily optimal. As defined by Osman and Laporte (1996), "a *metaheuristic* is an iterative generation process which guides a subordinate heuristic by combining intelligently different concepts for exploring and exploiting the search space, learning strategies are used to structure information in order to find efficiently near-optimal solutions". Many comparable definitions of metaheuristics can be found in the literature (Blum and Roli 2003), and the reader is referred to a recent book by Gendreau and Potvin (2019) on such methods. Local search algorithms (e.g. tabu search, simulated annealing, variable neighborhood search, and large neighborhood search) are popular metaheuristics. A local search starts from an initial solution. Next, at each iteration, the solution is modified with respect to predefined rules in order to hopefully generate an improved solution. This process is repeated until a stopping condition (e.g. a time limit) is satisfied.

Local search metaheuristics based on the *ruin and recreate* principle (Pisinger and Ropke 2007) are suitable to tackle the increased complexity of problem (P) when compared to the classical VRP. In particular, *Large Neighborhood Search*, LNS (Shaw 1998), aims at improving a current solution s by iteratively unbuilding and rebuilding it. At each step, q (parameter that is dynamically updated) jobs are removed randomly from solution s, and they are next reinserted (in a best-insertion fashion, as presented below) sequentially in order to obtain a new solution s'. For tackling (P), LNS is embedded into a simulated annealing framework to choose, with a certain probability, whether to move (or not) the search from s to s'. In our implementation of LNS, $|W|$ and $|K|$ are initially provided for each instance. At each step of LNS, an integer q is selected at random in interval $[1, ..., 0.2 \cdot n]$. The initial temperature of the simulated annealing process allows for a deterioration of 20% with a probability fixed to 0.5, and the cooling is determined such that the final temperature cannot lead to any deterioration. It has been shown by Shaw (1998) that LNS is able to produce good results for formulation (A).

The reader is referred to the work of Kirkpatrick *et al.* (1983) for having technical information related to the simulated annealing algorithm. The proposed solution method for (P) is summarized in Algorithm 4.1, where the best-encountered solution s^* is returned to the user at the end of the search process. Note that each parameter (say t) was tuned with respect to the following standard process. First, an interval $I = [a, b]$ is selected for some possible values of t. Second, several (e.g. 10) different equidistant values of t are selected in I. Third, the method is performed with the selected values of t in I. Finally, two cases (C1) and (C2) can occur: (C1) if the best results are obtained with a value of t that is not too close to a or b, then t is definitely fixed to its best value (i.e. the value that leads to the best solutions) and the tuning process is stopped for t; (C2) if the best results are obtained with t close to a (respectively, b), the interval I is enlarged with a smaller (respectively, larger) value of a (respectively, b), and the process is repeated.

Initialization

1. construct an initial solution s (e.g., by sequentially performing best insertions)
2. set $s^* = s$ (*initialization of the best-encountered solution*)

While a time limit is not reached, **do:**

1. remove at random an integer number $q \in [1, 0.2 \cdot n]$ of jobs from the current solution s (*ruin phase*)
2. reinsert sequentially the q removed jobs in order to generate a neighbor solution s' (*recreate phase*)
3. if the neighbor solution s' is better than the current solution s (with respect to the lexicographic preferences), set $s = s'$ (*s' becomes the new current solution*)
4. otherwise, set $s = s'$ with a certain probability (with respect to a simulated annealing rule)
5. if s is better than s^*, set $s^* = s$ (*the best-encountered solution is updated*)

Return the best-encountered solution s^*

Algorithm 4.1. *Ruin and recreate solution method for (P)*

To determine the best position for inserting a job, all the possible insertion positions are tested. Anytime a job is inserted, various situations must be considered depending on the insertion type (i.e. either in a passenger or in a driver planning). Each type of insertion leads to a dedicated method. First, we check whether the insertion can be scheduled by augmenting a loop that already exists, or if a new loop must be created. On the one hand, the feasibility of a loop extension can be quickly checked by simply updating the involved aggregated nodes at their specific positions in the route. On the other hand, when a new loop is created, the number of potential insertion positions increases significantly. Indeed, the new loop has to be first inserted in a worker planning (driver or passenger), and the quality of this insertion must then be evaluated with respect to the chosen route. Any insertion in a driver planning is the same as any insertion in the VRP context (i.e. add a node to a route). The number of tests to evaluate is in $O(n)$. In the passenger case, in contrast, the insertion is much more complicated. More precisely, one can assume that the new loop (denoted as ω_j) is added between loops ω_i and ω_{i+1} in a passenger planning. The transportation between the pick-up $A(\omega_i)$ at the end of ω_i and the delivery $B(\omega_{i+1})$ at the beginning of ω_{i+1} becomes obsolete, and thus, it must be removed from the partial solution. Consequently, two new transportation requests have to be performed: $(A(\omega_i) \rightarrow B(\omega_j))$ and $(A(\omega_j) \rightarrow B(\omega_{i+1}))$. In this case, the number of tests to be processed is in $O(n^4)$. This increased complexity is faced with an adaptation of the fast feasibility-check procedure designed by Masson *et al.* (2013), which is able to check in constant time if inserting two pick-up and delivery couples is feasible. To further reduce the number of feasible insertions to evaluate, necessary conditions and filters can be designed to focus on the most promising insertions (Hertz *et al.* 2005). For instance, one can only test the five positions i that minimize the distance to cover the two created pick-up and delivery couples $d_{A(\omega_i),B(\omega_j)} +$ $d_{A(\omega_j),B(w_{i+1})}$.

4.6. Results

To validate the efficiency of the used LNS, its results are compared to optimal VRP solutions where only heavy resources are used. Indeed, such experiments allow benchmarking the improvement gap of the proposed formulations with respect to the best solutions that the current practice of *EEP* could obtain. This managerial validation of the quality of the proposed solutions is sufficient from *EEP*'s perspective, and therefore, the development of other metaheuristics is left as an avenue of research.

The *Branch-And-Price* algorithm (BAP) developed by Desaulniers *et al.* (2008) is used to get optimal VRP solutions. Park-and-loop (i.e. allowing the workers to move without a vehicle) while enabling car sharing is likely to help managers reduce the number of employed cars (f_{car}) as well as the total driving distance (f_{dist}). Optimal values of f_{car} and f_{dist} (obtained by BAP) are denoted as f_{car}^* and f_{dist}^*, respectively. Depending on the instance, employing a light resource instead of a heavy one can either decrease or augment f_{dist}. First, f_{dist} decreases when the pooling of the heavy resources overcompensates the detours to carry the light resources. Second, f_{dist} augments when too many detours are needed to carry the light resources.

The computer used was a 3.4-GHz Intel Quad-core i7 with 8-GB DDR3 of RAM memory. The time limit of LNS is n minutes (where n is the number of jobs). Such a time limit meets *EEP* requirements, as day-ahead optimization is allowed (i.e. the routes can be built during the night before the considered planning horizon). For this reason, no additional information is given with respect to the speed of LNS (i.e. the computation time needed to generate s^*).

In section 4.6.1, we describe the results that were obtained when the workers are allowed to walk but are not equipped with an electric kick scooter. The latter extension is numerically investigated in section 4.6.2.

4.6.1. *Walking*

4.6.1.1. *Instances*

The instances have been generated based on the real cases faced by *EEP*. A square grid of 10 km × 10 km is used to capture the considered urban territory. The random locations of the n jobs are uniformly distributed in the grid. This configuration allows for walking between some pairs of jobs. For each job, its integer duration is randomly picked in the interval [15, 34] min, whereas its time window is always [8:00, 15:00]. Such a wide time window results in a rich solution space that augments the potential benefits offered by the original features of problem (P). In the chosen urban configuration, 30 km/h (respectively, 4 km/h) is the average vehicle (respectively, walking) speed. The daily walking distance cannot exceed 5 km, and not more than $Q = 2$ workers can be in the same vehicle. For each value n in the set {25, 45, 65, 85}, five instances are generated (with grids having various job configurations). Ten runs of LNS were performed for each instance. The smaller instances do not show enough potential for car sharing, whereas BAP is not able to provide optimal VRP solutions for the larger instances.

4.6.1.2. *Results*

Table 4.1 summarizes the results, where the above (respectively, below) part represents formulation (B) (respectively, (P)). First, the instance characteristics are given (i.e. n, $|W|$ and $|K|$). In other words, for each instance, the available resources W and K are initially provided. Consequently, only the transportation costs (i.e. f_{dist}) have to be minimized. $|W|$ is the smallest feasible value obtained for formulation (A) with respect to the considered instance size. Next, the average percentage gap is indicated with respect to the (A) solution values for f_{dist}. Each average is computed over the five configurations associated with each triplet $(n, |W|, |K|)$ and over the ten runs. For example, in the case $(n, |W|) = (25, 2)$: (1) no feasible solution was found for formulation (A) with $|K| = |W| = 1$; (2) formulation (B) reduces the transportation costs by 6.5% compared to f^*_{dist}; (3) formulation (P) leads to a 2.6%-augmentation of transportation costs (i.e. f_{dist} increases) but one vehicle is saved (i.e. f_{car} is reduced). Finally, in the last column, the same information (i.e. gaps) is given, but for the most clustered configuration. Such a configuration is likely to efficiently highlight the potential benefits associated with the park-and-loop and car-sharing features.

Consider column 5 of Table 4.1, involving all the configurations. For formulation (B), on the one hand, the f_{dist} improvement (with respect to the standard VRP formulation (A)) augments with n, which confirms the benefit of the park-and-loop feature. Considering formulation (P) (again versus (A)), on the other hand, a single car can only be saved (on average) if additional transportation costs are encountered. In other words, *EEP* cannot simultaneously improve f_{dist} and f_{car}. Column 6 of Table 4.1 provides the average value (over the 10 runs) obtained for the most clustered instance configuration. When considering column 6, the same trend is observed for formulation (B) versus (A), compared to column 5. Interestingly, it appears that formulation (P) can simultaneously reduce the number of vehicles (f_{car}) as well as the transportation costs (f_{dist}), hence improving on both the objectives lexicographically stated by *EEP*. This highlights the high potential of formulation (P) to diminish the environmental footprint of the considered transportation activities. For formulation (P), the quality of the results (i.e. of the solutions) decreases when n increases. This phenomenon is likely to result from the limited capacity of the employed straightforward metaheuristic rather than from the ability of synchronizing heavy and light resources to reduce the driving costs. Indeed, the complexity of managing passenger workers augments significantly with n, which directly impacts the efficiency of the solution method and its robustness. Developing additional metaheuristics is left here as an avenue of research.

Formulation	N	$\|W\|$	$\|K\|$	f_{dist} (five configurations)	f_{dist} (most clustered configuration)
(B)	25	2	2	−6.5%	−7.4%
	45	3	3	−8.7%	−7.5%
	65	4	4	−13%	−12.5%
	85	5	5	−11.2%	−9.3%
(P)	25	2	1	2.6%	−2.3%
	45	3	2	14.9%	−4.7%
	65	4	3	18.9%	−0.2%
	85	5	4	42.9%	22%

Table 4.1. *Park-and-loop and car pooling vs. classical VRP*

For $n = 45$ and the most clustered configuration, Table 4.2 gives the comparison of the average value, the best value, and the standard deviation σ (over the 10 runs). σ is low for formulations (A) and (B), which seems to indicate robust and efficient solutions. The larger σ-value for (P) is likely to show the need for a more focused metaheuristic and the raised additional complexity. Considering the best solutions (see column 5), we observe that increasing the use of light transportation resources can lead to both a shorter driving distance (the improvement gap of (P) can be up to 10.8% with respect to (A) and up to 3.6% with respect to (B)) and a reduced fleet of vehicles (one car is saved). Figure 4.2 represents these three best solutions. When compared to formulation (A), we can observe that (B) allows decreasing the driving distance, as some of the trips are walked instead of driven. The driving distance can be further reduced in formulation (P). Indeed, the generated detours required to drop off (respectively, pick-up) the passenger employee at job 15 (respectively, job 5) are overcompensated by the saving obtained by the presence of two employees in the same vehicle for part of the route.

Formulation	$|W|$	$|K|$	Average f_{dist} (km)	Best found f_{dist} (km)	σ
(A)	3	3	61.79	61.71	0.19
(B)	3	3	57.15	57.08	0.09
(P)	3	2	58.91	55.04	3.31

Table 4.2. *Results for the most clustered configuration (n = 45)*

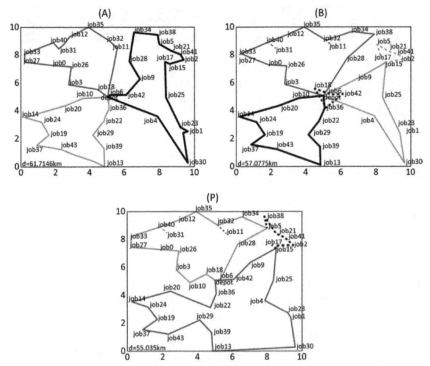

Dashed lines represent walking paths, whereas solid lines indicate travels by cars.

Figure 4.2. *Best solutions for formulations (A), (B), and (P) for the most clustered instance (n = 45)*

4.6.2. *Electric kick scooter*

4.6.2.1. *Instances*

We consider 60 instances (with $n \in \{20, 30, 40, 50\}$ jobs) derived from real data of *EEP* (as in section 4.6.1). In this case, the speed of the light resource is set to 15 km/h when a worker is equipped with an electric kick scooter (formerly 4 km/h when walking). We consider here three types of instances, depending on the considered time window size.

– *All-Day* instances: each job *j* has the same time window [8:00, 15:00].

– *Half-Day* instances: for each job *j*, we randomly assign time window [8:00, 11:30] or time window [11:30, 15:00].

– *Quarter-Day* instances: for each job *j*, we randomly assign one of the following time windows: [8:00, 9:45], [9:45, 11:30], [11:30, 13:15], and [13:15, 15:00].

Three service levels (that can be offered to *EEP* clients) are thus covered by these three instance types. Indeed, the smaller the assigned time window is, the better it is from the client standpoint (as s/he has to block a shorter time period to meet the *EEP* employee), but the worse it is from the route optimization perspective (indeed, additional constraints have to be satisfied).

4.6.2.2. *Results*

Table 4.3 gives the percentage of improvements obtained on the number of used cars (f_{car}) and on the transportation costs (f_{dist}) when workers are equipped with an electric kick scooter and when the following features are modified: range (i.e. 5 km vs. 10 km) and service level (i.e. *All-Day* vs. *Half-Day* vs. *Quarter-Day*). Average results (over all instances) are given in the last line. When simultaneously allowing car sharing and equipping workers with an electric kick scooter, we observe that a gain is reached, on average, for both objectives f_{car} and f_{dist}. Indeed, while f_{car} can be improved by 14.14%, f_{dist} can be decreased by 9.18%. These results highlight the importance of increasing the speed and range parameters of the light resource to magnify the gain offered by the synchronization of the light and heavy resources. We observe that increasing the service level (i.e. narrowing the time windows) obviously decreases the achieved gain in terms of driving distance or heavy-vehicle fleet size.

Range	5 km		10 km	
Objective	f_{car}	f_{dist}	f_{car}	f_{dist}
All-Day	−18.03%	−9.87%	−22.95%	−16.92%
Half-Day	−10.94%	−6.29%	−12.05%	−9.61%
Quarter-Day	−6.06%	−3.23%	−7.58%	−4.12%
Average	−7.91%	−5.92%	−14.14%	−9.18%

Table 4.3. *Gain if workers can move with an electric kick scooter*

4.7. Conclusion and future work

In this work, steps were performed toward synchronized multi-modal transportation, which was motivated by a real-case situation. Adopting a lexicographical ordering for the considered objectives, it was numerically shown that synchronizing two heterogeneous travel modes that vary in their characteristics (more precisely light and heavy resources that differ in their speed, autonomy, and operational costs) instead of only one can be an advantage with respect to the total transportation costs and to the employed resources (for instance, a smaller heavy-vehicle fleet). It is important to note that a conservative case was considered in this study: parking spot limitation and congestion were not taken into account and the job density was rather small (less than 1 job per km^2). One can reasonably expect that more favorable situations would be faced in other practical contexts (particularly, within cities), which would lead to higher gains than the ones observed in this study. We have measured that augmenting the light-resource speed and its associated range leads to larger gains. Therefore, ultimately, the resulting solutions would be similar to those which can be obtained by coordinating trucks and drones.

The following research directions can be envisioned. First, other transportation modes can be used. For instance, in the context of delivery, the next step, after having improved the situation by replacing walking by electric kick scooters, would be to consider drones as the light resource. Indeed, drones could even be faster than trucks, but additional constraints such as capacity and landing eligibility would have to be considered. Second, other efficient metaheuristics should be developed to tackle a larger variety of instances with a bigger number of jobs, even in the case where nonlinear costs occur (Bierlaire *et al.* 2010; Schindl and Zufferey 2015). Third, in addition to the already proposed heavy and light resources, one can also use an external taxi service in order to reduce the size of the employed fleet of vehicles at a reasonable additional cost. This is particularly appealing if a few isolated jobs require the need of an additional marginal resource. Finally, the robustness of our approach could be measured by introducing random fluctuations of the traveling and service times, as exposed by Respen *et al.* (2017a) for the VRP. In such a context, dynamic delays (e.g. traffic congestion and breakdowns) should be considered with care as they could lead to infeasible solutions with respect to the time window constraints.

4.8. References

Baldacci, R., Battarra, M., and Vigo, D. (2008). Routing a heterogeneous fleet of vehicles. In *The Vehicle Routing Problem: Latest Advances and New Challenges*, Golden, B. L., Raghavan, S., and Wasil, E. A. (eds.). Springer, Berlin.

Bierlaire, M., Thémans, M., and Zufferey, N. (2010). A heuristic for nonlinear global optimization. *INFORMS Journal on Computing*, 22(1), 59–70.

Blum, C. and Roli, A. (2003). Metaheuristics in combinatorial optimization: overview and conceptual comparison. *ACM Computing Surveys*, 35(3), 268–308.

Coindreau, M.-A., Gallay, O., and Zufferey, N. (2017a). Improved sustainability in vehicle routing via multimodality. *Proceedings of the 1st INFORMS Transportation and Logistics Society Conference (TSL 2017)*, Chicago, USA.

Coindreau, M.-A., Gallay, O., and Zufferey, N. (2017b). Vehicle routing with multi-modality: a practical application. *Proceedings of the 18th Annual Congress of the French Operations Research Society (ROADEF 2017)*, Metz, France.

Coindreau, M.-A., Gallay, O., and Zufferey, N. (2018). Synchronizing heterogeneous vehicles in a routing and scheduling context. *Proceedings of the 16th International Conference on Project Management and Scheduling (PMS 2018)*, Rome, Italy.

Desaulniers, G., Lessard, F., and Hadjar, A. (2008). Tabu search, partial elementarity, and generalized k-path inequalities for the vehicle routing problem with time windows. *Transportation Science*, 42(3), 387–404.

Drexl, M. (2012). Synchronization in vehicle routing: a survey of VRPs with multiple synchronization constraints. *Transportation Science*, 46(3), 297–316.

Fikar, C. and Hirsch, P. (2015). A matheuristic for routing real-world home service transport systems facilitating walking. *Journal of Cleaner Production*, 105, 300–310.

Gallay, O. and Zufferey, N. (2018). Metaheuristics for lexicographic optimization in industry. *Proceedings of the 19th Workshop on Metaheuristics for Industry (EU/ME 2018)*, Geneva, Switzerland.

Garey, M. and Johnson, D. S. (1979). *Computer and Intractability: A Guide to the Theory of NP-Completeness*. Freeman, San Francisco.

Gendreau, M. and Potvin, J.-Y. (2019). *Handbook of Metaheuristics*. Springer, Berlin.

Gussmagg-Pfliegl, E., Tricoire, F., Doerner, K., and Hartl, R. (2011). Mail-delivery problems with park-and-loop tours: a heuristic approach. *Proceedings of the ORP3 Meeting*, Cadiz, Spain.

Hertz, A., Schindl, D., and Zufferey, N. (2005). Lower bounding and tabu search procedures for the frequency assignment problem with polarization constraints. *4OR*, 3(2), 139–161.

Kirkpatrick, S., Gelatt, C. D., and Vecchi, M. (1983). Optimization by simulated annealing. *Science*, 220(5498), 671–680.

Koc, C., Bektas, T., Jabali, O., and Laporte, G. (2016). Thirty years of heterogeneous vehicle routing. *European Journal of Operational Research*, 249(1), 1–21.

Lin, C. K. Y. (2011). A vehicle routing problem with pickup and delivery time windows, and coordination of transportable resources. *Computers & Operations Research*, 38(11), 1596–1609.

Masson, R., Lehuédé, F., and Péton, O. (2013). Efficient feasibility testing for request insertion in the pickup and delivery problem with transfers. *Operations Research Letters*, 41(3), 211–215.

Masson, R., Lehuédé, F., and Péton, O. (2014). The dial-a-ride problem with transfers. *Computers & Operations Research*, 41, 12–23.

Murray, C. C. and Chu, A. G. (2015). The flying sidekick traveling salesman problem: optimization of drone-assisted parcel delivery. *Transportation Research Part C: Emerging Technologies*, 54, 86–109.

Osman, I. H. and Laporte, G. (1996). Metaheuristics: bibliography. *Annals of Operations Research*, 63, 513–623.

Pisinger, D. and Ropke, S. (2007). A general heuristic for vehicle routing problems. *Computers and Operations Research*, 34(8), 2403–2435.

Respen, J., Zufferey, N., and Potvin, J.-Y. (2017a). Impact of vehicle tracking on a routing problem with dynamic travel times. *RAIRO Operations Research*, 53(2), 401–414.

Respen, J., Zufferey, N., and Wieser, Ph. (2017b). Three-level inventory deployment for a luxury watch company facing various perturbations. *Journal of the Operational Research Society*, 68(10), 1195–1210.

Schindl, D. and Zufferey, N. (2015). A learning tabu search for a truck allocation problem with linear and nonlinear cost components. *Naval Research Logistics*, 62(1), 32–45.

Shaw, P. (1998). Using constraint programming and local search methods to solve vehicle routing problems. *Lecture Notes in Computer Science*, 1520, 417–431.

Thevenin, S., Zufferey, N., and Potvin, J.-Y. (2018). Graph multi-coloring for a job scheduling application. *Discrete Applied Mathematics*, 234, 218–235.

Zufferey, N. (2002). Heuristiques pour les problèmes de la coloration des sommets d'un graphe et d'affectation de fréquences avec polarités. PhD thesis, École Polytechnique Fédérale de Lausanne (EPFL), Switzerland.

5

An Overview of the Recent Solution Approaches in the Green Vehicle Routing Problem

The Green Vehicle Routing Problem (GVRP) is a branch of green logistics where the primary concern is the reduction of greenhouse gases (GHGs), next to other externalities caused by the intensive use of roads and other modes of transportation. From an operations research perspective, several exact and approximate methods were developed for different extensions of the GVRP since 2007. This chapter presents a brief review of the progress of the literature on GVRP as well as an up-to-date summary of the most frequently used solution approaches applied for the GVRP and its different variants from 2014.

5.1. Introduction

The Green Vehicle Routing Problem (GVRP) is an extension of the well-known Vehicle Routing Problem (VRP). The VRP was introduced by Dantzig and Ramser (1959) as the "Truck dispatching problem". It aims to find an optimal routing of a set of vehicles located at a central depot which aim to satisfy the demands of a set of dispersed customers. The primary objective of the first formulations of the VRP is the minimization of economic costs through the total traveled distance or the total time spent in the tour. Many variants of the VRP were conducted since its introduction, such as time window constraints, the congested period when defining time periods, split deliveries, simultaneous pickup and delivery, and so on. Lin *et al.* (2014) surveyed the numerous variants of the VRP that appeared from its introduction until 2013. The authors also summarized different studies dealing with

---

Chapter written by Emna MARREKCHI, Walid BESBES and Diala DHOUIB.

the GVRP from 2007 until 2013. They defined the GVRP as an extension of the VRP that considers an environmental objective. The authors propose a classification of the GVRP in three categories: the Pollution-Routing Problem (PRP) dealing with the minimization of emissions and speed in each arc, the G-VRP dealing with energy consumption, and the VRP in Reverse Logistics (VRPRL). The PRP concerns finding the optimal plan of vehicles' routing while minimizing the emissions of GHGs. A major objective of the G-VRP is the minimization of energy consumption (commonly expressed in terms of fuel consumption).

This classification of PRP and G-VRP for the GVRP in forward logistics was adopted in most of the research in this topic. In the same year, Park and Chae (2014) proposed a review of the adopted solution approaches for the GVRP in forward logistics. We extend this review by considering the works appearing after 2014. We divide the solution approaches into two classes: (i) exact methods leading to optimal solutions and (ii) approximate methods to find heuristics and metaheuristics.

Since the literature on GVRP is very rich and many surveys and papers described mathematical models, we exclude, in this chapter, this class of optimization approaches and expose the basic formulations of the PRP and G-VRP briefly.

The remainder of this chapter is organized as follows. In section 5.2, we present briefly the basic mathematical formulations of both GVRPs related to forward logistics with a description of the chronological progress of the literature on GVRP. In section 5.3, we summarize some interesting studies presenting solution methodologies. The most commonly used exact methods, heuristics, and metaheuristics are presented. Finally, general conclusions and some perspectives are given in section 5.4.

5.2. Chronological progress of the literature on the GVRP

5.2.1. *The Green-VRP*

Introduced by Kara *et al.* (2007) as the Energy Minimizing Vehicle Routing Problem (EMVRP), the first proposed model for the G-VRP is defined on a complete graph $G = (V, A)$, where $N = \{0, 1, ..., n\}$ is the node set and $A = \{(i,j): i, j \in V, i \neq j\}$ is the set of arcs, served by m identical vehicles constrained by capacity Q. Each vehicle has a tare (curb weight) Q_0. The set $N0 = N \setminus \{0\}$ is a customer set, and each customer $i \in N_0$ has a non-negative demand q_i. Binary variables x_{ij} are equal to 1 if and only if arc (i, j) is traversed and zero otherwise. Continuous variables f_{ij} represent the total amount of flow on each arc $(i, j) \in A$.

The model minimizes the emissions through what the authors called energy, which is the product of distance and weight of the visited arc. This weighted distance function reduces the energy used, which is considered at that stage to minimize the FC. The model is subject to some constraints. (i) Exactly m vehicles are used. (ii) Each node is served by one vehicle. (iii) Each route starts and ends at the depot. (iv) The flow equation balances the inflow and outflow of each node, prohibiting any illegal sub-tour. (v) The vehicle capacity is not exceeded. The related mathematical model is as follows:

$$Min \sum_{i=0}^{n} \sum_{j=0}^{n} d_{ij} f_{ij} \qquad [5.1]$$

s.t

$$\sum_{i=1}^{n} x_{oi} = m \qquad [5.2]$$

$$\sum_{i=1}^{n} x_{io} = m \qquad [5.3]$$

$$\sum_{i=0}^{n} x_{ij} = 1 \qquad j = 1,2,\dots,n \qquad [5.4]$$

$$\sum_{j=0}^{n} x_{ij} = 1 \qquad i = 1,2,\dots,n \qquad [5.5]$$

$$\sum_{j=0}^{n} f_{ij} - \sum_{j=0}^{n} f_{ji} = q_i \qquad i = 1,2,\dots,n \qquad [5.6]$$
$$\quad {\scriptstyle j \neq i} \qquad {\scriptstyle j \neq i}$$

$$f_{oi} = Q_o x_{oi} \qquad i = 1,2,\dots,n \qquad [5.7]$$

$$f_{ij} \leq (Q + Q_o - q_j) x_{ij} \qquad (i,j) \in A \qquad [5.8]$$

$$f_{ij} \geq (Q_o + q_i) x_{ij} \qquad (i,j) \in A \qquad [5.9]$$

$$x_{ij} \in \{0,1\} \qquad (i,j) \in A \qquad [5.10]$$

This paper presents a seminal contribution to the VRP with environmental considerations. Based on this, several studies built new extensions. Xiao *et al.* (2012) consider that Kara *et al.* (2007) did not discuss the formulation of fuel consumption carefully. They propose an MILP model for the Fuel consumption Capacitated VRP (FCVRP) in which the objective function minimizes both the sum of vehicles' fixed costs and the total fuel costs. A new linear expression linking the Fuel Consumption Rate (FCR) to the weight of vehicles was developed based on collected data from the Ministry of Land, Infrastructure, Transport, and Tourism of Japan. In this FCR formula, the authors fixed values for the fully-loaded and non-loaded vehicle FCRs. These values were criticized later by Ubeda *et al.* (2011) and Zhang *et al.* (2014). These parameters were updated as they are not representative of real situations, and they largely affect the final solution.

In Fukasawa *et al.* (2015), the EMVRP is studied with the assumption that the cost over each arc is the product of the arc length and the weight of the vehicle. A first formulation, called a two-index one-commodity flow formulation, is proposed. This model is the same one proposed initially by Kara *et al.* (2007). In addition, they introduced two other MILP models: an arc-load formulation and a set partitioning formulation. The arc-load formulation extends the version of 2007 by including a binary variable x_{ij}^q indicating whether or not a vehicle travels from customer i to customer j carrying a load that is exactly equal to q, where q is the load value. A branch-and-cut algorithm is applied and tested on the well-known CVRP instances. The results show that the algorithm can solve more instances to optimality compared to existent results in the literature.

Shijin and Xin (2016) extended the EMVRP by considering a mixed fleet, where it is not necessary to use all available vehicles. Two mixed-integer programs are presented. The first model minimizes the energy consumed based on the assumption of a cumulative energy function. The second formulation uses the parallel-machine scheduling problem where the machines represent the vehicles and the jobs represent the customers. The computational results show that the author' choice not to use all of the vehicles gives better results.

Recently, Ghannadpour (2019) proposed a multi-objective EMVRP with time windows and customers' priority for servicing. He develops a mathematical model that minimizes the total energy consumed, minimizes the total number of vehicles used, and maximizes the total satisfaction rate of customers. A multi-objective evolutionary algorithm is developed and tested on Solomon's instances (Solomon 1987). The comparison of the results with those obtained with the Non-dominated Sorting Genetic Algorithm II (NSGA II) and CPLEX Solver shows that the proposed method is of good quality.

5.2.2. The Pollution-Routing Problem

First introduced by Bektas and Laporte (2011), the PRP was extended by Demir *et al.* (2012) to consider the possibility of low travel speeds. The problem is defined on a complete graph $G = (N,A)$ with $N = \{0,1,...,n\}$ the set of nodes and $A = \{(i,j): i, j \in N, i \neq j\}$ the set of arcs visited by $K = \{1,2,.....,m\}$, a homogeneous and fixed size fleet of vehicles. The set $N_0 = N \setminus \{0\}$ is a customer set, and each customer $i \in N_0$ has a non-negative demand q_i. A service time interval $[a_i, b_i]$ is defined and the customer i must be served within this time interval. Early arrivals at the nodes are permitted but the vehicle has to wait until time a_i before service can start. The service time of customer i is denoted by t_i. The PRP considers the speed on each arc. For this, a discretized speed function is defined with R non-decreasing speed levels $\bar{v}^r$ $(r = 1,...,R)$. Binary variables x_{ij} are equal to 1 if and only if arc (i, j) is traversed. Continuous variables f_{ij} represent the total amount of flow on each arc $(i, j) \in A$. Continuous variables y_j represent the time at which the service starts at a node j. Finally, z_{ij}^r indicate whether or not an arc is traversed at a speed level r.

The PRP aims for the minimization of the GHG emissions incurred by the curb weight of the vehicle and the payload, in addition to the drivers' wages. The model is subject to some constraints stipulating that: (i) m vehicles depart from the depot. (ii) Each customer is visited exactly once. (iii) The balance flow (the flow is increased by the amount of demand of each visited customer) is guaranteed. (iv) The capacity restrictions are satisfied. (v) Time window constraints obtained through a linearization of some inequalities where $k_{ij} = max\{0, b_i + t_i + d_{ij}/v^l - a_j\}$. (vi) The total driving time restrictions for each vehicle are respected. (vii) Only one-speed level is selected for each arc and $z_{ii}^r = 1$ if $x_{ij}^r = 1$. The related mathematical model is detailed in what follows.

$$Min \sum_{(i,j)\in A} f_c KNV \lambda\, d_{ij} \sum_{r=1}^{R} z_{ij}^r / \bar{v}^r + \sum_{(i,j)\in A} f_c \omega\gamma\, \lambda\alpha_{ij}\, d_{ij} x_{ij} +$$
$$\sum_{(i,j)\in A} f_c\gamma\, \lambda\alpha_{ij}\, d_{ij} f_{ij} + \sum_{(i,j)\in A} f_c\beta\gamma\, \lambda d_{ij} \sum_{r=1}^{R} z_{ij}^r\, (\bar{v}^r)^2 + \sum_{j\in N_0} f_d s_j \quad [5.11]$$

s.t.

$$\sum_{j\in N} x_{0j} = m \qquad\qquad\qquad\qquad\qquad [5.12]$$

$$\sum_{j\in N} x_{ij} = 1 \qquad\qquad\qquad \forall i \in N_0 \quad [5.13]$$

$$\sum_{i\in N} x_{ij} = 1 \qquad\qquad\qquad \forall j \in N_0 \quad [5.14]$$

$$\sum_{j\in N} f_{ji} - \sum_{j\in N} f_{ij} = q_i \qquad\qquad \forall i \in N_0 \quad [5.15]$$

$$q_j\, x_{ij} \leq f_{ji} \leq (Q - q_i)\, x_{ij} \qquad\qquad \forall\, (i,j) \in A \quad [5.16]$$

$$y_i - y_j + t_i + \sum_{r \in R} d_{ij}\, Z_{ij}^r / \bar{v}^r \le k_{ij}\,(1 - x_{j0}) \quad \forall\, i \in N\,, \forall\, j \in N_0,\, i \ne j \quad [5.17]$$

$$a_i \le y_i \le b_i \qquad\qquad\qquad\qquad\qquad\qquad \forall\, i \in N_0 \quad [5.18]$$

$$y_j + t_j - s_j + \sum_{r \in R} d_{j0}\, z_{j0}^r / \bar{v}^r \le L\,(1 - x_{j0}) \qquad\qquad \forall\, j \in N_0 \quad [5.19]$$

$$\sum_{r \in R} z_{ij}^r = x_{ij} \qquad\qquad\qquad\qquad\qquad\qquad \forall\, (i,j) \in A \quad [5.20]$$

$$x_{ij} \in \{0,1\} \qquad\qquad\qquad\qquad\qquad\qquad \forall\, (i,j) \in A \quad [5.21]$$

$$f_{ij} \ge 0 \qquad\qquad\qquad\qquad\qquad\qquad\qquad \forall\, (i,j) \in A \quad [5.22]$$

$$y_i \ge 0 \qquad\qquad\qquad\qquad\qquad\qquad\qquad \forall\, i \in N_0 \quad [5.23]$$

$$z_{ij}^r \in \{0,1\} \qquad\qquad\qquad\qquad\qquad\qquad \forall\, (i,j) \in A,\, r \in R \quad [5.24]$$

Since that work, several extensions of the PRP have been studied. Franceschetti *et al.* (2013) considered the traffic congestion that significantly restricts vehicle speeds at peak periods and results in greater emissions. The proposed extension is a time-dependent PRP. Koc *et al.* (2014) studied the fleet size and mix PRP where the heterogeneous fleet is used instead of identical vehicles. In Demir *et al.* (2014), the bi-objective PRP was defined and both fuel consumption and driving time were minimized. Eshtehadi *et al.* (2017) included the stochastic demands and travel times in the PRP. Several extensions and solution approaches have been developed. In the following section, some other variants are surveyed.

5.3. Solution methodologies for the GVRP

In this section, we briefly present the most-used approaches for solving the GVRP with its different extensions. In Table 5.1, cited papers that present exact methods are grouped.

5.3.1. *Exact methods*

5.3.1.1. *Convex optimization*

By using the disjunctive convex programming tools, Fukasawa *et al.* (2016) proposed two mixed integer Convex Optimization (CO) models dedicated to PRP resolution with continuous speed. Both models are built on a naive nonconvex formulation of the PRP and a first disjunctive convex programming reformulation that was reformulated using a big-M formulation. A mixed-integer second-order cone programming model is also formulated with some valid inequalities. The proposed formulations of the big-M formulation and the mixed-integer second-order cone programming model were tested on the PRPLIB instances and on the instances of Kramer (2015b). Instances with 25 customers were optimally solved for the first time for such a problem.

5.3.1.2. Robust optimization

In Tajik *et al.* (2014), a MILP model is developed for the PRP with time windows and simultaneous pickup and delivery. The model minimizes a total cost including the cost of fuel consumption and CO_2 emissions, the payloads of the vehicles, acceleration, the driver wage, and penalty costs for tardiness and earliness in pickups. A Robust counterpart Optimization (RO) model is applied in order to take into account some stochastic parameters of the model, such as fuel consumption and emissions cost, travel, and service time. Sensitivity analysis and computational results show the effect of the number of pickups and deliveries on the objective function's value and that the capacity of the vehicles directly influences the routing plan and the fleet size. In Eshtehadi *et al.* (2017), the PRP with time windows was also studied. The proposed MILP minimizes the total cost of fuel consumption. The authors used the RO to deal with the demand uncertainty. A hard worst-case optimization approach was applied to the CVRP with demand uncertainty in order to compare it to deterministic solutions. A more flexible version, defined by the soft worst-case optimization approach leading to solving of the previous model but without satisfying all the constraints in their extreme worst-case values, was later proposed. The experimental results on the PRPLIB show that the proposed approaches lead to feasible solutions and that fuel savings are possible.

5.3.1.3. Dynamic programming

Xiao and Konak (2015b) studied the GVRSP that consists of not only finding the set of optimal routes but also returning the departure and arrival times of each vehicle at each node. The problem defined takes into account the time dependency and the possibility to schedule idle times anywhere in the tour in order to avoid congested periods. The proposed model minimizes the emissions and a tardiness penalty that depends on the customer importance. As the GVRP is NP-hard, more complicated extensions are also NP-hard. Based on this NP-hardness, the existing off-the-shelf solvers can solve, optimally, small-sized instances only. For this, the authors proposed two approaches to solve the GVRSP. A dynamic programming (DP) procedure was applied for the scheduling part of the GVRSP by calculating the optimal departure and arrival time of each vehicle at each node. The routing part was optimized using a metaheuristic method. Later, Xiao and Konak (2017) presented a more detailed and complex version: the time-dependent GVRSP with CO_2 minimization. The emissions were computed using the Comprehensive Modal Emissions Model (CMEM) and the developed MILP considers the payload of each vehicle on each arc as a decision variable and involves a mixed fleet. The routing phase of the problem was solved using a DP. The DP was able to find optimal schedules for all traveled arcs with discrete departure/arrival times.

5.3.1.4. Branch-and-Price algorithm

Dabia *et al.* (2016) applied the Branch-and-Price algorithm (BPA) for a different problem: the PRP. The pricing problem is a speed- and departure time-dependent elementary shortest path problem with resource constraints, while the master problem is a set partitioning solved using column generation. This approach is applied for the first time for this problematic concerned with PRP in the green context. The computational results on Solomon's instances (Solomon 1987) showed that the algorithm can solve instances with up to 100 customers; to optimality, however, many instances with only 25 customers were not solved.

Dellaert *et al.* (2018) studied the two-echelon vehicle routing problem constrained by time windows. The 2E-VRP consists of a first echelon where freight is transferred from depots to intermediate facilities (generally by means of large-capacitated vehicles) and a second echelon where the freight is moved from these facilities to final customers (commonly small capacitated vehicles are used). The authors proposed two mathematical formulations for the problem: the first formulation considers the paths of both first- and second-echelon tours, while the second formulation decomposes the first- and second-echelon paths. Both formulations were solved using BPAs. The BPAs were tested on newly generated instances for the two-echelon vehicle routing problem with time windows. The proposed solution approach is the first to be able to solve large instances composed of five satellites and 100 customers to optimality.

References	Variants	Solution approaches
Tajik *et al.* (2014)	PRPTWSPD	MM+RO
Xiao and Konak (2015b)	GVRSP	MM+DP
Dabia *et al.* (2016)	PRP	BPA
Fukasawa *et al.* (2016)	PRP	CO

Eshtehadi *et al.* (2017)	PRP	MM+RO
Xiao and Konak (2017)	TD-VRSP-CO$_2$	MM+DP
Dellaert *et al.* (2018)	2E-VRPTW	MM+BPA

PRPTWSPD: PRP with Time Windows and Simultaneous Pickup and Delivery; *GVRSP*: Green Vehicle Routing and Scheduling Problem; *TD-VRSP-CO$_2$*: Time-Dependent Vehicle Routing and Scheduling Problem with CO$_2$ consideration

Table 5.1. *The most-used exact methods for the GVRP. "MM" refers to the development of a mathematical model*

5.3.2. *Metaheuristics*

Heuristics and metaheuristics are both approximate methods that do not guarantee optimal solutions but give feasible and good solutions in reasonable computational time. The suffix "meta" added to heuristic means higher and biggest level. Metaheuristics are more performant and practical in solving combinatorial problems than heuristics. They can be applied to a wide range of problems, in contrast with heuristics, which are customized for the treated problem. There is a large diversity in metaheuristics. We describe the most-used methods in GVRPs and related variants in the following.

5.3.2.1. *Genetic algorithm*

The genetic algorithm (GA) is an evolutionary metaheuristic inspired by the process of Darwin's natural evolution. This theory stipulates that all species increase their ability to survive and reproduce by developing the natural selection of small and inherited variations. The GA imitates this theory by starting with a population (this population is usually randomly generated), called a generation, which undergoes an iterative process. At each generation, a fitness representing the value of an objective function is evaluated. New generations are created based on bio-inspired operators: mutation, crossover, and selection.

El Bouzekri El Idrissi and El Hilali Alaoui (2014) proposed a bi-GVRP that minimizes emissions and total traveled distance representing transportation cost. A GA was applied to a multi-objective optimization weighted linear aggregation. At each iteration, the authors applied two operators, – mutation and crossover – to select the best individuals based on their fitness. The fitness is defined as the inverse of the distance, so the lower the distance, the higher the fitness. The selection is made based on the roulette operator. This operator consists of selecting individuals proportionally to their fitness: survival of the fittest. A step of replacement is also applied to select the individuals that will figure in the next generation. The GA was tested on Eilon data (Christofides and Elion 1969) and the Fisher Problem (Fisher *et al*. 1981), and it proves its efficiency compared to existent results.

In Chu-Fu Hsueh (2016), a GVRP with stochastic travel speeds and the mixed fleet was proposed. A GA was applied with two chromosomes encoded: the first one represents the sequence of customers and so has a length equal to the number of customers. The second chromosome represents the index of the last served customer for each vehicle and so its length is equal to the number of vehicles. The fitness function is expressed through the problem objective function of total fixed costs of dispatching and emissions minimization. The selection process is based on the tournament method in which the fittest individuals from a random picking are selected. The crossover is applied to the first chromosomes only. To widen the research space, a mutation operator is used. The new two-part chromosome was tested on the PRPLIB of Demir *et al*. (2012) and was proved to be able to efficiently solve other extensions of VRPs.

In Xiao and Konak (2015b, 2017), a DP was defined next to a GA for solving large-sized instances of a GVRSP. In the latest version (2017) with heterogeneous fleet, the choice of the GA metaheuristic is based on the dependency of routing and scheduling in this particular problem. In fact, the GA is able to combine, through the crossover phase, feasible and unfeasible solutions and create new ones. A dynamic fitness function is defined as a penalty function that helps the search for best solutions that can reside in boundaries of feasible and infeasible solutions. Computational experiments on 30 randomly generated instances and 14 well-known CVRP benchmark instances (up to 199 customers) show the effectivity and efficiency of the proposed approach.

Oliveira da Costa *et al*. (2017) applied the GA for a real case study of parcel deliveries in Bristol, in the UK. The initialization of the population is done with the Clark Wright and random insertion construction heuristics that return three initial members of the population. The remaining is randomly generated. Tournament method is used for the selection phase. New offspring is only selected if it has better a fitness value than current chromosomes. The proposed algorithm was tested on the instances proposed by Christofides (1976) and Christofides and Elion (1969). Comparisons between solving m Traveling Salesman Problems (where m designates drivers pre-assigned to regions) and GVRPs (with environmental concerns) show that the applied approach leads to gains in the distance traveled and in emissions.

5.3.2.2. *Simulated annealing*

This probabilistic metaheuristic is known for its usefulness in finding global rather than local optima. It is inspired by the thermodynamics where metals cool and anneal; however, instead of the energy of a material, simulated annealing (SA) uses the objective function of an optimization problem. This method is straightforward in its application. It chooses a random move. If this move improves the solution, it is accepted. Otherwise, a probability function (analogous to temperature in thermodynamics) is applied in order to make the next unguided move. The objective of SA is to move from high-energy spaces to low-energy spaces.

Xiao and Konak (2015a) proposed an SA for the GVRSP. The proposed algorithm was tested on 30 small-sized instances, and the results show that optimal solutions were found for more than two-thirds of the GVRSPs, with less than 1% of the average deviation.

Feng *et al.* (2017) proposed a GVRP with stochastic speeds and an improved SA. The proposed solution approach acts based on four axes: construction of the initial solution with depot index 0 and series of positive numbers for customers, generation of neighborhood solutions based on exchange rules (swap, relocation, and 2-opt), local search, and replacement of the current best solution (based on a memory array that records the best solutions). Experiments on the PRPLIB show that the improved SA is effective for large-sized instances.

Dagne *et al.* (2019) studied a multi-depot GVRP. A modified SA is proposed. The initial solution is generated following three steps: clustering (customers are grouped according to a distance factor), routing (insured based on a distance matrix), and path optimization (starting from the nearest customers to the depot). Neighborhood search is based on the 2-opt and 3-opt methods. The criteria for accepting a solution are made based on a modified probability of accepting criteria. The approach proposed is tested on the instances of Cordeau (Cordeau *et al.* 1997), and comparisons between the improved SA and other metaheuristics show the efficiency of this approach in terms of solution quality.

5.3.2.3. Tabu search

Fakhrizada and Esfahani (2013) had demonstrated that this metaheuristic is an efficient solution approach for VRP issues. The Tabu search (TS) relies on memory structures. It memorizes the last changes of recent moves and prevents future moves from undergoing these changes.

Gang *et al.* (2016) proposed a TS for the GVRSP constrained by time windows, time dependency, and simultaneous pickup and delivery of an airline ticketing company. The customer satisfaction is stated as an objective to be maximized, with an emissions objective to be minimized. The hybridization of the TS with an heuristic algorithm shows that this approach finds a green routing and scheduling plan that respects the environment.

Setak *et al.* (2017) applied the TS to a time-dependent PRP that minimizes travel time, toll fees, and emissions. The problem is defined in a multi-graph, allowing the existence of more than one edge between any two nodes. The TS is defined according to three main parameters: its length, its tenure, and the maximum number of iterations. Tested on 28 generated instances, the TS proves its efficiency and effectiveness.

5.3.2.4. *Particle swarm optimization*

Particle swarm optimization (PSO) is inspired by the behavior of social organisms living in groups, such as birds and fish. These particles have stochastic trajectories influenced by the best-recorded position and the best-achieved group position. Each particle has a position and a velocity, which both change at each iteration. In the standard PSO, all particles are forced to follow the same strategy. This leads to the fact that the standard PSO is a monotonic learning pattern. This monotonicity makes the standard PSO algorithm sometimes unable to deal with complex situations. From this, modified and new extensions of the PSO have been developed to fight this lack.

Naderipour and Alinaghian (2016) studied the open time-dependent VRP in which the vehicles are not constrained to return to the depot after completing their tour. To solve the problem, an improved PSO is developed and tested on Augerat's instances (Augerat *et al.* 1995). The improved PSO extends the original PSO by exploring the neighbor particle to find global optima. The results show that the proposed solution approach leads to a 16% reduction in emissions.

Kumar *et al.* (2016) studied multi-objective, multi-vehicle production routing and the PRP with time windows. The objective function is to minimize the total operational costs and emissions. For this multi-objective case, the authors proposed a self-learning PSO. Contrary to the standard monotonic PSO, the self-learning PSO relies on four learning operators that help the particle in: (i) converging to the current global best solution, (ii) exploiting a local optimum, (iii) exploring new promising areas, and (iv) jumping-out of a local optimum. The proposed metaheuristic is tested on the PRPLIB and compared to the performance of the performant Non-dominated Sorting Genetic Algorithm II (NSGA II). The proposed multi-objective self-learning PSO is proved to perform better than the NSGA II. Besides, the proposed metaheuristic can solve large instances, while the NSGA II deteriorates.

Li *et al.* (2018) proposed an extension of the GVRP: green vehicle routing for cold chain logistics. Cold chain logistics needs an environment with a low temperature maintained, which consumes more fuel in comparison to ordinary logistics. The proposed model minimizes a total cost related to the vehicle operating, quality loss, product freshness, penalty, and energy, in addition to GHG emissions. A Chinese real-life case study was defined and both standard and modified PSOs were applied to solve it. The modified MPSO, with the advantage of preventing the solutions from being embedded into local optima, leads to better routing decisions and is also faster.

5.3.2.5. *Adaptive large neighborhood search*

The adaptive large neighborhood search (ALNS) metaheuristic extends the large neighborhood search (LNS) by modifying an initial solution using operators of destruction and repair. This iterative metaheuristic consists of destroying part of the current solution and then reconstructing it in the hope of finding a better solution.

Demir *et al.* (2014) proposed an enhanced PSO for the bi-objective PRP with two objectives: minimizing emissions and minimizing total driving time. At each iteration of the ALNS, a speed optimization algorithm is applied. The authors also defined four *a posteriori* methods, namely, the weighting method, the weighting method with normalization, the epsilon-constraint method, and a new hybrid method. These methods were tested with the proposed ALNS to their well-known PRPLIB instances. Later, Majidi *et al.* (2017) used the PRPLIB and the instances to test the proposed ALNS dedicated to solving the PRP with simultaneous pickup and delivery. The proposed metaheuristic can find good-quality solutions. It is highly efficient for small- and large-scale instances. Franceschetti *et al.* (2017) proposed a time-dependent PRP where the objective is to minimize the emissions and driver wages. An ALNS is proposed and tested on the PRPLIB instances. The proposed ALNS combines pre-existing removal and insertion operators with newly developed ones that are significantly efficient for medium- and large-scale instances (with up to 200 nodes).

In Zhang *et al.* (2018), a joint optimization model of the green vehicle scheduling and routing problem with time-varying speeds is defined. Soft time window constraints and driver wage are taken into consideration. The proposed model and an ALNS metaheuristic were tested on a real Chinese case study. A study is conducted on the effects of different optimal objectives on the delivery routes and departure time, and useful insights were stated.

References	Variants	Solution approaches
El Bouzekri El Idrissi and El Hilali Alaoui (2014)	GVRP	MM+GA
Demir *et al.* (2014)	PRP	MM+ALNS
Xiao and Konak (2015a)	GVRSP	MM+SA
Xiao and Konak (2015b)	GVRSP	MM+GA
Gang *et al.* (2016)	GVRSP	MM+TS
Hsueh (2016)	GVRP	MM+TS
Kumar *et al.* (2016)	MMPPRP-TW	MM+PSO
Naderipour and Alinaghian (2016)	OTDVRP	PSO
Feng *et al.* (2017)	VRPFSV	MM+SA
Majidi *et al.* (2017)	PRPSPD	MM+ALNS
Oliveira da Costa *et al.* (2017)	CVRP	GA
Setak *et al.* (2017)	TDPRP	TS
Xiao and Konak (2017)	TD-VRSP-CO$_2$	GA
Li *et al.* (2018)	GVRPCCL	MM+PSO
Zhang *et al.* (2018)	GVRSP	MM+ALNS
Dagne *et al.* (2019)	G-VRPMD	MM+SA

MMPPRP-TW: Multi-objective Multi-vehicles Production routing and PRP with Time Windows; *OTDVRP*: Open Time-Dependent VRP; *VRPFSV*: VRP with Fuel consumption and Stochastic travel speeds; *PRPSPD*: PRP with Simultaneous Pickup and Delivery; *CVRP*: Capacitated VRP*; TDPRP*: Time-Dependent PRP; *TD-VRSP-CO$_2$*: Time-Dependent Vehicle Routing and Scheduling Problem with CO$_2$ consideration; *GVRPCCL*: Green Vehicle Routing for Cold Chain Logistics; *G-VRPMD*: Green VRP with Multi-Depots.

Table 5.2. *The most-used metaheuristics for GVRP*

5.3.3. *Heuristics*

Similarly to metaheuristics, the heuristic approach does not guarantee the optimal solution. This approach is generally customized for a particular problem and is not applicable for others, contrary to the wide range of applicability of metaheuristics. It is an approach that speeds up the process of finding a satisfactory solution.

5.3.3.1. *Speed optimization algorithm*

This heuristic has been intensively used in the new research area in GVRP regarding the interest in optimizing this factor of fuel consumption and increasing emissions. Several extensions of the GVRP and especially the PRP have been handled with the speed optimization algorithm (SOA). Koc *et al.* (2014) applied the SOA for the fleet size and mix PRP. The PRP combined with an SOA has received intensive attention (Saka *et al.* 2017). Kramer *et al.* (2015a) combined the SOA with a departure-time optimization algorithm.

5.3.3.2. *Savings heuristics of Clarke and Wright (1964)*

Molina *et al.* (2014) proposed a GVRP with mixed fleet and time windows. The model is multi-objective: minimizing the total internal costs and minimizing emissions. The savings heuristic was applied for the heterogeneous case of GVRP. After each route, the algorithm calculates the savings for each vehicle and objective function from connecting two customers. Then these two customers are allocated to a route by further savings. The application of the proposed heuristic to a Spanish case study demonstrates the efficiency of the solution method.

Alinaghian and Zamani (2016) applied the savings (Sv) algorithm for the fleet size and mix GVRP. A savings algorithm is proposed with a giant tour heuristic. The computational results on Augerat instances (Augerat *et al.* 1995) show the efficiency of the proposed heuristics with a low percentage of error.

References	Variants	Solution approaches
Koc *et al.* (2014)	FSMPRP	MM+SOA
Molina *et al.* (2014)	HVRP	MM+Sv
Kramer *et al.* (2015a)	PRP	SDTOA
Alinaghian and Zamani (2016)	FSMGVRP	MM+Sv
Saka *et al.* (2017)	PRP	MM+SOA

FSMPRP: Fleet Size and Mix PRP; *HVRP*: Heterogeneous VRP; *FSMGVRP*: Fleet Size and Mix GVRP; *SDTOA*: Speed and Departure Time Optimization Algorithm.

Table 5.3. *The most-used heuristics for GVRP*

5.4. Conclusion

Nowadays, the transportation sector is one of the main contributors to GHG emissions. Since its introduction in 2007, the GVRP has received considerable attention, and several reviews have covered the existing literature, especially between 2007 and 2014. In this chapter, we have covered the most-used methods of optimization dedicated to the GVRP starting from 2014. As the GVRP is an NP-hard problem, efforts had been concentrated on developing approximate methods rather than exact methods. We remarked that the genetic algorithm is the most commonly used metaheuristic. This observation could be explained by the efficiency of this type of algorithm in solving different extensions of the GVRP. This review sheds light on the opportunities to develop approximate methods for the GVRPs and related extensions. Concerning other well-known heuristics such as local search, variable neighborhood search, and so on, we think that these methods need to be explored, tested, and hybridized with other exact/approximate approaches on different extensions of the GVRP.

As the GVRP is closely related to real situations, efforts to test and develop models with real-life applications are always encouraged. Finally, we believe that the consideration of real GVRP problems has not received, until now, the attention that it deserves.

5.5. References

Alinaghian, M. and Zamani, M. (2016). Three new heuristic algorithms for the fleet size and mix green vehicle routing problem. *Journal of Industrial and Systems Engineering*, 9(2), 88–101.

Augerat, P., Belenguer, J.M., Benavent, E., Corberan, A., and Rinaldi, G. (1995). Computational results with a branch and cut code for the capacitated vehicle routing problem. Research Report 949-M, University Joseph Fourier, Saint-Martin-d'Hères, France.

Bektas, T. and Laporte, G. (2011). The pollution routing problem. *Transportation Research Part B*, 45, 1232–1250.

Bektas, T., Ehmke, J.F.N., Psaraftis, H., and Puchinger J. (2019). The role of operational research in green freight transportation. *European Journal of Operational Research*, 274(3), 807–827.

Christofides, N. (1976). The vehicle routing problem. *Revue Française d'Automatique, d'Informatique et de Recherche Opérationnelle*, 10, 55–70.

Christofides, N. and Elion, S. (1969). An algorithm for the vehicle dispatching problem. *Operational Research Quarterly*, 20, 309–318.

Clarke, G. and Wright, J.W. (1964). Scheduling of vehicles from a central depot to a number of delivery points. *Operations Research*, 12, 568–581.

Cordeau, J.F., Gendreau, M., and Laporte, G. (1997). A Tabu search heuristic for periodic and multi-depot vehicle routing problems. *Networks*, 30, 105–119.

Dabia, S., Demir, E., and Van Woensel. (2016). An exact approach for the pollution-routing problem. *Transportation Science*, 51(4), 607–628.

Dagne, T.B., Jayaprakash, J., Haile, B., and Geremew, S. (2019). Optimization of green logistic distribution routing problem with multi depot using improved simulated annealing. In *6th EAI International Conference, ICAST 2018, Bahir Dar, Ethiopia*, Zimale, F.A., Enku, T., and Fanta, S.W. (eds). Springer.

Dantzig, G.B. and Ramser, J.H. (1959). The truck dispatching problem. *Management Science*, 6(1), 80–91.

Dellaert, N., Saridarq, F.D., Woensel, T.V., and Crainic, T.G. (2018). Branch-and-price based algorithms for the two-echelon vehicle routing problem with time windows. *Transportation Science*. doi: 10.1287/trsc.2018.0844.

Demir, E., Bektas, T., and Laporte, G. (2012). An adaptive large neighborhood search heuristic for the Pollution-Routing Problem. *European Journal of Operational Research*, 223, 346–359.

Demir, E., Bektas, T., and Laporte, G. (2014). The bi-objective Pollution-Routing Problem. *European Journal of Operational Research*, 232, 464–478.

El Bouzekri El Idrissi, A. and El Hilali Alaoui, A. (2014). Evolutionary algorithm for the bi-objective green vehicle routing problem. *International Journal of Scientific & Engineering Research*, 5(9), 70–77.

Eshtehadi, R., Fathian, M., and Demir, E. (2017). Robust solutions to the pollution-routing problem with demand and travel time uncertainty. *Transportation Research Part D*, 51, 351–363.

Fakhrizada, M. and Esfahanib, A.S. (2013). Modeling the time windows vehicle routing problem in cross-docking strategy using two meta-heuristic algorithms. *International Journal of Engineering-Transactions A: Basics*, 27(7), 1113–1126.

Feng, Y., Zhang, R.Q., and Jia, G. (2017). Vehicle routing problems with fuel consumption and stochastic travel speeds. *Mathematical Problems in Engineering*, Article ID 6329203.

Fisher, M., Jaikumar, R., and Van Wassenhove, L. (1981). A generalized assignment heuristic for vehicle routing. *Networks*, 11, 109–124.

Franceschetti, A., Demir, E., Honhon, D., Woensel, T.V., Bektas, T., and Laporte, G. (2013). The time-dependent pollution-routing problem. *Transportation Research Part B*, 56, 265–293.

Franceschetti, A., Demir, E., Honhon, D., Woensel, T.V., Laporte, G., and Stobbe, M. (2017). A metaheuristic for the time-dependent pollution-routing problem. *European Journal of Operational Research*, 259(3), 972–991.

Fukasawa, R., He, Q., and Song, Y. (2015). A branch-cut-and-price algorithm for the energy minimization vehicle routing problem. *Transportation Science*, 50(1), 23–34.

Fukasawa, R., He, Q., and Song, Y. (2016). A disjunctive convex programming approach to the pollution-routing problem. *Transportation Research Part B*, 94, 61–79.

Gang, H., Meiling, F., Hainan, Z., and Junqing, S. (2016). Research on green vehicle scheduling of free picking up and delivering customers for airlines ticketing company. *Chinese Control and Decision Conference (CCDC)*, IEEE.

Ghannadpour, S.F. and Zarrabi, A. (2019). Multi-objective heterogeneous vehicle routing and scheduling problem with energy minimizing. *Swarm and Evolutionary Computation*, 44, 728–747.

Hsueh, C.-F. (2016). The green vehicle routing problem with stochastic travel speeds. *16th COTA International Conference of Transportation Professionals, CICTP 2016*, ASCE, Reston, USA.

Kara, I., Kara, B.Y., and Kadri Yetis, M. (2007). *Combinatorial Optimization and Applications*. Springer.

Koc, C., Bektas, T., Jabali, O., and Laporte, G. (2014). The fleet size and mix pollution-routing problem. *Transportation Research Part B*, 70, 239–254.

Kramer, R., Maculan, N., Subramanian, A., and Vidal, T. (2015a). A speed and departure time optimization algorithm for the pollution-routing problem. *European Journal of Operational Research*, 247, 782–787.

Kramer, R., Subramanian, A., Vidal, T., and Cabral, L.D.A.F. (2015b). A matheuristic approach for the pollution-routing problem. *European Journal of Operational Research*, 243(2), 523–539.

Kumar, R.S., Kondapaneni, K., Dixit, V., Goswami, A., Thakur, L.S., and Tiwari, M.K. (2016). Multi-objective modeling of production and pollution routing problem with time window: a self-learning particle swarm optimization approach. *Computers & Industrial Engineering*, 99, 29–40.

Li, Y., Lim, M.K., and Tseng, M.L. (2018). A green vehicle routing model based on modified particle swarm optimization for cold chain logistics. *Industrial Management & Data Systems*, 119(1), 89–110.

Lin, C., Choy, K.L., Ho, G.T.S., Chung, S.H., and Lam, H.Y. (2014). Survey of green vehicle routing problem: past and future trends. *Expert Systems With Applications*, 41(4, Pt. 1), 1118–1138.

Majidi, S., Hosseini-Motlagh, S.M., Yaghoubi, S., and Jokar, A. (2017). Fuzzy green vehicle routing problem with simultaneous pickup delivery and time windows. *RAIRO – Operations Research*, 51, 1151–1176.

Molina, J.C, Eguia, I, Racero, J., and Guerrero, F. (2014). Multi-objective vehicle routing problem with cost and emission functions. *Procedia – Social and Behavioral Sciences*, 160, 254–263.

Naderipour, M. and Alinaghian, M. (2016). Measurement, evaluation and minimization of CO2, NOx, and CO emissions in the open time dependent vehicle routing problem. *Measurement*, 90, 443–452.

Oliveira da Costa, P.R., Mauceri, S., Carroll, P., and Pallonetto, F. (2017). A genetic algorithm for a green vehicle routing problem. *Electronic Notes in Discrete Mathematics*, 64, 65–74.

Park, Y. and Chae, J. (2014). A review of the solution approaches used in recent GVRP (Green Vehicle Routing Problem). *International Journal of Advanced Logistics*, 3(1–2), 27–37.

Saka, O.C., Gurel, S., and Van Woensel, T. (2017). Using cost change estimates in a local search heuristic for the pollution routing problem. *OR Spectrum*, 39(2), 557–587.

Setak, M., Shakeri, Z., and Pathoghi, A. (2017). A time dependent pollution routing problem in multi-graph. *IJE Transactions B: Applications*, 30(2), 234–242.

Shijin, W. and Liu, X. (2016). Energy minimization vehicle routing problem with heterogeneous vehicles. *13th International Conference on Service Systems and Service Management* (ICSSSM), IEEE.

Solomon, M.M. (1987). Algorithms for the vehicle routing and scheduling problems with time window constraints. *Operations Research*, 35(2), 254–265.

Tajik, N., Tavakkoli-Moghaddam, R., Vahdani, B., and Mousavi, S.M. (2014). A robust optimization approach for pollution routing problem with pickup and delivery under uncertainty. *Journal of Manufacturing Systems*, 33, 277–286.

Ubeda, S., Arcelus, F.J., Faulin, J. (2011). Green logistics at Eroski: a case study. *International Journal of Production Economics*, 131(1), 44–51.

Xiao, Y. and Konak, A. (2015a). A simulating annealing algorithm to solve the green vehicle routing & scheduling problem with hierarchical objectives and weighted tardiness. *Applied Soft Computing*, 34, 372–388.

Xiao, Y. and Konak, A. (2015b). Green vehicle routing problem with time-varying traffic congestion. *14th INFORMS Computing Society Conference*, Richmond, USA, 134–148.

Xiao, Y. and Konak, A. (2017). A genetic algorithm with exact dynamic programming for the green vehicle routing and scheduling problem. *Journal of Cleaner Production*, 167, 1450–1463.

Xiao, Y., Zhao, Q., Kaku, I., and Xu, Y. (2012). Development of a fuel consumption optimization model for the capacitated vehicle routing problem. *Computers & Operations Research*, 39, 1419–1431.

Zhang, S., Lee, C.K.M., Hoy, K.L, Ho, W., and Ip, W.H. (2014). Design and development of a hybrid artificial bee colony algorithm for the environmental vehicle routing problem. *Transportation Research Part D*, 31, 85–99.

Zhang, D., Wang, X., Li, S., Ni, N., and Zhang, Z. (2018). Joint optimization of green vehicle scheduling and routing problem with time-varying speeds. *PLOS ONE*, 13(2), e0192000.

6

Multi-Criteria Decision Aid for Green Modes of Crude Oil Transportation Using MACBETH: The Sfax Region Case

The hazardous materials transportation is a problem of growing interest worldwide, mainly due to the increasing volumes of goods transported and the risks generated. Transport is, therefore, both a logistical and a safety issue. In this context, the modal choice is a logistical choice that integrates several criteria and can influence the long-term sustainability and competitiveness of a company. This modal choice decision is not only influenced by the criteria of cost, time, and quality, but also by a wide range of social and environmental criteria. In this chapter, we focus on a specific activity in Tunisia. This activity is the transport of crude oil from the Sfax region to the port of Skhira. The problem to be solved in this research regards choosing the most appropriate mode(s) of transport for carrying crude oil while also considering economic, social, and environmental factors.

In order to achieve these objectives, we used the multi-criteria *MACBETH* method to find the appropriate mode of crude oil transportation that represents the compromise solution. To better validate our contribution, we conducted sensitivity analyses and a comparison with the *AHP* multi-criteria method.

6.1. Introduction

Transport is a key activity throughout the supply chain. It is part of a logistic process that is often multi-stakeholder and multi-activity. In fact, it can be considered as a strategic tool for linking various operators of a supply chain.

Chapter written by Nouha HAMMAMI, Mohamed Haykal AMMAR and Diala DHOUIB.

Freight transport is an intermediate activity in the process of supply, production, and distribution of products–the aim of which is to ensure that the different phases of product development, up to the final consumption stage, are synchronized.

However, the transport of hazardous materials differs from that of ordinary goods. In fact, the transport of hazardous materials is an issue of growing interest worldwide, mainly due to the increasing volumes of transported materials and the risks generated, in addition to the global challenge in terms of freight transport performance. These expeditions are made every day by rails, roads, planes, sea, canals and rivers.

Consequently, the transport of dangerous materials is a complex social and ecologically-sensitive problem involving a multitude of economic, social, and environmental parameters. It is, therefore, green transport that effectively integrates social and environmental concerns with dangerous materials transport logistics issues.

Among the green initiatives, we can mention:

– The use of green fuels such as low sulfur products and alternative fuels such as liquefied natural gas;

– Order consolidation and route optimization reducing distribution frequency, energy consumption, and CO_2;

– Concerns related to community/environment, employee health, and safety during transportation.

In the case of hazardous materials, the transport comes as both a logistical and safety challenge. We understand the importance of maintaining green transport management in a good state according to the right regulations, all the while not losing sight of the logistical constraints of the supply chain.

One of the company's major challenges is the implementation of an appropriate green transport system for hazardous materials, which is adapted to regulatory requirements and normative recommendations. The latter now require economic development that is more aware of the environment and society, in order to deal with ecological damage and social problems.

In this context, the mode of transport is a crucial element of the transport system, and the modal choice is a logistical choice that can influence the long-term sustainability and competitiveness of a company. Due to the advantages and disadvantages of each mode of transport, the modal choice is always a very important problem for companies, particularly in the case of the transportation of hazardous materials. This modal choice decision is generally not taken for each individual instruction, but incorporates several criteria. It is not only influenced by cost, time, and quality criteria, but also by a wide range of social and environmental criteria.

This chapter is divided into four sections: the first section presents a bibliographical study of the issues concerning the transport of hazardous materials, more particularly the issues regarding the design of green transport networks for hazardous materials, integrated problems of location and routing of the transport of hazardous materials, and the risk assessment issues for the transport of hazardous materials. The second section presents the *MACBETH* multi-criteria method, its concept and its steps. The third section shows our issues and objectives. The fourth section presents our methodological approach based on the *MACBETH* multi-criteria method, as well as the results obtained, sensitivity analyses, comparative analysis and discussions carried out.

6.2. State-of-the-art

According to Erkut and Alp (2007), most of the hazardous materials transport studies can generally be classified into the following groups: Vehicle Routing Issue, Network Design Issue, Risk Assessment Issue, and Integrated Location Issue and Routing.

6.2.1. *Hazardous materials transportation integrated location and routing problem*

Current and Ratick (1995) conducted one of the first studies to jointly model the location of facilities and the routing of dangerous materials. They proposed a mixed-integer multi-purpose programming model, and solved it using a business optimization tool in order to help decision makers locate and transport facilities handling dangerous materials to these facilities. In this model, the authors consider unit transport costs, fixed and variable facility costs, in addition to overall and individual risk and equity.

Xie *et al.* (2012) address the issue of locating transfer grounds and the routing of multi-modal transport networks. They present a linear programming model in mixed multi-purpose and multimodal (rail/road) integers, capable of simultaneously optimizing transfer ground locations and transport routes for dangerous materials subject to risk and cost constraints. They applied it to two transport networks of different sizes in Guangdong, China.

Inspired by the work of Xie *et al.* (2012), Yang Jiang *et al.* (2014) developed a similar model by adding a 0–1 decision variable that could generate optimization results that reflect the routing of dangerous materials' flows in accordance with rail transport organization principles.

6.2.2. *Hazardous materials transportation risk assessment problem*

Bubbico *et al.* (2004) propose a risk assessment tool for the transport of dangerous materials by road, rail, and combined rail–road transport. This tool takes into account the product database, accident statistics, and the selection of mean values that are typical of the parameters related to the type of transport activity and route. It relies on the geographic information system to help the decision maker to choose the route, resulting in the risk analysis. To better understand how this instrument works, the researchers promoted two examples and highlighted the benefits of this tool, which is not limited to road selection and risk analysis, but also allows the visualization of routes and impact areas for different disaster scenarios and the assessment of risk mitigation possibilities arising from route selection or mode of transport.

Koen Van Raemdonck *et al.* (2013) propose an assessment framework to map global and local risks for the area under consideration, and develop a methodology, for calculating local accident risk that takes local infrastructure parameters and accident data into account. The proposed framework would make it possible to estimate, visualize and compare the risk of transporting dangerous materials in Flanders, Belgium on a specific route by road, train, inland waterways, and even by pipeline.

Ammar *et al.* (2014) propose a risk analysis related to the road transport of dangerous materials from a company in Sfax, Tunisia. They focused on human, mechanical, and terrorist risks. They used the *FMECA* method and a multi-agent system in order to help make decisions to control and anticipate risks.

Luca Talarico *et al.* (2015) present a multi-modal transport safety model in a chemical supply chain. This model is based on game theory and allows safety measures to be allocated for each route belonging to a specific mode of transport. This is in order to prevent and detect terrorist attacks and avoid human and economic losses.

6.2.3. *Hazardous materials transportation network design problem*

Kara and Verter (2004) address the road network design problem of hazardous materials shipments when the government designates a network and transporters choose a route on that network. Indeed, they propose a two-level linear integer programming model (the role of transporters and government authorities) based on geographic information systems in order to design a road transport network so as to minimize the total risk resulting from the choice that transporters make regarding the cheapest route. The proposed model is being applied to the dangerous materials road transportation network in West Ontario, Canada.

On the other hand, Erkut and Alp (2007) simplify the issue of designing a road network for the transport of hazardous materials by using a tree structure so that there is only one path between each origin and destination, and this restriction removes the second level (transporter role). First, they formulated a mathematical programming model using integers with a single objective (minimization of total transport risk). Then, they developed a simple heuristic construction so as to extend the solution of the tree design issue by adding the shortest paths to the tree. These additions keep risks to a minimum and also provide carriers with the opportunity to choose less costly routes. The researchers use the road network of the city of Ravenna in Italy in order to illustrate the two solutions (integer programming model and heuristic resolution method).

Berman *et al.* (2007) are developing a method for determining the optimal design of a specialized emergency road network response for hazardous materials incidents. This is to maximize the ability to respond to incidents in a region, using a maximum arc recovery model. The application of the proposed methodology in Quebec and Ontario has improved emergency response capacity.

Erkut and Gzara (2008) consider a similar problem to that of Kara and Verter (2004). In fact, they generalized their model by considering the case of an unmanaged network and generated the same network for all hazardous materials shipments. In a first phase, the authors model the problem as a two-level network system and then analyze it by comparing it to three other scenarios. However, the two-level model is difficult to solve and can be ill-conceived, so in a second phase, the researchers put forward a heuristic algorithm that always looks for a stable solution to protect the government from the worst-case scenario so as to achieve a cost/risk trade-off.

Verter and Kara (2008) address the problem of road network design through road-based modeling, whose objective is to minimize the risk of road transport of dangerous materials according to government authorities, without threatening the economic viability of transporters' activities. The authors generate several solutions by varying the number of routing options in the formulated model until they reach a certain compromise between the regulator and the transporters. Two applications were illustrated: the first case focuses on shipments of dangerous goods by the road network in West Ontario, Canada, and the second case examines the issue in a much larger geographical area covering the Ontario and Quebec regions.

Bianco *et al.* (2009) address the hazardous materials road network design problem by involving both regional and local authorities when regulating shipments of dangerous materials in Italy. In fact, they proposed a two-level linear programming model. This model aims to minimize the total risk of the regional area and to ensure equity of risk of the populated links in the local area, by imposing restrictions on the volume of dangerous materials traffic on road network links. Since the two-level model is difficult to solve in an optimal fashion and its optimal solution may not be stable, the authors provide a heuristic method for finding a stable solution. The proposed two-level model and heuristic algorithm are being tested on real scenarios in an Italian regional network.

Leal Junior and D'Agosto (2011a) are developing a modal choice method consisting of seven steps that have been prepared on the basis of bibliographic research results and knowledge from experts. This approach allows a dynamic assessment of modal choice performance, all the while considering economic criteria (cost, safety, and relative deviation in delivery time) and socio-environmental criteria (energy consumption, *GHG* emissions, and liquid waste emissions), in order to prioritize alternatives for land (road/rail) and pipeline transport modes for the shipment of dangerous materials. They applied it to a real situation through a case study of bioethanol transport in the south-central region of Brazil to a port of export. The results indicate that road transport, although most often used, is not the best option compared to trains or pipelines (or a combination of three methods) from a socio-environmental perspective. However, in environmental terms, pipeline transport is the most appropriate method for long distances.

In the same context, Leal Junior and D'Agosto (2011b) use another modal choice method of theorem (2011a) to choose between the possible modes of transport (road, rail, sea, and pipeline) and substitute road transport, while considering economic (cost, reliability, and safety) and socio-environmental (energy consumption, greenhouse gas emissions, and solid and liquid waste emissions) aspects. According to a field study, the authors find that long-distance road transport is the worst of all the options considered.

Kazemi and Szmerekovsky (2015) examined a multi-modal network design problem in a downstream oil supply chain. To solve this problem, the authors propose multi-level, multi-product, and multi-modal mixed-variable linear mathematical programming in order to optimize distribution center locations and capacities, oil allocation, routes, modes of transport, and transfer volume so as to minimize the total cost of the chain. This model is characterized by the integration of multi-modal transport planning into the strategic design of the downstream supply chain. The authors have thus demonstrated that this multi-modal model has a lower total cost and a more appropriate design. The article presents a realistic case study of a downstream oil chain in two regions of the United States in order to illustrate the efficiency and improve performance measures of the chain.

Belaid *et al.* (2016) solve the problem of designing a bimodal network (road and pipeline) for transporting oil in the Sfax region of Tunisia using two objectives. The authors look for trees that cover the minimum construction cost and they also look for accident risk that links the various oil fields to the port of Skhira, using a constraint resolution technique. The results show that pipeline network solutions outperform road solutions.

Juliana Monteiro Lopes *et al.* (2016) present a comparative study of scenarios with which they can identify the most appropriate mode of transport in a bioethanol supply chain, aimed at reducing greenhouse gas emissions and total energy consumption. Using a life cycle analysis (*LCA*) and part of the lifecycle inventory (*LCI*), the authors identify the most appropriate scenario while taking into account total energy consumption, percentage of renewable energy used, and CO_2 emissions. This work shows the impact of modal choice and the use of renewable energies with regards to the environmental performance of the bioethanol supply chain.

A literature review was conducted by Strogen *et al.* (2016) on the assessment of external effects of the main modes of fuel transport on the environment, public health and safety. The aim was to present a framework for assessing new infrastructure projects and encouraging long-term thinking toward pipeline development, as the latter has lower impacts than other modes–particularly in terms of public health management and the monetary value of risks that could be potentially avoided.

A recent study by Siddiqui *et al.* (2017) addresses an integrated problem of inventory management and the choice of the mode of transport (marine/pipeline) for transporting refined oil products between refineries and distribution centers. It should be noted that transportation decisions are not only dictated by the refinery's production schedule, inventory levels, and customer demand, but also by environmental risks. As a result, the authors propose a mixed-integer linear planning with two objectives: to minimize the cost resulting from the use of ships and pipelines and the fixed operating costs of these ships and to minimize the risks associated with the use of both modes of transport when transporting refined oil products solved by a time-based heuristic solution. To validate their model, a realistic infrastructure in the United States was analyzed. The results show that pipeline transportation is the preferred mode for all refined oil products if cost is the only consideration. However, if environmental risks are considered, marine transportation is the preferred mode for most refined oil products, with the exception of heavier oils.

Based on our previous literature review, our work pertains to the network design problem, as the selection of an appropriate mode of transport is an important element in the design of the transportation network of *Hazmat*, as specified by Jayaraman (1998).

6.3. Real case: choice of crude oil transportation modal from the Sfax region to the Skhira port

Tunisia is located in a region that is rich in natural resources (such as crude oil, natural gas, iron mines, and phosphate). It operates a significant number of oil projects, in excess of 75 oil fields. The annual activity report (ETAP 2017) points out that the crude oil and condensate production of *ETAP* concessionaires were 11 261 705 barrels in 2017 (compared to 13 365 146 barrels in 2016), of which 34% was transported by tanker truck. However, despite the large number of oil projects, oil fields in Tunisia are characterized by limited reserves in terms of the vast majority of Tunisian oil deposits and can be identified by their high quality.

In this regard, it should be noted that the use of road transport for crude oil is a specific activity in Tunisia. The responsible authorities explained that the limited reserves, in terms of the vast majority of Tunisian oil fields, are transported by tanker truck to gas and liquefied gas gathering stations, and this being the only mode that can ensure economic efficiency as confirmed by Ammar *et al.* (2016) and Ammar *et al.* (forthcoming).

However, despite the decline in international barrel prices, in recent years, we have seen projects to transport crude oil by pipeline instead of by road. Regarding this, several questions were asked about this project:

– Can pipeline transportation ensure economic efficiency?

– Have decision makers favored factors other than cost?

– What are the specificities of crude oil's green transport?

– What is/are the most appropriate mode(s)?

6.3.1. *Identification of the problem*

The problem to be solved in this research is the choosing of the most appropriate mode(s) of crude oil transport from the Sfax region to the Skhira port, all the while considering economic factors, as well as social and environmental factors, as the latter now take on the same or even greater importance than economic sustainability.

Referring to our bibliographical study, let us note that the solution of an issue in the design of a network for transporting hazardous materials is mainly ensured by mathematical optimization methods and, more precisely, mathematical programming with multiple objectives, which aims to simultaneously optimize multiple objectives at the same time while under constraints. However, these methods require, first, that the assessments of actions be crucial and, second, that the criteria should be of a genuine nature. In addition, the decision maker is involved in defining the issue, or after the issue has been solved, but does not contribute to the construction of solutions.

To fill these gaps and to adapt to our real context, we have instead used multi-criteria decision support methods, considered as one of the most important branches of operational research to establish (or model) the preparation of decisions and the preferences of decision makers in order to move toward a compromise solution while taking into account various heterogeneous, conflicting, and contradictory criteria. In our research, we chose the *MACBETH* multi-criteria method to find the compromised way to transport crude oil from the Sfax region to the Skhira port, based on economic, environmental and social criteria.

6.3.2. *Method for Measuring Attractiveness by a Categorical-Based Evaluation Technique (MACBETH)*

MACBETH was developed in 1990, in collaboration with Professors C. A. Bana e Costa, J. Cl. Vansnick, and J. M. De Corte. This has led to the development of software that allows the proposed methodology to be tested in real-world practical applications. It is the *M-MACBETH* software (Bana e Costa *et al.* 2006).

The *MACBETH* method, as its name suggests, is an approach to measure attractiveness by way of an evaluation technique that is based on semantic categories, which is used to develop performance expectations that are consistent with their aggregation. The aggregation factor used is the weighted average. It adopts an initial repetitive questioning procedure in order to compare two elements using qualitative preferences alone.

Indeed, this method makes it possible to translate the semantic judgments made by a decision maker on a numerical scale through comparisons by experts in different situations.

The semantic categories (also called preference levels) are:

– C_0: No difference in attractiveness.

– C_1: Very weak difference in attractiveness.

– C_2: Weak difference in attractiveness.

– C_3: Moderate difference in attractiveness.

– C_4: Strong difference in attractiveness.

– C_5: Very Strong difference in attractiveness.

– C_6: Extreme difference in attractiveness.

The method recommends a structured procedure with five main steps:

– Step 1: The acquisition of preferred information.

– Step 2: The proposal of a scale.

– Step 3: The scale adjustment.

– Step 4: The determination of the weight.

– Step 5: The performance aggregation.

6.3.3. *Research methodology: MACBETH application*

To solve our modal choice problem, we used the multi-criteria *MACBETH* method to find the best way to transport crude oil from the Sfax region to the Skhira port, based on economic, environmental and social criteria.

6.3.3.1. *Structuring phase: identification of alternatives and criteria*

To transport crude oil from the Sfax region to the Skhira port, four alternatives have been selected, namely: Truck-Tanker, Pipeline, Train and Truck-Tanker,

Pipeline and Truck-Tanker, in order to arrange them from the best to the least good according to multiple criteria.

The criteria to be taken into account in the modal choice are determined through our literature review and expert opinion. These 12 criteria are as follows: Economic Risk (Specific Infrastructure Cost (C1) and Variable Costs (C2)) determined by Belaid *et al.* (2016), and the remaining criteria, determined by Ammar *et al.* (2014): Human Risk (Loss of Control (C3), Inappropriate Parking (C4), Occupational Disease (C5), Passage by a High Risk Area (C6) and Damage of Product Transported (C7)), Mechanical Risk (Mechanical Breakdown (C8) and Explosion Wheel (C9)), Environmental Risk (Overflowing of the Dangerous Products (C10) and Rupture within the Tank Degasser (C11)) and Terrorism Risk (C12).

6.3.3.2. *Matrices of attractiveness differences*

After having identified the criteria and alternatives considered, for each criterion, the decision maker will verbally judge the difference in attractiveness between, two actions, x and y of S (where x is more attractive than y), using semantic categories (also called preference levels), as shown in Figures 6.1–6.12.

At each judgment, the program checks the consistency of the new data with the previous data (consistency in *MACBETH*). The results of the decision maker's judgments are presented as a matrix.

Once all judgments have been entered, for any criteria, the software builds a numerical scale to translate ordinal preferences (verbal expressions) on a cardinal scale. This step is based on the resolution of a linear program.

This scale is proposed to the decision maker, and if this scale does not seem correct, the scores are adjusted in accordance with the judgment data (preference levels) that are provided in the matrix.

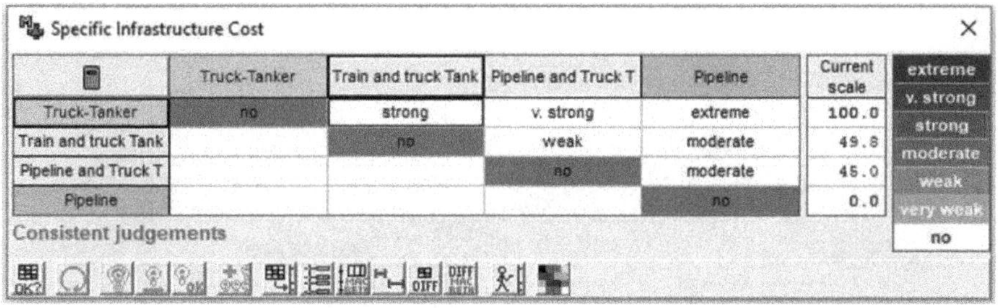

Figure 6.1. *Matrix of attractiveness differences (specific infrastructure cost criterion)*

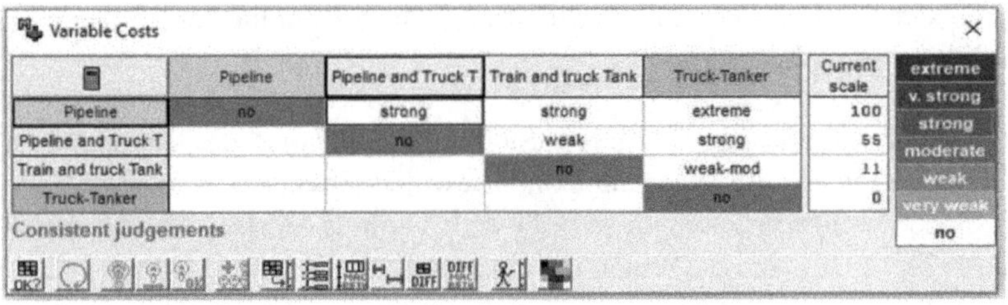

Figure 6.2. *Matrix of attractiveness differences (variable cost criterion)*

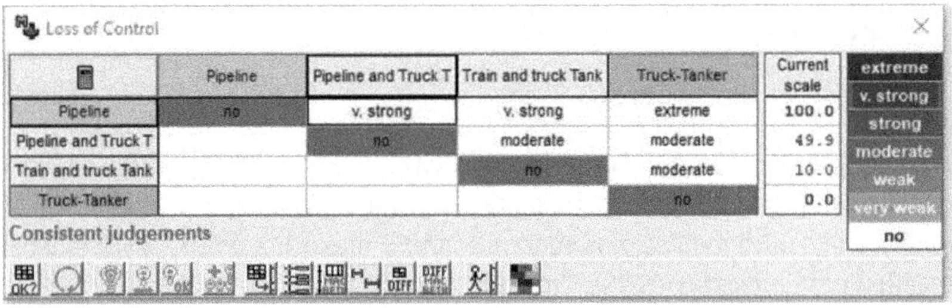

Figure 6.3. *Matrix of attractiveness differences (loss of control criterion)*

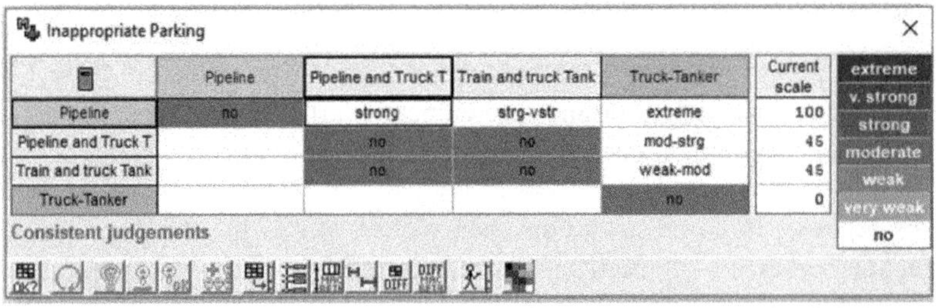

Figure 6.4. *Matrix of attractiveness differences (inappropriate parking criterion)*

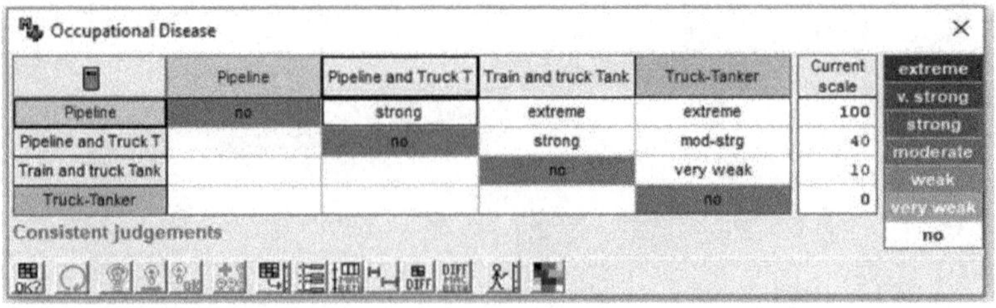

Figure 6.5. *Matrix of attractiveness differences (occupational disease criterion)*

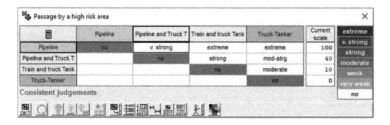

Passage by a high risk area ✕

	Pipeline	Pipeline and Truck T	Train and truck Tank	Truck-Tanker	Current scale	
Pipeline	no	v. strong	extreme	extreme	100	extreme
Pipeline and Truck T		no	strong	mod-strg	40	v. strong
Train and truck Tank			no	moderate	10	strong
Truck-Tanker				no	0	moderate
						weak
						very weak
Consistent judgements						no

Figure 6.6. *Matrix of attractiveness differences (passage by a high risk area criterion)*

Damage of Product Transported ✕

	Pipeline	Pipeline and Truck T	Train and truck Tank	Truck-Tanker	Current scale	
Pipeline	no	strong	v. strong	v. strong	100	extreme
Pipeline and Truck T		no	strong	mod-strg	50	v. strong
Train and truck Tank			no	very weak	10	strong
Truck-Tanker				no	0	moderate
						weak
						very weak
Consistent judgements						no

Figure 6.7. *Matrix of attractiveness differences (damage of product transported criterion)*

Mechanical breakdown ✕

	Pipeline	Pipeline and Truck T	Truck-Tanker	Train and truck Tank	Current scale	
Pipeline	no	strong	v. strong	vstrg-extr	100	extreme
Pipeline and Truck T		no	mod-strg	strong	40	v. strong
Truck-Tanker			no	very weak	5	strong
Train and truck Tank				no	0	moderate
						weak
						very weak
Consistent judgements						no

Figure 6.8. *Matrix of attractiveness differences (mechanical breakdown criterion)*

Explosion wheel ✕

	Pipeline	Pipeline and Truck T	Train and truck Tank	Truck-Tanker	Current scale	
Pipeline	no	strg-extr	strong	v. strong	100	extreme
Pipeline and Truck T		no	mod-strg	mod-strg	50	v. strong
Train and truck Tank			no	mod-strg	10	strong
Truck-Tanker				no	0	moderate
						weak
						very weak
Consistent judgements						no

Figure 6.9. *Matrix of attractiveness differences (explosion wheel criterion)*

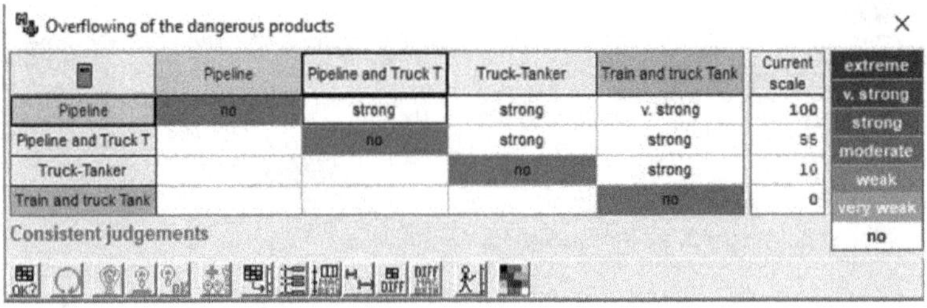

Figure 6.10. *Matrix of attractiveness differences (overflowing of the dangerous products criterion)*

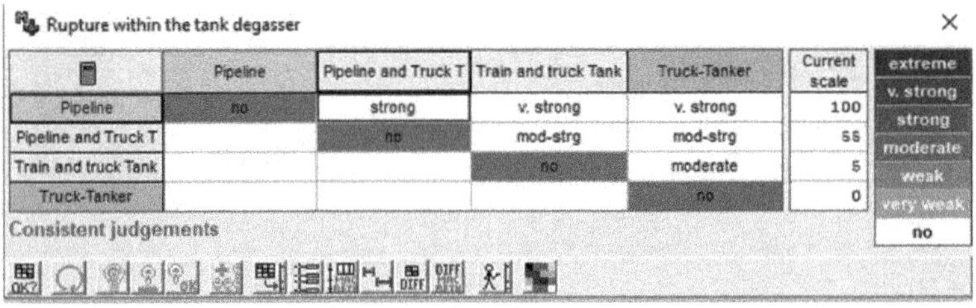

Figure 6.11. *Matrix of attractiveness differences (rupture within the tank degasser criterion)*

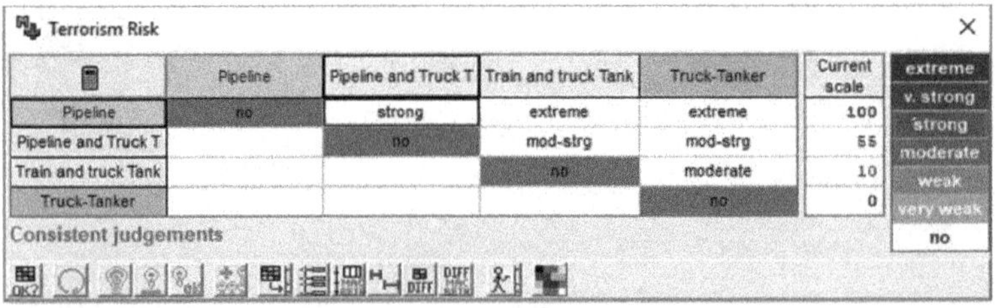

Figure 6.12. *Matrix of attractiveness differences (terrorism risk criterion)*

6.3.3.3. *Determination of the criteria weights*

This step allows the decision maker to weigh up the performance expressions. This is a key step in the procedure. The idea is to have a number of relationships between performance expression vectors and their associated aggregate performance expressions. In fact, the criteria are all assessed while checking the consistency of the response with the data that have already been entered. Then, a weight scale is created for the criteria (see Figure 6.13). Obviously, the decision maker is asked to check this weight scale and any necessary modifications are made.

To determine these weights, a system of equations must be solved, where w_i corresponds to the weight associated with the performance P_i of criterion i:

$$Pag_2 - Pag_1 = k\alpha \Leftrightarrow (w_1 P_{12} + \cdots + w_i P_{i2} + \cdots + w_n P_{n2}) - (w_1 P_{11} + \cdots + w_i P_{i1} + \cdots + w_n P_{n1}) = k\alpha \qquad [6.1]$$

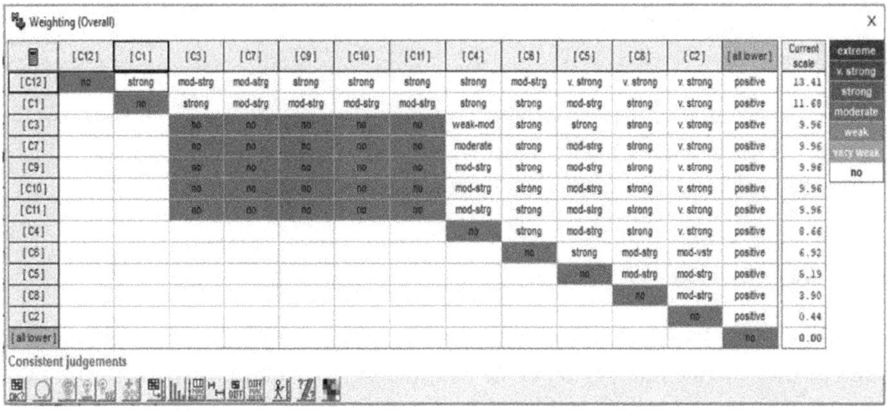

	[C12]	[C1]	[C3]	[C7]	[C9]	[C10]	[C11]	[C4]	[C6]	[C5]	[C8]	[C2]	[all lower]	Current scale
[C12]	no	strong	mod-strg	mod-strg	strong	strong	strong	strong	mod-strg	v. strong	v. strong	v. strong	positive	13.41
[C1]		no	strong	mod-strg	mod-strg	mod-strg	mod-strg	strong	strong	mod-strg	strong	v. strong	positive	11.68
[C3]			no	no	no	no	no	weak-mod	strong	strong	strong	v. strong	positive	9.96
[C7]			no	no	no	no	no	moderate	strong	mod-strg	strong	v. strong	positive	9.96
[C9]			no	no	no	no	no	mod-strg	strong	mod-strg	strong	v. strong	positive	9.96
[C10]			no	no	no	no	no	mod-strg	strong	mod-strg	strong	v. strong	positive	9.96
[C11]			no	no	no	no	no	mod-strg	strong	mod-strg	strong	v. strong	positive	9.96
[C4]								no	strong	mod-strg	strong	v. strong	positive	8.66
[C6]									no	strong	mod-strg	mod-vstr	positive	6.92
[C5]										no	mod-strg	mod-strg	positive	5.19
[C8]											no	mod-strg	positive	3.90
[C2]												no	positive	0.44
[all lower]													no	0.00

Figure 6.13. *Criteria weight matrix based on attractiveness differences*

6.3.3.4. *Performance aggregation*

The last step consists in aggregating the performance expressions by the weighted average. Each of the alternatives considered is then assigned an overall score, its aggregate performance expression. If this expression effectively reflects the decision maker's knowledge, the elaboration of the performance expressions and the weights of the aggregation operator are validated. Otherwise, the determination of weights and the elaboration of performance expressions are reconsidered.

The aggregate performance P^{ag} is equal to the sum of the weighted performances of the option for each criterion.

$$P^{aggregate} = w_1 P_1 + \cdots + w_i P_i + \cdots + w_n P_n \qquad [6.2]$$

The result obtained, following the final aggregation, is shown in Figure 6.14. At the end of this step, the decision maker can classify the alternatives selected during the structuring phase of the method.

Table of scores													X
Options	Overall	C1	C2	C3	C4	C5	C6	C7	C8	C9	C10	C11	C12
Truck-Tanker	12.87	100.00	0.00	0.00	0.00	0.00	0.00	0.00	5.00	0.00	10.00	0.00	0.00
Pipeline	88.32	0.00	100.00	100.00	100.00	100.00	100.00	100.00	100.00	100.00	100.00	100.00	100.00
Train and truck Tank	15.80	49.80	11.00	10.00	45.00	10.00	10.00	10.00	0.00	10.00	0.00	5.00	10.00
Pipeline and Truck T	49.06	45.00	55.00	49.90	45.00	40.00	40.00	50.00	40.00	50.00	55.00	55.00	55.00
[all upper]	100.00	100.00	100.00	100.00	100.00	100.00	100.00	100.00	100.00	100.00	100.00	100.00	100.00
[all lower]	0.00	0.00	0.00	0.00	0.00	0.00	0.00	0.00	0.00	0.00	0.00	0.00	0.00
Weights :		0.1168	0.0044	0.0996	0.0866	0.0519	0.0692	0.0996	0.0390	0.0996	0.0996	0.0996	0.1341

Figure 6.14. *Aggregation matrix of performance expressions*

Figure 6.14 shows that the pipeline is the best solution for transporting oil from the Sfax region to the Skhira port with a percentage rate of 88.32%, which represents the overall transport mode scores.

6.3.4. *Results and discussions*

First, it should be recalled that this study was actually carried out on the transport of crude oil from the Sfax region to the Skhira port. To better understand the results, we will present alternative profiles that provide a graphical representation of the performance obtained by the modes on each of the criteria, sensitivity analyses and a comparative analysis, using the *AHP* method.

6.3.4.1. *Profiles of alternatives related to all criteria*

The alternative profiles give a graphical representation of the performance obtained by the modes on each of the criteria. Figure 6.15 shows that the tanker truck is the preferred mode of transport, but only when the cost of the specific infrastructure is taken into account. However, based on socio-environmental factors, the pipeline is the best alternative among the transport modes for transporting oil from the Sfax region to the Skhira port (see Figure 6.16).

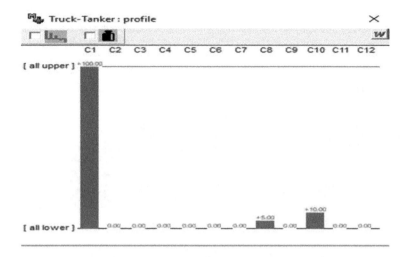

Figure 6.15. *Tanker Truck Profile related to all criteria*

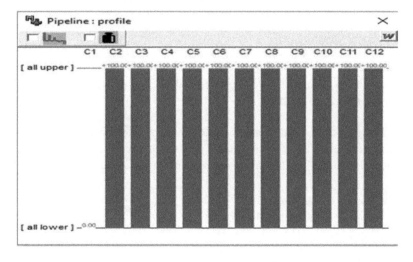

Figure 6.16. *Pipeline Profile related to all criteria*

Figure 6.17 shows that the "Specific Infrastructure Cost (C1)" and "Terrorism Risk (C12)" criteria have a strong influence over the choice of crude oil transport, in addition to other criteria such as "Loss of Control (C3)", "Damage of Product Transported (C7)", "Explosion Wheel (C9)", "Overflowing of the Dangerous Products (C10)", and "Rupture within the Tank Degasser (C11)" which are also significant to the choice of crude oil transport.

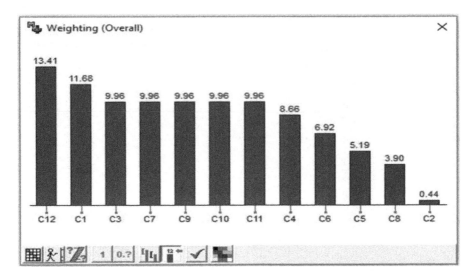

Figure 6.17. *Criteria weight based on attractiveness differences between criteria*

6.3.4.2. *Sensitivity analysis*

A sensitivity analysis that concerns criteria weights makes it possible to study the effect that a change in the weighted value of a criterion may have on the recommendation from the model.

By changing the weight of the "Specific Infrastructure Cost (C1)" factor from 0 to 100%, the overall Tanker-Truck and Train-Truck Tanker scores increase and the Pipeline and Pipeline-Truck Tanker scores decrease (see Figure 6.18).

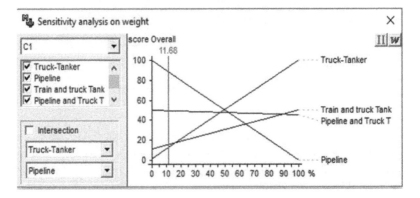

Figure 6.18. *Sensitivity analysis on the weight of the "Cost of Specific Infrastructure (C1)" criterion*

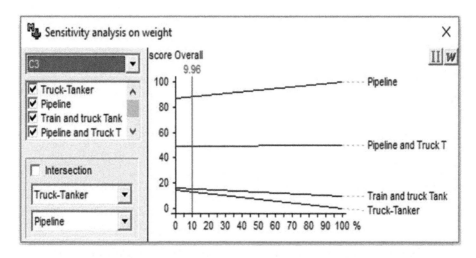

Figure 6.19. *Sensitivity analysis on the weight of the "Loss of Control (C3)" criterion*

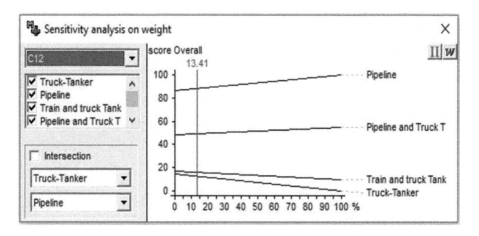

Figure 6.20. *Sensitivity analysis on the weight of the "Terrorism Risk (C12)" criterion*

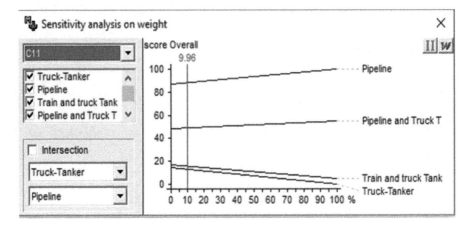

Figure 6.21. *Sensitivity analysis on the weight of the "Rupture within the Tank Degasser (C11)" criterion*

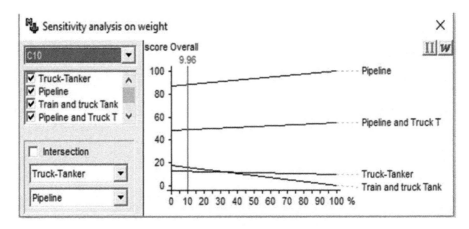

Figure 6.22. *Sensitivity analysis on the weight of the "Overflowing of Dangerous Products (C10)" criterion*

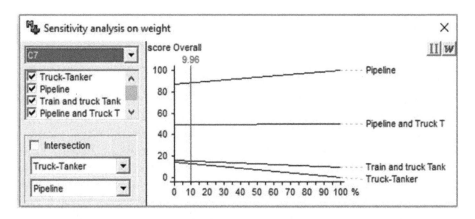

Figure 6.23. *Sensitivity analysis on the weight of the "Damage to the Product Transported (C7)" criterion*

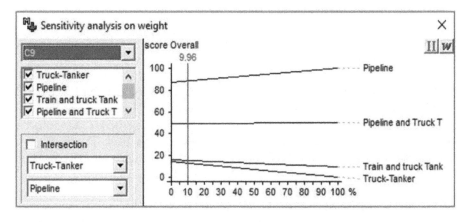

Figure 6.24. *Sensitivity analysis on the weight of the "Explosion Wheel (C9)" criterion*

However, for the following criteria: Loss of Control (C3), Rupture within the Tank Degasser (C11), Overflowing of the Dangerous Products (C10), Terrorism Risk (C12), Damage of Product Transported (C7) and Explosion Wheel (C9), the overall Truck-Tanker and Train-Truck Tanker scores decrease, but the Pipeline and Pipeline-Truck Tanker scores increase (see Figures 6.19–6.24).

The comparison between the results shows that most of the storage is the same and is only different for two alternatives: Pipeline and Truck-Tanker. This is due to the large difference between the two alternatives according to the specific Infrastructure Cost (C1) criterion.

6.3.4.3. *Comparison with the AHP method*

A comparison of the results obtained using the *MACBETH* method with those found using the *AHP* method is made. *AHP* is one of the multi-criteria analysis methods. The basis of this method is to represent a decision-making problem through a hierarchical structure that reflects the interactions between various aspects, criteria, indicators, and alternatives of the problem, then to make paired comparisons of the elements of the hierarchy, and finally, to determine the priorities for action. The objective of the *AHP* is to define the optimal alternative and to rank the others according to the criteria that describe them. The steps to solve a multi-criteria problem using the *AHP* method are:

– Step 1: Hierarchical decomposition;

– Step 2: Perform binary comparisons;

– Step 3: Determine priorities;

– Step 4: Consistency of judgments.

Based on the judgments provided by decision makers, the third step is to calculate the relative importance of each element of the hierarchy. The decision maker must complete a binary comparison matrix for each criterion. Each matrix compares the choices two by two, according to the criterion passed. The next step is to calculate the priority vector $V = (V_1, ..., V_n)$. The calculation of product V makes it possible to obtain a vector that contains the final weights of each choice.

In Table 6.1, we must calculate the overall priority for each mode of transport; in other words, priorities that take not only consider the preferences of alternatives for each criterion but also the different weights of each criterion.

After determining the *AHP* steps, we can now list the modes of transport classified by their overall priority or preference as follows:

Priorities for action:

$$\begin{matrix} A_1 \\ A_2 \\ A_3 \\ A_4 \end{matrix} \begin{pmatrix} 0.45 \\ 0.22 \\ 0.17 \\ 0.16 \end{pmatrix} \qquad [6.3]$$

	N1	N2	N3	N4	N5	N6	N7	N8	N9	N10	N11	N12
Criteria priorities	0.265	0.193	0.074	0.084	0.075	0.083	0.078	0.037	0.047	0.019	0.032	0.013
Pipeline (A1)	0.088	0.599	0.655	0.478	0.605	0.610	0.602	0.521	0.321	0.621	0.458	0.532
Pipeline and Truck (A2)	0.223	0.221	0.104	0.154	0.223	0.218	0.219	0.262	0.321	0.130	0.284	0.238
Train and Truck (A3)	0.052	0.130	0.182	0.319	0.124	0.126	0.127	0.158	0.321	0.206	0.166	0.172
Tanker Truck (A4)	0.637	0.050	0.059	0.049	0.048	0.046	0.052	0.060	0.036	0.043	0.092	0.058

Table 6.1. *Model summary*

According to the priority vector of the actions, we end up obtaining the same order obtained by *MACBETH*; therefore, the pipeline mode of transport (A1) is the most preferable (global priority = 0.45).

6.4. Conclusion

In this chapter, we have examined a range of problems regarding the transport of dangerous materials. We were particularly interested in the problem of designing a network for the transport of dangerous materials and, more specifically, in the problem of choosing the best mode of transport for dangerous materials.

The modal choice is a logistical choice that integrates several criteria and can influence the long-term sustainability and competitiveness of a company. This modal choice decision is not only influenced by the criteria of cost, time, and quality but also by a wide range of social and environmental criteria. In this chapter, we focused on a particular activity in Tunisia. This involved the transport of crude oil from the Sfax region to the Skhira port, taking economic, social, and environmental factors into account.

To achieve these objectives, we used the *MACBETH* method to find the best way to transport crude oil from the Sfax region to the Skhira port. The results of the case study indicated that using the pipeline as a mode of transport is the best solution for transporting oil from the Sfax region to the Skhira port with a percentage rate of 88.32%.

The Tanker-Truck is the preferred mode of transport, but only when the cost of the specific infrastructure is taken into account. However, based on socio-environmental factors, pipeline is the best solution among the transport modes for transporting oil from the Sfax region to the Skhira port.

The results obtained during this work are rather encouraging. Our study confirms that the Specific Infrastructure Cost and Terrorism Risk criteria have a strong influence over the choice of crude oil transport from the Sfax region to the Skhira port. Thus, other criteria such as the Overflowing of the Dangerous Products, Rupture within the Tank Degasser, Explosion Wheel, Loss of Control and Damage of Product Transported are also sensitive to choose the mode of crude oil transport.

The most striking conclusion of this study is the relative superiority of the pipeline over other modes of transport due to the monetary value of potentially avoided environmental and social risks.

To ensure the performance of the approach studied, we conducted sensitivity and comparative analyses that showed satisfactory results.

6.5. References

Ammar, M. H., Benaissa, E., and Chabchoub, H. (forthcoming). Design of a digital traceability system for road crude oil transport (DiTSyRoCOT): Tunisian case study. *World Review of Intermodal Transportation Research*.

Ammar, M. H., Benaissa, M., and Chabchoub, H. (2014). Risk assessment of hazard material transportation using FMECA approach: case study in a Tunisian company. *2014 IEEE International Conference on Advanced Logistics and Transport (ICALT)*, Tunisia.

Ammar, M. H., Benaissa, M., and Chabchoub, H. (2016). Preliminary study on stakeholders needs and requirements in the development of a traceability system for road transport of crude oil. *International Conference on Advanced Logistics and Transport (ICALT)*, 87–92.

Bana e Costa, C. A., Oliveira, C. S., and Vieira, V. (2006). Prioritization of bridges and tunnels in earthquake risk mitigation using multicriteria decision analysis: application to Lisbon. *The International Journal of Management Science (omega)*, 36(3), 442–450.

Belaid, E., Limbourg, S., and Mostert, M. (2016). Bi-objective road and pipe network design for crude oil transport in the Sfax region in Tunisia. *Procedia Engineering*, 142, 108–115.

Berman, O., Verter, V., and Kara, B. Y. (2007). Designing emergency response networks for hazardous materials transportation. *Computers & Operations Research*, 34(5), 1374–1388.

Bianco, L., Caramia, M., and Giordani, S. (2009). A bilevel flow model for hazmat transportation network design. *Transportation Research Part C: Emerging Technologies*, 17(2), 175–196.

Bubbico, R., Di Cave, S., and Mazzarotta, B. (2004). Risk analysis for road and rail transport of hazardous materials: a GIS approach. *Journal of Loss Prevention in the Process Industries*, 17(6), 483–488.

Current, J. and Ratick, S. (1995). A model to assess risk, equity and efficiency in facility location and transportation of hazardous materials. *Location Science*, 3(3), 187–201.

Erkut, E. and Alp, O. (2007). Designing a road network for hazardous materials shipments. *Computers & Operations Research*, 34(5), 1389–1405.

Erkut, E. and Gzara, F. (2008). Solving the hazmat transport network design problem. *Computers & Operations Research*, 35(7), 2234–2247.

ETAP. (2017). Annual Activity Report. Report European Commission, Tunisia.

Jayaraman, V. (1998). Transportation, facility location and inventory issues in distribution network design: an investigation. *International Journal of Operations & Production Management*, 18(5), 471–494.

Jiang, Y., Zhang, X., and Rong, Y. (2014). A multimodal location and routing model for hazardous materials transportation based on multi-commodity flow model. *Procedia-Social and Behavioral Sciences*, 138, 791–799.

Kara, B. Y. and Verter, V. (2004). Designing a road network for hazardous materials transportation. *Transportation Science*, 38(2), 188–196.

Kazemi, Y. and Szmerekovsky, J. (2015). Modeling downstream petroleum supply chain: the importance of multi-mode transportation to strategic planning. *Transportation Research Part E: Logistics and Transportation Review*, 83, 111–125.

Leal Junior, I. C. and D'Agosto, M. A. (2011a). Modal choice evaluation of transport alternatives for exporting bio-ethanol from Brazil. *Transportation Research Part D: Transport and Environment*, 16(3), 201–207.

Leal Junior, I. C. and D'Agosto, M. A. (2011b). Modal choice for transportation of hazardous materials: the case of land modes of transport of bio-ethanol in Brazil. *Journal of Cleaner Production*, 19(2–3), 229–240.

Lopes, J. M., Leal Junior, I. C., and Guimarães, V. A. (2016). Impact of modal choice in energy consumption and carbon dioxide emissions: analysis of Brazilian bioethanol supply chain. *Brazilian Journal of Operations & Production Management*, 13(2), 138–148.

Siddiqui, A., Verma, M., and Verter, V. (2017). An integrated framework for inventory management and transportation of refined petroleum products: pipeline or marine? *Applied Mathematical Modelling*, 55, 224–247.

Strogen, B., Bell, K., and Breunig, H. (2016). Environmental, public health, and safety assessment of fuel pipelines and other freight transportation modes. *Applied Energy*, 171, 266–276.

Talarico, L., Reniers, G., Sörensen, K., and Springael, J. (2015). MISTRAL: a game-theoretical model to allocate security measures in a multi-modal chemical transportation network with adaptive adversaries. *Reliability Engineering & System Safety*, 138, 105–114.

Van Raemdonck, K., Macharis, C., and Mairesse, O. (2013). Risk analysis system for the transport of hazardous materials. *Journal of Safety Research*, 45, 55–63.

Verter, V. and Kara, B. Y. (2008). A path-based approach for hazmat transport network design. *Management Science*, 54(1), 29–40.

Xie, Y., Lu, W., Wang, W., and Quadrifoglio, L. (2012). A multimodal location and routing model for hazardous materials transportation. *Journal of Hazardous Materials*, 227, 135–141.

7

Green Reverse Logistics: Case of the Vehicle Routing Problem with Delivery and Collection Demands

This chapter discusses the developments in the area of the vehicle routing problem (VRP) and more specifically VRPs which feature both delivery and collection demands, and their relevance and contribution to the go green reverse logistics polices. This chapter initially elaborates on the VRP and its variants involved in reverse logistics, then highlights the significance and ecological relevance of the VRP delivery and collection models and provides information concerning freight transport CO_2 conversions and computations. Finally, this chapter describes green VRP models, showing the link between traditional and green VRP models and how principles from both could be combined in order to achieve better economic and environmental gains.

7.1. Introduction and significance

The discipline of logistics and supply chain management has seen a continuous and rapid development in recent years due to its importance in the economies of organizations and countries. Typically, most companies perceive the role of supply chain management as an activity that adds value to their markets; hence, it has become very significant to their strategic decision-making. Due to evolving customer demand, companies strive to achieve efficient delivery service without compromising the customer service quality and the profitability of the business. On the other hand, issues around the management of the operational physical distribution and collection activities are also seen from an environmental perspective, especially by big organizations, as part of corporate social

Chapter written by Naveed WASSAN, Niaz WASSAN, Lina SIMEONOVA and Walid BESBES.

responsibility, and governments and public service institutions (such as councils) as a part of their political agenda. Hence, these institutions would like to see less traffic on the roads, meaning less pollution. These evolving demands have put constant pressure on logistics operations to be more efficient and to satisfy these agendas. As a result, researchers and practitioners around the globe are inspired to address these economically and environmentally important logistical issues more and more efficiently. The issue of transforming transportation into a more environmentally friendly industry is a global issue, it requires tangible efforts from all stakeholders at a persistent level as road traffic activities and greenhouse gases are increasing constantly. For example, "the UK emissions data from the National Atmospheric Emissions Inventory (NAEI), DECC/DEFRA, estimate greenhouse gas emissions from HGVs to have increased by 1% to 18.7 million tons CO_2 equivalent between 2013 and 2014". The main findings of the estimated figures published by the UK Department of Transport show a continuous significant yearly increase in all types of traffic, particularly light goods vehicles (LGV). Comparison trends of 2014 and 2015 show that all motor vehicle traffic increased by 1.8%, LGV traffic increased by 5.1%, and car traffic increased by 1.3%. Traffic volumes increased across all road classifications, and minor rural road traffic increased the most by 4.9% (Department for Transport 2015).

Table 7.1 shows an example of increasing road freight activity of heavy goods vehicles (HGVs) in the UK. This table shows that domestic road freight activity increase in 2015 compared to 2014 as published in the UK Department for Transport statistical release in August 2016 (Department for Transport 2016).

		% increase
Lifted goods	1.65 billion tons	11%
Moved goods	152 billion ton kilometers	12%
Vehicle distance	18.4 billion kilometers	9%

Table 7.1. *Domestic road freight activity increases in 2015 (HGVs in 2015 compared to 2014) (Department for Transport 2015)*

Interestingly, the Department for Transport estimates of GDP in the UK show an increase in the year ending March 2015. In particular, the four goods traffic-related industrial groupings in the economy, i.e. production, construction, services, and agriculture, showed an increase in their output over the same period. Considering the above information, there is a noticeable positive correlation between the GDP growth and increasing traffic volumes. The above findings become very vital if the

GDP versus traffic relationship is associated with emerging developing countries like China and India whose economies are growing much faster than the UK. The above statistics pinpoint the importance of this growing global issue and trigger a need to address the problem on a priority basis to achieve a balance between the economic gains versus ecological and social concerns.

Vehicle routing as a physical distribution problem is considered one of the important modes of transportation; hence, it has been enormously studied in the literature. However, there is still a wide gap between the assumption-based theoretical studies carried out in academia and the reality of the industry. The research carried out in the area of the vehicle routing problem (VRP) is concentrated mainly on reducing the total distance traveled by a fleet of vehicles (e.g. less fuel costs) and efficient fleet management (e.g. less vehicles on roads and better customer service). Obviously, both of these objectives would serve to reduce CO_2 emissions as a by-product because CO_2 generation is shown to be proportional to fuel consumption. Along those lines, another important aspect of the vehicle routing studied in the literature is called the vehicle routing problem with delivery and collection demands. This aspect of the vehicle routing literature can be attributed rather directly to the reverse logistics due to its collection component (Dethloff 2001). The other attributes that are addressed in the VRP literature include the use of heterogeneous fleets, load management, speed, and so on, which are also considered to be related to CO_2 reduction. For example, for a given task, a mix of small, medium and large vehicles in a fleet is considered to be less costly (due to fuel costs) as compared to utilizing a fleet of identically size large vehicles for the same task. Similarly, in some vehicle routing studies, fuel consumption is shown to be directly related to the vehicle load, type, and speed factors. Therefore, in this chapter, we discuss the developments in the area of vehicle routing and, more specifically, the VRPs, which feature both delivery and collection demands and their relevance and contribution to go green reverse logistics polices. In the following sections, we briefly elaborate on the VRP and its variants involved in reverse logistics. The chapter highlights the significance and ecological relevance of the VRP delivery and collection models and provides information concerning freight transport CO_2 conversions and computations. Finally, we briefly describe green VRP models, showing the link between traditional and green VRP models and how principles from both could be combined in order to achieve better economic and environmental gains.

7.2. The Vehicle Routing Problem and its variants

7.2.1. *The evolution of the Vehicle Routing Problem*

The evolution story of the VRP starts with the generalization of the classical Traveling Salesman Problem (TSP) by Dantzig and Ramser (1959). The TSP is typically described as a salesman who has to start a tour from his/her home city and visit all customers at different locations before returning back to his/her home city. The problem is to find the order in which the salesman is to visit all customers to minimize the total distance traveled (Bai *et al.* 2005; Gamboa *et al.* 2006; Gendreau *et al.* 1992; Lawler *et al.* 1985). Special cases of the TSP arise in terms of its applications (e.g. the Chinese Postman Problem where it is not necessary for the salesman to return home (Eiselt *et al.* 1995)). For instance, the problem may have special properties where the distance between the pairs of nodes is assumed to be asymmetric (not the same in both directions). The story then moves to the extension of the TSP, i.e. the Multiple-Traveling Salesman Problem (mTSP), which involves the use of exactly *m* salesmen (Bektas 2006; Bodin *et al.* 1983; Lawler *et al.* 1985). The extension of the mTSP model then took the shape of the classical vehicle routing problem (VRP) in the work of Dantzig and Ramser (1959) with the incorporation of some additional aspects such as vehicle capacity restrictions.

7.2.2. *The Vehicle Routing Problem*

The VRP is a general name devoted to a whole set of problems. In its simplest form, the VRP involves a set of customers with deterministic demands, a fleet of vehicles (normally homogeneous in physicality and unlimited in number), and a depot. The problem is to design a set of routes (starting and ending at the depot) to serve all the customers at a minimum cost while satisfying the vehicle capacity and (in some cases) route-length constraints. Figure 7.1 shows an illustrative example of the classical VRP. For detailed information on the subject of VRP, see the works of Toth and Vigo (2002), Mester and Braysy (2007), Bin *et al.* (2009), and Fleszar *et al.* (2009).

7.2.3. *VRP variants*

In the field of transportation and distribution logistics, the vehicle routing problem has evolved as a pivotal problem since Dantzig and Ramser (1959) first introduced it as the Truck Dispatching Problem. Since then, especially in the past three decades, the *VRP* has emerged as one of the most studied problems in the area of combinatorial optimization. Numerous variants of the VRP have been introduced, and hundreds of papers have been written on this subject with new efficient solution methodologies in the literature.

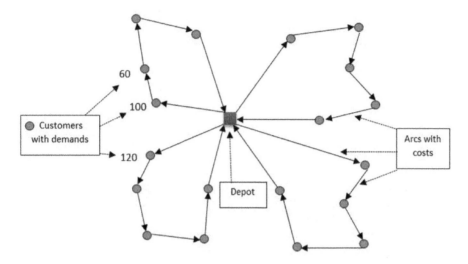

Figure 7.1. *An illustrative example of the VRP. For a color version of this figure, see www.iste.co.uk/besbes/transport.zip*

Conventionally, the primary objective behind the development of numerous variants of the VRP models is to bring the problem closer to the requirements of real-world applications. Consequently, by taking advantage of the studies around the VRP and its different versions, public or private transportation companies in the real world can save substantial transportation costs (e.g. combining delivery and pickup operations, using a mix of smaller and bigger vehicles, serving from more than one depot, etc.). Ganesh and Nallathambi (2007) presented a broad review of the Vehicle Routing Problem, its variants, solution approaches, and applications. It has been reported that, on average, the transportation of goods or material accounts for the highest proportion of logistics costs. The authors argue that the VRP has been assumed to be a deterministic and static problem traditionally; however, in the present-day context, VRP takes account of collecting and processing information and takes decisions accordingly within certain time span. However, it should be noted that around the time when the study by Ganesh and Nallathambi (2007) was published, another class of the VRP emerged, referred to as "rich" VRPs, inspired by real applications (Gribkovskaia *et al.* 2006). A large number of such studies exist in the literature, and the reader is referred to Goel and Gruhn (2008), Vidal *et al.* (2014), and a recent review of Lahyani *et al.* (2015). On the other hand, the counter argument to the study by Ganesh and Nallathambi (2007) and the fact behind the evolution of VRP variants is that these are inspired by real-life operations. The literature on the VRP shows a clear trend toward bringing it closer to reality. We believe the research work of Wassan (2016) is yet another step to bringing the VRP closer to reality by addressing multiple uses of fleets with backhauling in a time span, which is very much in practice.

In the following sections, some of the main variants of the VRP and those which are relevant to this study are briefly described and useful references are provided.

7.3. The VRP with delivery and collection demand models

7.3.1. *The VRP with Mixed Deliveries and Pickups*

The Vehicle Routing Problem with Mixed Deliveries and Pickups (VRPMDP) is another backhauling version in which the order of the pickup and delivery customers is not important when it comes to serving their demand. That is, linehaul and backhaul customers can be mixed freely within a route in a way that customers are either delivery or pickup locations. The VRPMDP is studied further with the extensions such as "multi-depot" and "time windows" (Jarpa *et al.* 2010; Zhong and Cole 2005). The following studies can be a useful start for understanding this version of backhauling VRPs: Halse (1992), Salhi and Nagy (1999), Salhi and Wade (2001), Wade and Salhi (2002), Nagy and Salhi (2005), Ropke and Pisinger (2006), Tutuncu *et al.* (2009), and Lin and Tao (2011). Moreover, a recent paper by Wassan and Nagy (2014) provides a comprehensive discussion on the modeling issues and the metaheuristics developments around this problem.

7.3.2. *The VRP with Simultaneous Deliveries and Pickups*

The Vehicle Routing Problem with Simultaneous Deliveries and Pickups (VRPSDP) was introduced by Min (1989). In VRPSDP, a vehicle can serve a linehaul customer only, a backhaul customer only, or it can serve a customer both with linehaul and backhaul demands simultaneously. Taking into account the fact that serving customers simultaneously can lead to a problem of rearranging the load on a vehicle, it is assumed that the physical design of a vehicle is designed in such way that it can be accessed from several sides in order to accommodate the load. For more information on the VRPSDP, see Salhi and Nagy (1999), Dethloff (2001), Nagy and Salhi (2005), Chen and Wu (2006), Ganesh and Narendran (2007), Wassan *et al.* (2008a, 2008b), Gajpal and Abad (2009), Zachariadis and Kiranoudis (2012), Wassan and Nagy (2014), and Nagy *et al.* (2015).

Other notable related models include the Vehicle Routing Problem with Restricted Mixing of Deliveries and Pickups (Nagy *et al.* 2013), the Vehicle Routing Problem with Divisible Deliveries and Pickups (Nagy *et al.* 2013), and the Vehicle Routing with Restricted Mixing of Divisible Deliveries and Pickups (Wassan and Nagy 2014). It should be noted that some authors refer to the vehicle routing problem with delivery and pickup (VRPDP) as the vehicle routing problem with pickup and delivery (VRPPD). The VRPDP assume that goods stored at some customer location cannot be transported directly to another customer. Hence, problems such as the dial-a-ride problem (Cordeau and Laporte 2007) are excluded in this chapter.

7.3.3. *The VRP with Backhauls*

The Vehicle Routing Problem with Backhauls (VRPB) is an extension of the VRP, often termed as the classical VRPB. It is one of the most studied problems among the class of backhauling VRPs in the reverse logistics area. The customers in this variant are divided into two groups known as the linehaul (delivery) and the backhaul (pickup). Hence, in the VRPB, the vehicles are also used for picking up goods to bring back to the depot after all the deliveries are made. Figure 7.2 shows an illustrative example of the VRPB. The objective of the VRPB is to minimize the total (cost) distance traveled while satisfying demands of both types of customers. However, a VRPB solution must satisfy the following main characteristic, i.e. each vehicle must make all the deliveries before making any pickups. This characteristic is encouraged by the fact that delivery of goods to the customers is considered to be the most profitable activity in many practical situations, and the fact that some vehicles are rear-loaded and it is difficult to rearrange the delivery load on board in order to adjust the new pickup load. The VRPB has been studied extensively in the literature, and the reader may refer to the studies of Goetschalckx and Jacobs-Blecha (1989), Toth and Vigo (1996), Toth and Vigo (1997), Mingozzi and Baldacci (1999), Toth and Vigo (1999), Osman and Wassan (2002), Toth and Vigo (2003), Wassan (2007), Salhi *et al.* (2013), Wassan *et al.* (2013), and Wu *et al.* (2016).

The VRPB arises in many real-life applications such as delivery and pickup of mail to/from customers or post offices, delivery of drink bottles to shops and pickup of empty bottles, and delivery of new household appliances and removal of old ones. Another application of the VRPB can be found in the grocery distribution industry, where groceries are distributed to stores (considered as linehaul customers) from distribution centers; pickups of groceries are carried from the production sites (considered as backhaul customers) to the distribution centers (Ropke and Pisinger

2006). Moreover, the applications of the VRPB can be found in many other real-world scenarios where return of commodities to the distribution center is involved, i.e. reverse logistics (Cuervo *et al.* 2014).

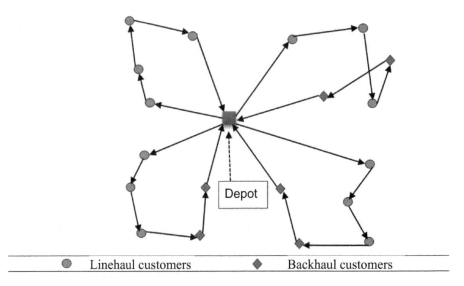

| ● Linehaul customers | ◆ Backhaul customers |

Figure 7.2. *An illustrative example of the VRPB. For a color version of this figure, see www.iste.co.uk/besbes/transport.zip*

There are also some other versions of the VRPB which have been are modeled and studied in the literature. In this section, we present brief descriptions of those relevant VRPB variants, along with some useful references.

7.3.4. *The Multiple-Trip Vehicle Routing Problem with Backhauls*

While the VRPB has already been explained earlier in this section, the MT-VRP model is an extension of the classical VRP in which a vehicle may perform several routes (trips) within a given time period. Along with the typical VRP constraints, an additional aspect is included in the model, which involves the assignment of the optimized set of routes to the available fleet (Taillard *et al.* 1996). Both the MT-VRP and the VRPB are considered more valuable than the classical VRP in terms of cost savings and placing fewer numbers of vehicles on the roads. The MT-VRP could save a considerable number of vehicles where each vehicle of the given fleet may be used more than once in a given planning period (Taillard *et al.* 1996). On the other hand, as mentioned earlier, in the VRPB, a vehicle is used to serve collection demands after it has served the delivery demands rather than using separate vehicles to serve both demands separately. The above characteristics are established in the literature for the MT-VRP and the VRPB (Wassan 2016). However, these characteristics are application dependent. For instance, Ong and Suprayogi (2011) studied the vehicle routing problem with backhaul, multiple trips, and time windows (VRPBMTTW). Further possibilities could include the consideration of a heterogeneous fleet instead of a homogeneous one; and vehicles which could be allowed to serve backhaul customers only. However, all these features are very important from both the managerial and the ecological perspectives.

Wassan (2016) studied comprehensively the Multiple-Trip Vehicle Routing Problem with Backhauls (MT-VRPB). The MT-VRPB combines the characteristics of the classical versions of two problems studied in the literature; therefore, in the MT-VRPB, a vehicle may not only make more than one trip in a given planning period but it can also collect goods at each trip. The objective is to minimize the total cost by reducing the total distance traveled and the number of vehicles used. It is evident by combining the aspects of the above two models into a single model, i.e. the Multiple-Trip Vehicle Routing Problem with Backhauls adds even further value to the practice of the vehicle routing. These kinds of models are more relevant, especially when it comes to the need for optimizing a fixed or limited availability fleet and utilizing fully the driver time to achieve strategic competitive advantage, resulting in reduction in CO_2 emissions as a premium by-product objective. For further information, the reader is referred to a recent review of Koc and Laporte (2018).

7.4. Studies in VRPB-related areas

There are many studies in the literature, which are related to the VRPB; however, we exclude them because these studies are special cases of the VRPB. Nevertheless, we would like to provide some references here for the interested readers.

Notable instances include the vehicle routing problem with delivery and backhaul options by Anily (1996); the vehicle routing problem with backhauls and inventory (VRPBI) by Liu and Chung (2009); the mixed vehicle routing problem with backhauls (MVRPB) by Wade and Salhi (2002), Lin and Tao (2011), and Wassan et al. (2013); the vehicle routing problem with restricted mixing of deliveries and pickups by Nagy et al. (2013); the fleet size and mix vehicle routing problem with backhauls by Salhi et al. (2013); and the vehicle routing problem with divisible deliveries and pickups by Nagy et al. (2015). For more information on the modeling issues and metaheuristics solution approaches on the vehicle routing problems involving pickups and deliveries, we refer the reader to Wassan and Nagy (2014).

7.4.1. *Significance of the VRP models with delivery and collection demands*

In the above VRP models, distance/cost minimization has been the key objective besides the maximization of fleet utility and service. In the literature, the VRP models with delivery/collection demands such as VRPDP, VRPB, and the MT-VRPB are considered very important on the operational level since backhauling and multiple scheduling are seen in many real-life applications. By using these models, significant cost savings (e.g. operational and fixed costs) can be achieved by reducing the number of vehicles and hence drivers (Chbichib *et al.* 2011; Wassan 2007; Wassan *et al.* 2017). Studying them simultaneously seems even more pragmatic with regard to many real-life situations in order to enhance the overall distribution logistics efficiency. The MT-VRPB appears in many real-world applications such as distribution of groceries, couriers who offer same day collection, and delivery services. Moreover, the MT-VRPB especially arises in urban areas where travel times (distances) are rather small, and the light load vehicles are reloaded after performing the short tours and used again. The growing examples of those cases arise in online business such as retail markets, i.e. grocery stores, cafes, supermarkets, restaurants, and so on. The model may cater largely for those small, medium, or large logistics companies that wish to use a limited/fixed fleet or strategically want to reduce the vehicle fleet size.

However, a popular criticism concerning the VRP models is that such models rely on a variety of assumptions and there is a perception of these models as being far from reality. This is because there is still a considerable gap between the existing models and the reality, which needs to be bridged by developing more integrated models that fulfill the contemporary demands of the industry. However, the economic and ecological relevance of those models is undeniable, and it is noticeable from the literature that research has been continuously trying to develop models that are closer to the real applications of the vehicle routing. More recently, a good development and increasing interest in the applications of VRPs in real-life situations have been present in the literature. These models are being termed as "Rich" VRP models (Battara *et al.* 2009). Simeonova *et al.* (2018) introduce a real-life VRP, with an interesting notion of light loads, where load restrictions force given customers to be serviced later on the route when the lorry is sufficiently light. However, so far, these models seem to be specific to individual applications. The main difficulty of designing the VRP models and solving them in an integrated manner by considering various real-life routing requirements is the complex nature of those instances of the problem and the fact that these models belong to the category of hard combinatorial optimization (*CO*) problems.

7.4.2. Ecological relevance of the VRP models

As described in section 7.1, the amount of emissions produced by a vehicle are shown to be proportional to fuel/energy consumption, and the fuel/energy consumption is proportional to several factors such as distance traveled, load, speed, and so on (Xiao *et al.* 2012). Pradenas *et al.* (2013) show that the environmental impact of vehicle routing planning is related to the rate of vehicle use, load, distances traveled, appropriate vehicle type, and a cooperative game approach. The backhaul-based cooperative and non-cooperative scenarios in terms of both routing and emission costs are further discussed by Juan *et al.* (2014). In some studies, there is also evidence that factors such as road inclination (Tavares *et al.* 2008), and traffic disturbances (Ericsson *et al.* 2006) can also affect fuel consumption and emissions. The study of the importance of considering fuel efficiency is critical because studies have shown that, in real-life applications, the minimum cost or minimum distance routes are not always optimal when fuel consumption and emissions are concerned. An example of this is a recent paper by Ehmke *et al.* (2018), where the authors clearly show the differences between optimizing time, cost, and fuel efficiency. In some cases, significant fuel savings can come only at a small increase in cost.

In the classical VRP-based studies, typically only delivery demand is considered. Once the demand is fulfilled, vehicles used in service return to the depot(s) empty. Darvish *et al.* (2017) found "empty running of vehicles" as an important factor in reducing the emissions, although the return journeys with empty vehicles would consume less fuel as established in the study of Sahin *et al.* (2009). However, if the returning vehicles are utilized efficiently for the purpose of collection demand, then this tactic approach could save much more cost (fuel) as shown in the studies of Toth and Vigo (1999), Ropke and Pisinger (2006), Nagy *et al.* (2013), Salhi *et al.* (2013), and Wassan *et al.* (2017). Moreover, due to the boom in internet shopping and great competition, companies use services such as free returns as a competitive advantage and even, in the case of Royal Mail in the UK, as "a statement of confidence in the brand" (Royal Mail 2019). This emphasizes the need for more efficient incorporation of goods collections and the potential of VRPB reverse logistics studies toward reducing emissions as a by-product as compared to the classical VRP models without backhauls. For example, more recently, the results provided by Wassan *et al.* (2017) show clear advantages for logistics companies and their management decisions. The results demonstrate that a logistic company adopting a multi-trip routing strategy can utilize fully all working hours in a planning period. The results also show that the multi-trips with backhauling provide a clear advantage in reducing fixed costs by reducing the number of vehicles used, which can be very much relevant for those companies which depend on hiring a fleet for the distribution and/or reverse logistics reasons. Making deliveries in a given planning period is especially relevant for those companies which are involved in supplying fresh/perishable goods, and in urban area distribution logistics such as online deliveries. Such developments can be vital from the ecological perspective because these tactical (procurement) gains and fleet management (operational) decisions may be translated into greenhouse gas reduction.

7.4.3. *Computation of freight transport greenhouse gas emissions*

In this study, we mainly reflect on the CO_2 emission factor of the greenhouse gases; however, other pollution factors such as methane (CH_4) and nitrous oxide (N_2O) could be considered alongside this appropriately. As for the freight transportation, CO_2 emission generation is related to various factors such as vehicle type (HGV, LGV, Rigid, and Articulated), load, fuel used, and so on. For example, Table 7.2 gives the effect of the loading factor on CO_2 emission as published by the UK Department for Business, Energy and Industrial Strategy (2017). The data in Table 7.2 show that the effect of load is symmetrical and independent of driving cycle. Thus, for example, a <33t Arctic HGV emits 20% more CO_2 per/km when fully loaded and 20% less CO_2 per/km when empty relative to emissions at half-load. Moreover, refrigerated/temperature-controlled Rigid and Arctic HGVs demonstrated of statistics 19% and 16%, respectively. For more information, see the UK Department for Business, Energy and Industrial Strategy (2017).

Fuel/energy consumption is regarded as related to direct and/or indirect/Well-to-Tank (*WTT*) emissions. Tables 7.3 and 7.4 give the calculation of CO_2 and transport conversion of CO_2, respectively. Considering that, the Rigid/Articulated diesel engine lorries/vans are considered mostly in the VRP models, and fuel/energy consumption is proportional to the distance traveled. Equation [7.1] can be used to calculate the CO_2 emission for the results produced by the VRP models. However, additional calculations are needed to assess the impact of other factors such as, load, speed, refrigeration, and so on.

	Gross Vehicle Weight (GVW)	% change in CO_2 emissions
	<7.5t	8%
Rigid	7.5–17t	12.5%
	>17t	18%
Articulated	<33t	20%
	>33t	25%

Table 7.2. *Change in CO_2 emissions caused by ±50% change in load from average loading factor of 50% (Department for Business, Energy and Industrial Strategy 2017)*

Based on Tables 7.1 and 7.2, the emission can be calculated as follows. For example, an Articulated lorry with diesel engine would consume 0.35 L fuel per km (for a Rigid Van with diesel engine, this factor is 0.097 L/km) and generates 2.68 kg (0.00263 tons) of CO_2 per liter of diesel. The calculation of CO_2 can be shown as follows by denoting these factors as:

– Fuel consumption per/km = $x1$

– CO_2 emission per/litre = $x2$

– Distance traveled = d

$$Total\ CO_2\ emission = x1 * x2 * d \qquad\qquad [7.1]$$

Fuel type	Kilogram of CO_2 per unit of consumption
Grid electricity	43 per kWh
Natural gas	3,142 per ton
Diesel fuel	2.68 per liter
Petrol	2.31 per liter
Coal	2,419 per ton
LPG	1.51 per liter

Table 7.3. *Calculation of CO_2 emissions (Davies 2003)*

Vehicle type	Kilogram CO_2 per liter
Small petrol car 1.4 L engine	0.17/km
Medium car (1.4–2.1 L)	0.22/km
Large car	0.27/km
Average petrol car	0.20/km
Small diesel car (>2 L)	0.12/km
Large car	0.14/km
Average diesel car	0.12/km
Articulated lorry, diesel engine	2.68/km (0.35 L fuel per km)
Rail	0.06 per person per km
Air, short haul (500km)	0.18 per person per km
Air, long haul	0.11
Shipping	0.01 per ton per km

Table 7.4. *Transport CO_2 emission conversion (Davies 2003)*

Looking at the above information, one can calculate the emission savings that could be obtained using combined demand (delivery and collection) models. Since the VRP models with combined delivery and collection use the same vehicle for both demands (instead of just considering deliveries, the case for classical VRPs where a vehicle comes back to depot empty), the savings in CO_2 emission would be significant. The correlation between empty running vehicles and emission has been established by Darvish *et al.* (2017). According to the UK Department of Business, Energy and Industrial Strategy (2017), empty running (carrying 0 tons for the whole journey from origin to destination) among heavy goods vehicles has increased recently. Hence, the increasing number of empty vehicles on roads highlights the role and the importance of the VRP models with backhauling in terms of both economic and environmental concerns.

7.4.4. *Vehicle routing models directly focused on green transportation*

As stated in section 7.1 of this chapter, traditionally the literature on road freight transportation has mainly concentrated on efficient fleet management to achieve economic benefits and better-quality service. The green benefits have been perceived as a secondary objective achieved as a by-product of those studies. Within this domain of research, the prominent examples include the vehicle routing problem

(VRP) and its variants including VRP with backhauls, and so on. However, since the start of this decade, the VRP literature has seen some studies directly addressing green issues. The reasons for such interest and attention are well recognized and noted earlier in this chapter. In this section, we briefly describe the vehicle routing models that are directly focused on green transportation. Broadly speaking, the literature on such environmentally-friendly models may be divided into two categories – green VRPs; and those comprising electric vehicles. We briefly review some relevant studies to keep the reader up-to-date about the recent developments in this research area. The following section shows the link between traditional and green VRP models and the significance of their integration, in order to achieve better economic and ecological gains. The green VRPs and the electric vehicles modeling studies are presented in chronological order of their publication year for ease.

7.4.5. *Green VRP models*

The literature on green road transportation has mainly concentrated on the issue of emissions. McKinnon and Piecyk (2009) were among those who started to highlight the issue by presenting a review of the UK's road freight transport CO_2 emissions. The same authors (Piecyk and McKinnon 2010) presented a scenario-based forecasting study to assess CO_2 emission levels from road freight transport in 2020. However, Bektas and Laporte (2011) presented a study based on the classical Vehicle Routing Problem (VRP), called the Pollution-Routing Problem (PRP) with an extended objective function accounting for greenhouse emissions, along with traditional input parameters such as travel distance and so on. Demir *et al.* (2011) presented a review and a numerical comparison of several freight transportation vehicle emission models from the literature. Their study also reflects on the outputs of those models in relation to field studies. Xiao *et al.* (2012) developed a fuel consumption model for the capacitated vehicle routing problem to minimize fuel consumption by considering the "Fuel Consumption Rate, a factor considered as a load-dependent function". Lin *et al.* (2014) presented a literature review of Green Vehicle Routing Problems (GVRP) categorizing the GVRP into Green-PRP, Pollution Routing Problem, and VRP in Reverse Logistics. The paper also includes discussion on research gaps between the classes of models in terms of the complexity issues in real-world VRPs. Demir *et al.* (2014) presented a review of green road freight transportation. This study is predominantly focused on the models that address emission and CO_2 savings. Ehmke *et al.* (2016) studied data-driven approaches for optimizing emissions in an urban area considering the variability in the speed of traffic on arcs in the network. Poonthalir and Nadarajan (2018) conducted research on fuel consumption and concluded that greater efficiency can be achieved under varying speed limits. Bektas *et al.* (2019) present an overview and discussion on the contribution of operational research-based methodologies toward greening freight transportation. The study mainly focuses on two aspects: road (including urban and electric vehicles) and maritime transportation.

7.4.6. *Electric vehicles modeling*

Fuel costs accounts for 39%–60% of a company's operating costs, and the introduction of electric vehicles (EVs) can reduce this cost significantly, as they are much more energy efficient (Sahin *et al.* 2009). However, being more efficient than the conventional petroleum fuel does not mean that EVs do not produce any emissions which affect the environment. They may not contribute to CO_2 emissions directly, but they require energy, which could be counted as emission depending on the energy production methods. Therefore, in addition to simply introducing EVs, there is also a need to optimize their utilization by efficient routing, charging, and so on. There are some relevant recent studies which consider some of the most important aspects of EV routing. For instance, Erdogan and Miller-Hooks (2012) proposed an electric VRP, where the vehicles have limited driving range and limited refueling infrastructure, but vehicles can visit more than one station along the route. Badin *et al.* (2013) presented a simulation-based study that quantifies the influence of different energy consumption influencing factors such as driving conditions, auxiliaries' impact, driver's aggressiveness, and braking energy recovery strategy on an electric vehicle. Wua *et al.* (2015) proposed an analytical electric vehicle power estimation model based on a practical analysis, showing an EV is more efficient when driving on in-city routes than driving on motorway routes. Goeke and Schneider (2015) studied a variant of the vehicle routing problem with a mixed fleet of commercial electric and conventional vehicles. The authors claim to have studied different electric commercial vehicle routing models that assume energy consumption to be a linear function of traveled distance and incorporate speed, gradient, and cargo load distribution. Jochem *et al.* (2015) developed an optimizing energy system model, called "PERSEUS-NET-TS", to analyze the corresponding CO_2 emissions in Germany in 2030. Their finding is based on four assessment methods: average annual electricity mix, average time-dependent electricity mix, marginal electricity mix, and balancing zero emissions. Keskin and Çatay (2016) studied an electric vehicle routing problem with time windows with partial recharging of electric vehicles. According to their findings, shorter recharging duration is more practical than longer charging duration as it may significantly improve the routing decisions. Lin *et al.* (2016) studied a general Electric Vehicle Routing Problem (EVRP) that addresses certain aspects such as the travel time and energy costs while considering the load effect on battery consumption in their model. Their optimal routing strategy also includes decisions on the electric vehicle fleet size. Hiermann *et al.* (2016) introduce an Electric Fleet Size and Mix Vehicle Routing Problem with Time Windows and Recharging Stations (E-FSMFTW), where in addition to optimizing the fleet and routes, a choice of recharging times and locations is also included in the decision, due to the limited battery power. Jeong *et al.* (2019) studied dynamic wireless charging (DWC) technology that enables the batteries of EVs to charge automatically while traveling on road. Their findings provide insight into the relationship between the battery lifetime and the DWC from the charging arrangement.

Based on the arguments discussed earlier in this chapter, the above two categories of the vehicle routing models can be enriched with the inclusion of both delivery and collection demands. Moreover, with increasing developments in battery power, such modeling accompaniments can contribute significantly toward saving indirect/Well-to-Tank (WTT) emissions produced during power generation.

7.5. Conclusion

This chapter studied some important VRP models meticulously to gain a better understanding of the main issues in this subject area, especially in terms of their contribution to reducing CO_2 emissions. The literature of the VRP models appears to be concentrated mainly on developing the variant models that are closer to reality and can be applied and tested in practice. There is ample evidence of developments of more realistic models in terms of reducing the gap between the assumption-based theoretical VRP models conducted by academics and the actual practices in industry. Hence, the study in this chapter provides insights concerning the relevance of such models to address the issues (e.g. routing cost, maximizing the fleet usage, fewer vehicles on roads, environmental, etc.) which are of growing importance to the industry, governments, and other stakeholders. The references provided in this chapter support our argument of developing research that is more conclusive based on integrated modeling in the area of green reverse logistics. Within this domain, the VRP models optimizing delivery and collection demands simultaneously are more environmentally friendly routing models due to better utilization of vehicles and avoiding empty returning trips.

Overall, it can be concluded that designing and solving efficient vehicle routing models has a great role in minimizing greenhouse gas emissions. Studying the objectives of traditional VRPs and Green VRPs along with the considerations of electric vehicles in an integrated manner allows us to create powerful models that not only optimize economic gains but also contribute to a cleaner environment.

7.6. References

Anily, S. (1996). The vehicle routing problems with delivery and back-haul options. *Naval Research Logistics*, 43, 415–434.

Badin, F., Berr, F. L., Briki, H., Dabadie, J.-C., Petit, M., Magand, S., and Condemine, E. (2013). Evaluation of EVs energy consumption influencing factors, driving conditions, auxiliaries use, driver's aggressiveness. *World Electric Vehicle Journal*, 6, 112–123.

Bai, Y., Zhang, W., and Jin, Z. (2005). A new self-organizing maps strategy for the solving the travelling salesman problem. *Chaos, Solution and Fractals*, 28(1), 1082–1089.

Battara, M., Monaci, M., and Vigo, D. (2009). An adaptive guidance approach for the heuristic solution of a minimum multiple trip vehicle routing problem. *Computers and Operations Research*, 36, 3041–3050.

Bektas, T. (2006). The multiple traveling salesman problem: an overview of formulations and solution procedures. *Omega*, 34, 209–219.

Bektas, T. and Laporte, G. (2011). The pollution-routing problem. *Transportation Research Part B*, 45, 1232–1250.

Bektas, T., Ehmke, J. F., Psaraftis, H. N., and Puchinger, J. (2019). The role of operational research in green freight transportation. *European Journal of Operational Research*, 274, 807–823.

Bin, Y., Zhen, Y. Z., and Baozhen, Y. (2009). An improved ant colony optimisation for vehicle routing problem. *European Journal of Operational Research*, 196, 171–176.

Bodin, L., Golden, B., Assad, A., and Ball, M. (1983). Routing and scheduling of vehicles and crews: the state of the art. *Computers and Operations Research*, 10(2), 63–211.

Chbichib, A., Mellouli, R., and Chabchoub, H. (2011). Profitable vehicle routing problem with multiple trips: modelling and constructive heuristics. *4th International Conference on Logistics*, May 31–June 3, Hammamet, Tunisia.

Chen, J. F. and Wu, T. H. (2006). Vehicle routing problem with simultaneous delivery and pickups. *Journal of the Operational Research Society*, 57, 579–587.

Cordeau, J.-F. and Laporte, G. (2007). The dial-a-ride problem: models and algorithms. *Annals of Operations Research*, 153, 29–46.

Cuervo, D. P., Goos, P., Sorensen, K., and Arraiz, E. (2014). An iterated local search algorithm for the vehicle routing problem with backhauls. *European Journal of Operational Research*, 237(2), 454–464.

Dantzig, G. B. and Ramser, J. H. (1959). The truck dispatching problem. *Management Science*, 6, 80–91.

Darvish, M., Archetti, C., and Coelho, L. C. (2017). Minimizing emissions in integrated distribution problems. Report, CIRRELT, University of Laval. Available at: https://www.cirrelt.ca/DocumentsTravail/CIRRELT-2017-41.pdf.

Davies, T. (2003). Calculation of CO_2 emissions. Available at: https://people.exeter.ac.uk/ TWDavies/energy_conversion/Calculation%20of%20CO2%20emissions%20from%20fue ls.htm.

Demir, E., Bektas, T., and Laporte, G. (2011). A comparative analysis of several vehicle emission models for road freight transportation. *Transportation Research Part D*, 16, 347–357.

Demir, E., Bektas, T., and Laporte, G. (2014). A review of recent research on green road freight transportation. *European Journal of Operational Research*, 237, 775–793.

Department for Business, Energy and Industrial Strategy (2017). Greenhouse gas reporting: conversion factors 2017. Report, Department for Business, Energy and Industrial Strategy, UK. Available at: https://www.gov.uk/government/publications/greenhouse-gas-reporting-conversion-factors-2017.

Department for Transport. (2015). Road traffic estimates for Great Britain: January to March 2015. Report, Department for Transport, UK. Available at: https://www.gov.uk/ government/statistics/road-traffic-estimates-for-great-britain-january-to-march-2015.

Department for Transport. (2016). Domestic Road Freight Statistics, United Kingdom 2015. Report, Department for Transport, UK. Available at: https://assets.publishing.service. gov.uk/government/uploads/system/uploads/attachment_data/file/546346/domestic-road-freight-statistics-2015.pdf.

Dethloff, J. (2001). Vehicle routing and reverse logistics: the vehicle routing problem with simultaneous delivery and pick-up. *OR Spektrum*, 23, 79–96.

Ehmke, J. F., Campbell, A. M., and Thomas, B. W. (2016). Data-driven approaches for emissions-minimized paths in urban areas. *Computers & Operations Research*, 67, 34–47.

Ehmke, J. F., Campbell, A. M., and Thomas, B. W. (2018). Optimizing for total costs in vehicle routing in urban areas. *Transportation Research Part E*, 116, 242–265.

Eiselt, H. A., Gendreau, M., and Laporte, G. (1995). Arc routing problems, part I: the Chinese Postman Problem. *Operations Research*, 43(2), 231–242.

Erdogan, S. and Miller-Hooks, E. (2012) A green Vehicle Routing Problem. *Transportation Research Part E: Logistics and Transportation Review*, 48(1), 100–114.

Ericsson, E., Larsson, H., and Brundell-Freij, K. (2006). Optimizing route choice for lowest fuel consumption – potential effects of a new driver support tool. *Transportation Research Part C – Emerging Technologies*, 14, 369–383.

Fleszar, K., Osman, I. H., and Hindi, K. S. (2009). A variable neighbourhood search algorithm for the open vehicle routing problem. *European Journal of Operational Research*, 195, 803–809.

Gajpal, Y. and Abad, P. L. (2009). Multi-ant colony system (MACS) for a vehicle routing problem with backhauls. *European Journal of Operational Research*, 196, 102–117.

Gamboa, D., Rego, C., and Glover, F. (2006). Implementation analysis of efficient heuristic algorithms for the traveling salesman problem. *Computers and Operations Research*, 33, 1154–1172.

Ganesh, K. and Nallathambi, A. S. (2007). Variants, solution approaches and applications for vehicle routing problems in supply chain: agile framework and comprehensive review. *International Journal of Agile Systems and Management*, 2(1), 50–72.

Gendreau, M., Hertz, A., and Laporte, G. (1992). New insertion and post-optimisation procedures for travelling salesman problem. *Operations Research*, 40(6), 1086–1094.

Goel, A. and Gruhn, V. (2008). A general vehicle routing problem. *European Journal of Operational Research*, 191, 650–660.

Goeke, D. and Schneider, M. (2015). Routing a mixed fleet of electric and conventional vehicles. *European Journal of Operational Research*, 245, 81–99.

Goetschalckx, M. and Jacobs-Blecha, C. (1989). The vehicle routing problem with backhauls. *European Journal of Operational Research*, 42, 39–51.

Gribkovskaia, I., Gullberg, B. O., Hovden, K. J., and Wallace, S. W. (2006). Optimization model for a livestock collection problem. *International Journal of Physical Distribution & Logistics Management*, 36, 136–152.

Halse, K. (1992). Modelling and solving complex vehicle routing problems. PhD thesis, Technical University, Denmark.

Hiermann, G., Puchinger, J., Ropke, S., and Hartl, R. F. (2016). The electric fleet size and mix vehicle routing problem with time windows and recharging stations. *European Journal of Operational Research*, 252, 995–1018.

Jarpa, G. G., Desaulniers, G., Laporte, G., and Marianov, V. (2010). A branch-and-cut algorithm for the vehicle routing problem with deliveries, selective pickups and time windows. *European Journal of Operational Research*, 206, 341–349.

Jeong, S., Jang, Y. J., Kum, D., and Lee, M. S. (2019). Charging automation for electric vehicles: is a smaller battery good for the wireless charging electric vehicles? *IEEE Transactions on Automation Science and Engineering*, 16(1), 486–497.

Jochem, P., Babrowski, S., and Fichtner, W. (2015). Assessing CO_2 emissions of electric vehicles in Germany in 2030. *Transportation Research Part A*, 78, 68–83.

Juan, A. A., Faulin, J., Perez-Bernabeu, E., and Jozefowiez, N. (2014). Horizontal cooperation in vehicle routing problem with backhauling and environmental criteria. *Procedia – Social and Behavioral Sciences*, 111, 1133–1141.

Keskin, M. and Çatay, B. (2016). Partial recharge strategies for the electric vehicle routing problem with time windows. *Transportation Research Part C*, 65, 111–127.

Koc, C. and Laporte, G. (2018). Vehicle routing with backhauls: review and research perspectives. *Computers and Operations Research*, 91, 79–91.

Lahyani, R., Khemakhem, M., and Semet, F. (2015). Rich vehicle routing problems: from a taxonomy to a definition. *European Journal of Operational Research*, 241, 1–14.

Lawler, E. L., Lenstra, J. K., and Rinnooy Kan, A. H. G. (1985). *The Travelling Salesman Problem: A Guided Tour of Combinatorial Optimisation*. Wiley, New York.

Lin, L. and Tao, L. (2011). Solving mixed vehicle routing problem with backhauls by adaptive memory programming methodology. *Third International Conference on Measuring Technology and Mechatronics Automation*, Shanghai, China.

Lin, C., Choy, K. L., Ho, G. T. S., Chung, S. H., and Lam, H. Y. (2014). Survey of green vehicle routing problem: past and future trends. *Expert Systems With Applications*, 41, 1118–1138.

Lin, J., Zhou, W., and Wolfson, O. (2016). Electric vehicle routing problem. *Transportation Research Procedia*, 12, 508–521.

Liu, S.-C. and Chung, C.-H. (2009). A heuristic method for the vehicle routing problem with backhauls and inventory. *Journal of Intelligent Manufacturing*, 20(1), 29–42.

McKinnon, A. C. and Piecyk, M. I. (2009). Measurement of CO_2 emissions from road freight transport: a review of UK experience. *Energy Policy*, 37, 3733–3742.

Mester, D. and Braysy, O. (2007). Active-guided evolution strategies for large-scale capacitated vehicle routing problem. *Computers and Operations Research*, 34, 2964–2975.

Min, H. (1989). The multiple vehicle routing problem with simultaneous delivery and pickup. *Transportation Research*, 23, 377–386.

Mingozzi, A. and Baldacci, R. (1999). An exact method for the vehicle routing with backhauls. *Transportation Science*, 33(3), 315–329.

Nagy, G. and Salhi, S. (2005). Heuristic algorithms for single and multiple depot vehicle routing problems with pickups and deliveries. *European Journal of Operational Research*, 162(1), 126–141.

Nagy, G., Wassan, N. A., and Salhi, S. (2013). The vehicle routing problem with restricted mixing of deliveries and pickups. *Journal of Scheduling*, 16(2), 199–213.

Nagy, G., Wassan, N. A., Speranza, M. G., and Archetti, C. (2015). The vehicle routing problem with divisible deliveries and pickups. *Transportation Science*, 49(2), 271–294.

Ong, J. O. and Suprayogi (2011). Vehicle routing problem with backhauls, multiple trips and time windows. *Journal Teknik Industri*, 13(1), 1–10.

Osman, I. H. and Wassan, N. A. (2002). A reactive tabu meta-heuristic for the vehicle routing problem with back-hauls. *Journal of Scheduling*, 5, 263–285.

Piecyk, M. I. and McKinnon, A. C. (2010). Forecasting the carbon footprint of road freight transport in 2020. *International Journal of Production Economics*, 128, 31–42.

Poonthalir, G. and Nadarajan, R. (2018). A fuel efficient green vehicle routing problem with varying speed constraint (F-GVRP). *Expert Systems With Applications*, 100, 131–144.

Pradenas, L., Oportos, B., and Parada, V. (2013). Mitigation of greenhouse gas emissions in vehicle routing problems with backhauling. *Expert Systems With Applications*, 40, 2985–2991.

Ropke, S. and Pisinger, D. (2006). A unified heuristic for a large class of vehicle routing problems with backhauls. *European Journal of Operational Research*, 171(3), 750–775.

Royal Mail (2019). Can free returns drive sales? Available at: https://www.royalmail.com/business/insights/business-trends/free-returns.

Sahin, B., Yilmaz, H., Ust, Y., Guneri, A. F., and Gulsun, B. (2009). An approach for analysing transportation costs and a case study. *European Journal of Operational Research*, 193(1), 1–11.

Salhi, S. and Nagy, G. (1999). A cluster insertion heuristic for the single and multiple depot vehicle routing problems with backhauling. *Journal of Operational Research Society*, 50, 1034–1042.

Salhi, S. and Wade, A. (2001). An ant system algorithm for the vehicle routing problem with backhauls. *4th International Conference on Metaheuristics*, Porto, Portugal.

Salhi, S., Wassan, N. A., and Hajarat, M. (2013). The fleet size and mix vehicle routing problem with backhauls: formulation and set partitioning-based heuristics. *Transportation Research Part E*, 56, 22–35.

Simeonova, L., Wassan, N., Salhi, S., and Nagy, G. (2018). The heterogeneous fleet vehicle routing problem with light loads and overtime: formulation and population variable neighbourhood search with adaptive memory. *Expert Systems With Applications*, 114, 183–195.

Taillard, E., Laporte, G., and Gendreau, M. (1996). Vehicle routing with multiple use of vehicles. *Journal of the Operational Research Society*, 47(8), 1065–1070.

Tavares, G., Zsigraiova, Z., Semiao, V., and da Grac, M. (2008). A case study of fuel savings through optimization of MSW transportation routes. *Management of Environmental Quality*, 19(4), 444–454.

Toth, P. and Vigo, D. (1996). A heuristic algorithm for the vehicle routing problem with backhauls. In *Advanced Methods in Transportation Analysis*, Bianco, L. and Toth, P. (eds). Springer, Berlin, 585–608.

Toth, P. and Vigo, D. (1997). An exact algorithm for the vehicle routing problem with backhauls. *Transportation Science*, 31, 372–385.

Toth, P. and Vigo, D. (1999). A heuristic algorithm for the symmetric and asymmetric vehicle routing problems with backhauls. *European Journal of Operational Research*, 113, 528–543.

Toth, P. and Vigo, D. (eds). (2002). *The Vehicle Routing Problem*. Siam, USA.

Toth, P. and Vigo, D. (2003). The granular tabu search and its application to the vehicle routing problems. *INFORMS Journal of Computing*, 15(4), 333–346.

Tutuncu, G. Y., Carreto, C. A. C., and Baker, B. M. (2009). A visual interactive approach to classical and mixed vehicle routing problems with backhauls. *Omega*, 37, 138–154.

Vidal, T., Crainic, T., Gendreau, M., and Prins, C. (2014). A unified solution framework for multi-attribute vehicle routing problems. *European Journal of Operational Research*, 234, 658–673.

Wade, A. C. and Salhi, S. (2002). An investigation into a new class of vehicle routing problem with backhauls. *The International Journal of Management Science*, 30, 479–487.

Wassan, N. (2007). Reactive tabu adaptive memory programming search for the vehicle routing problem with backhauls. *Journal of Operational Research Society*, 58, 1630–1641.

Wassan, N. (2016). Meta-heuristics for the multiple trip vehicle routing problem with backhauls. PhD thesis, University of Kent, UK.

Wassan, N. A. and Nagy, G. (2014). Vehicle routing problem with deliveries and pickups: Modelling issues and meta-heuristics solution approaches. *International Journal of Transportation*, 2(1), 95–110.

Wassan, N. A., Nagy, G., and Ahmadi, S. (2008a). A heuristic method for the vehicle routing problem with mixed deliveries and pickups. *Journal of Scheduling*, 11, 149–161.

Wassan, N. A., Wassan, A. H., and Nagy, G. (2008b). A reactive tabu search algorithm for the vehicle routing problem with simultaneous pickups and deliveries. *Journal of Combinatorial Optimization*, 15, 368–386.

Wassan, N. A., Salhi, S., Nagy, G., Wassan, N., and Wade, A. (2013). Solving the mixed backhauling vehicle routing: problem with ants. *International Journal of Energy Optimisation and Engineering*, 2(2), 62–77.

Wassan, N., Wassan, N. A., Nagy, G., and Salhi, S. (2017). The multiple trip vehicle routing problem with backhauls: formulation and a two-level variable neighbourhood search. *Computers & Operations Research*, 78, 454–467.

Wu, W., Tian, Y., and Jin, T. (2016). A label based ant colony algorithm for heterogeneous vehicle routing with mixed backhaul. *Applied Soft Computing*, 47, 224–234.

Wua, X., Freese, D., Cabrera, A., and Kitch, W. A. (2015). Electric vehicles' energy consumption measurement and estimation. *Transportation Research Part D*, 34, 52–67.

Xiao, Y., Zhao, Q., Kaku, I., and Xu, Y. (2012). Development of a fuel consumption optimization model for the capacitated vehicle routing problem. *Computers & Operations Research*, 39, 1419–1431.

Zachariadis, E. and Kiranoudis, C. (2012). An effective local search approach for the vehicle routing problem with backhauls. *Expert Systems With Applications*, 39(3), 3174–3184.

Zhong, Y. and Cole, M. H. (2005). A vehicle routing problem with backhauls and time windows: a guided local search solution. *Transportation Research Part E: Logistics and Transportation Review*, 41(2), 131–144.

8

An Improved DTC Induction Motor for Electric Vehicle Propulsion: An Intention to Provide a Comfortable Ride

In this chapter, the behavior of a Direct Torque Control (DTC)-based induction motor (IM) for an electric vehicle (EV) is studied through simulation. We will compare two DTC approaches: i) the basic DTC approach with uncontrolled switching frequency using hysteresis controllers and ii) a proposed strategy with fixed switching frequency using a PI-PWM torque controller. The first approach is penalized by the uncontrolled switching frequency of the inverter, which, in the case of electric propulsion applications, induces vibration and therefore compromises the comfortable ride. The second DTC approach is developed in order to minimize the torque ripples and to fix the torque switching frequency. The obtained simulation results, dealing with both transient and steady-state operations, are presented and discussed.

8.1. Introduction

In view of several reasons such as air pollution, greenhouse gas emissions, rapid depletion, investigation of natural resources, and rising oil prices, humanity needs to exploit a greener solution for transportation (Afroditia *et al.* 2014; US Environmental Protection Agency 2016). For the greener tomorrow in terms of automotive solutions, electric vehicles (EVs) represent a gratifying alternative (Erdogan and Hooks 2012; Felipe *et al.* 2014; Serra 2013). Leaping into the era of EVs will benefit both humanity and the environment (Struben and Sterman 2008). In fact, governments around the world are encouraging the transition to EVs and are investing a great deal of effort in popularizing them as a means of dealing with global warming problems, thus extricating themselves from their dependence on oil,

---

Chapter written by Fatma BEN SALEM and Moez FEKI.

and addressing energy conservation. But at the same time, many challenges are waiting to be resolved. Conception, adaptation, dissemination, and penetration of EVs will not be an easy job.

As advantages of EVs, we can mention energy efficiency, virtual lack of pollution, and the availability of electric energy through electric distribution systems. The other major features include the optimum design of the motor, selection of a proper drive system, and optimal control strategy.

In this case, it is important to select appropriate traction motors for the EV propulsion systems (Xue *et al.* 2008). The process of selecting the right electric propulsion system is, however, not trivial and should be carried out at the system level. In fact, the choice of electric propulsion systems for EVs mainly depends on three factors: driver expectation, vehicle constraints, and energy source. For the propulsion of EVs, the induction motor (IM) seems to be the candidate that best fulfills their major requirements. This is mainly due to its low cost, robustness, high reliability, and maintenance-free properties (Tabbache *et al.* 2010).

Among the various control techniques available, Direct Torque Control (DTC) appears to be very convenient for EV propulsion (Ben Salem and Masmoudi 2006; Faiz *et al.* 2003; Liu and Zhang 2016; Ronanki *et al.* 2013; Singh *et al.* 2006). The reference speed, which is directly applied by the pedal of the vehicle, is the input for the motor controller. Furthermore, EVs require fast torque response and high drive efficiency. Without mechanical speed sensors at the motor shaft, DTC IM drives have features such as low cost, quick response, and high reliability in EV applications.

Nevertheless, it is well known that DTC strategies are penalized by the uncontrolled switching frequency of the inverter yielding high torque ripples, which, in the case of electric propulsion applications, induces vibration and therefore compromises passenger comfort (Ben Salem and Masmoudi 2007a). However, in DTC strategies, the hysteresis bandwidths of both torque and flux regulators, which are generally chosen arbitrarily, greatly influence the drive performance.

This chapter presents a comparison study between two DTC strategies dedicated to EV applications: i) the basic DTC strategy with uncontrolled switching frequency using hysteresis controllers and ii) a new strategy with fixed switching strategy using PWM torque controller.

The proposed DTC strategy is developed in order to gain reduction of torque ripples and to fix torque switching frequency. For the sake of comparison, the above-described DTC strategies are implemented in the same simulation environment. The obtained simulation results, dealing with both transient and steady-state operations, are presented and discussed.

8.2. Several components of EV motor drive

The major electric propulsion system of EVs consists of the motor, controller, power source, charger, transmission device, and wheels (Figure 8.1). The majority of EVs developed so far are based on DC motors, induction motors or permanent magnetic motors. The maintenance-free low-cost induction machines became an attractive alternative to many developers. Three-phase IMs are best suited to EV drive applications. In fact, IMs are cost-effective and are suitable in terms of size and weight, speed rotation, efficiency, controllability, and reliability.

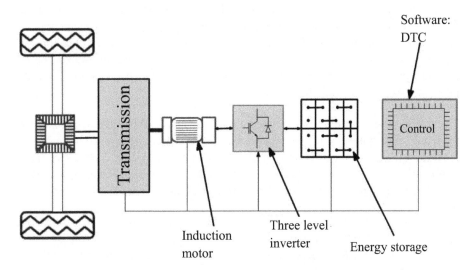

Figure 8.1. *Components of an EV propulsion system. For a color version of this figure, see www.iste.co.uk/besbes/transport.zip*

The proposed motor drive includes the electric motor (induction motor), power converter (three-phase voltage inverter), energy storage (battery), and electronic controller (DTC). These components are the core of the EV propulsion system. Among the desired features of the propulsion system for an EV are high ratio of "torque/inertia" and "power/weight", high maximum torque capability, high speed, low level of audible noise (low torque ripples), low maintenance, small size, low weight, reasonable cost, high efficiency over low- and high-speed ranges, energy recovery on braking, and non-sensitivity to acceleration forces.

Special attention is focused upon the influence of the hysteresis controller of the electromagnetic torque regulator on the average switching frequency of the voltage inverter feeding the IM under conventional DTC strategy (Ben Salem and Masmoudi 2006, 2007b).

8.3. An overview of induction motor control strategies

The induction motor currently, occupies a place of choice in industrial applications such as speed variator. The simplicity of the IM is paid for by the complexity of its control. In fact, obtaining high performance in terms of dynamic response and accuracy of the desired torque requires the implementation of sophisticated control algorithms. Indeed, the absence of a linear relationship between the stator currents and the torque and the flow of the machine, to control the electromagnetic torque, requires the development of control laws that cover a wide range of speeds (Chan and Shi 2011).

Several research works have been developed and published concerning the modeling and synthesis of the appropriate control laws. These techniques are progressing due to the evolution of digital computers. The scalar control technique (V/f control) is the oldest method of control of speed drives that remain limited to steady-state operation, with notably low performance at low speed (Bose 1980).

The Field Oriented Control (FOC) strategy makes it possible to emulate the operation of a DC motor (Blaschke 1972). The basics of FOC theory were introduced by German researchers (Blaschke 1972). The realization of the FOC for IMs powered by the PWM inverter presents a remarkable dynamic improvement compared to the scalar control based only on linear models in steady state. The FOC uses a nonlinear coordinate transformation with a nonlinear state feedback for achieving an asymptotic decoupling between the variables and making it possible to obtain the best dynamic performance from this machine (Ben Salem and Derbel 2007). Nevertheless, this control technique remains very sensitive to parametric variations, particularly for rotor resistance, which are difficult to identify during operation. Since 1990, researchers using this high-performance control strategy have been focusing on the problem of the sensitivity of the strategy to the resistance variation (Ben Salem and Derbel 2007) or the rotor time constant.

Recently, a new control family called DTC has appeared. It was introduced by Depenbrock *et al.* (1988, 1992) in Germany and by Takahashi and Noguchi (1986), Takahashi and Asakawa (1987), Takahashi and Ohmori (1988), and Noguchi *et al.* (1999) in Japan. DTC is based on the fast-dynamic response of the stator flux vector when applying a voltage to machine terminals. By choosing the right switch combinations on the inverter device, DTC drives the stator flux vector to the desired position such that the desired torque and stator flux are achieved.

8.4. DTC strategies

Two major classes of DTC (direct torque control) strategies can be distinguished: i) strategies without controlled switching frequency (Ben Salem and Masmoudi 2007a, 2007c; Takahashi and Asakawa 1987; Takahashi and Noguchi 1986; Takahashi and Ohmori 1988; Noguchi *et al.* 1999) and ii) strategies with controlled switching frequency (Arunadevi *et al.* 2011; Ben Hamed *et al.* 2008; Ben Salem and Derbel 2014, 2016; Chlebis *et al.* 2010; Meroufel *et al.* 2012; Silva *et al.* 2004). Evidently, the second class of DTC strategies offers higher performance in terms of torque ripple reduction and efficiency improvement. Nevertheless, these strategies would certainly require control systems with higher CPU frequencies in so far as their implementation schemes are more complicated than those of the first class. The major drawbacks of strategies without controlled switching frequency are their high torque ripples and switching losses.

8.4.1. *Conventional DTC fundamentals*

The basic idea of DTC strategy is to choose a suitable voltage vector to keep the machine's electromagnetic torque and the stator flux magnitude within predefined hysteresis bounds.

8.4.1.1. *Voltage inverter description*

Considering a three-phase two-level voltage source inverter, there are six non-zero voltage vectors and two zero voltage vectors which can be applied to the machine terminals.

The voltage vector of a three-phase voltage inverter can be expressed as follows:

$$\overline{V}_s = \sqrt{\frac{2}{3}\left[S_a + S_b e^{j\frac{2\pi}{3}} + S_c e^{j\frac{4\pi}{3}}\right]} \qquad [8.1]$$

where S_a, S_b, and S_c are three-phase inverter switching functions, which can take a logical value of either 1 or 0.

Figure 8.2 shows the connections of a three-phase two-level inverter.

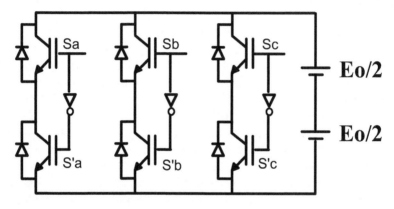

Figure 8.2. *Two-level inverter*

8.4.1.2. *Mathematical model of IMs*

An accurate dynamic model of the IM is necessary to study the dynamic behavior of the motor under both transient and steady-state conditions. Indeed, the dynamic behavior of an IM is described in terms of space variables as follows:

$$\begin{cases} \frac{d}{dt}\phi_{\alpha s} = v_{\alpha s} - R_s i_{\alpha s} \\ \frac{d}{dt}\phi_{\beta s} = v_{\beta s} - R_s i_{\beta s} \\ \frac{d}{dt}\phi_{\alpha r} = -R_r i_{\alpha r} + \omega_m \phi_{\beta r} \\ \frac{d}{dt}\phi_{\beta r} = -R_r i_{\beta r} + \omega_m \phi_{\alpha r} \end{cases} \qquad [8.2]$$

where subscripts s and r refer to stator and rotor; subscripts α and β refer to components in (α, β) frame; v, i, and ϕ refer to voltage, current, and flux, respectively; R_s and R_r refer to stator and rotor resistances; and ω_m refers to the machine speed ($\omega_m = N_p \Omega_m = \omega_s - \omega_r$ and N_p is the pole pair number).

The relationships between currents and flux are:

$$\begin{cases} \phi_{as} = L_s i_{as} + M i_{\alpha r} \\ \phi_{\alpha r} = M i_{as} + L_r i_{\alpha r} \\ \phi_{\beta r} = M i_{\beta s} + L_r i_{\beta r} \\ \phi_{\beta s} = L_s i_{\beta s} + M i_{\beta r} \end{cases} \qquad [8.3]$$

where L and M refer to the inductance and the mutual inductance.

The mechanical part of the machine is described by:

$$J \frac{d}{dt} \Omega_m = T_{em} - T_l \qquad [8.4]$$

where J is the motor inertia and T_l is the load torque.

8.4.1.3. *Conventional EV-DTC scheme*

The implementation scheme of the conventional DTC strategy of an IM drive dedicated to EV applications is shown in Figure 8.3.

The stator flux amplitude and phase are expressed using *Concordia* quantities, as follows:

$$\begin{cases} |\Phi_s| = \sqrt{\phi_{as}^2 + \phi_{\beta s}^2} \\ \theta_s = \arctan\left(\frac{\phi_{\beta s}}{\phi_{as}}\right) \end{cases} \qquad [8.5]$$

The electromagnetic torque can be expressed in terms of stator current and flux as:

$$T_{em} = N_p \left(\phi_{as} i_{\beta s} - \phi_{\beta s} i_{as} \right) \qquad [8.6]$$

where N_p is the pole pair.

Furthermore, the electromagnetic torque T_{em} can be written as a function of stator and rotor flux as follows:

$$T_{em} = N_p \frac{M}{L_s L_r - M^2} |\Phi_r||\Phi_s| \sin\delta \qquad [8.7]$$

where Φ_r is the rotor flux; δ is the angle between the stator and rotor flux-linkage space vectors; L_s, L_r, and M are the stator self-inductance, the rotor self-inductance, and the mutual inductance, respectively.

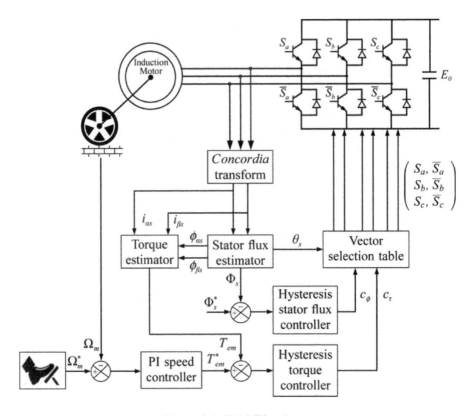

Figure 8.3. *EV-DTC scheme*

The set of combinations of the outputs of the flux and torque hysteresis regulators (c_ϕ, c_r), proposed by Takahashi, are classified in Table 8.1.

The reference speed, which is directly applied by the pedal of the vehicle, is the input for the motor controller.

c_ϕ	+1			−1		
c_r	+1	0	−1	+1	0	−1
S_1	V_2	V_7	V_6	V_3	V_0	V_5
S_2	V_3	V_0	V_1	V_4	V_7	V_6

S_3	V_4	V_7	V_2	V_5	V_0	V_1
S_4	V_5	V_0	V_3	V_6	V_7	V_2
S_5	V_6	V_7	V_4	V_1	V_0	V_3
S_6	V_1	V_0	V_5	V_2	V_7	V_4

Table 8.1. *Conventional DTC strategy switching table*

The stator flux vector can be estimated using measured current and voltage vectors:

$$\frac{d}{dt}\overline{\Phi}_s = \overline{V}_s - R_s\overline{I}_s \qquad [8.8]$$

The electromagnetic torque can be expressed in terms of stator current and flux as:

$$T_{em} = N_p Im\left(\overline{\Phi}_s\overline{I}_s^*\right) \qquad [8.9]$$

where N_p is the pole pair number.

8.4.2. *An improvement of DTC strategy: fixed torque switching frequency*

This approach differs from the basic DTC approach by using a new torque controller with fixed switching frequency replacing the torque hysteresis controller that is penalized by the uncontrolled switching frequency of the inverter yielding high torque ripples, which, in the case of EV propulsion applications, induces vibration and therefore compromises ride comfort.

8.4.2.1. *Modeling of the new torque controller*

Based on the study done by Ben Salem and Masmoudi (2007b), it has been detailed that the inverter average switching frequency F_c, which is the result of the addition of the switching frequency due to the flux hysteresis regulator F_ϕ and the switching frequency due to the torque hysteresis regulator F_τ (Kang *et al.* 1999; Kang and Sul 2001), depends more on the value of F_τ. Within this idea, the switching frequency could be kept constant by fixing F_τ. The proposed controller requires the determination of the power switch conduction times in each modulation period T_0, leading to controlled switching frequency.

The scheme of the considered torque controller fixing F_τ is illustrated in Figure 8.4. F_τ is controlled by fixing the frequency of the PWM block T_0. The synthesis of the PI controller, included in the torque loop, is a specific issue of the DTC strategy considered.

In what follows, we are interested in the synthesis of the proposed torque controller which is presented in Figure 8.4.

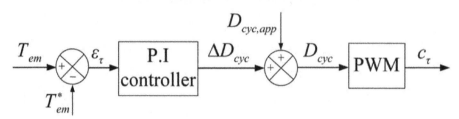

Figure 8.4. *Proposed torque loop*

where the transfer function between torque error ε_τ and the duty cycle variation ΔD_{cyc} is $K_p \frac{T_i s+1}{T_i s}$ where K_p is the proportional gain and T_i is the integration time. In what follows, the centered PWM case is considered with $D_{cycapp} = 0.5$, as shown in Figure 8.5.

Furthermore, the output c_τ can be obtained using the following algorithm:

$$c_r \begin{cases} 0 & \text{if } T_n < t < \frac{T_0}{2}\left(1 - D_{cyc}\right) \\ 1 & \text{if } \frac{T_0}{2}\left(1 - D_{cyc}\right) < t < \frac{T_0}{2}\left(1 + D_{cyc}\right) \\ 0 & \text{if } \frac{T_0}{2}\left(1 + D_{cyc}\right) < t < T_{n+1} \end{cases} \qquad [8.10]$$

The output of the proposed torque controller is similar to that produced by the two-level hysteresis comparator. An active forward voltage is selected when the output of the controller $c_\tau = 1$ in order to increase the torque. A zero voltage vector (which will reduce the torque) is selected when torque status is $c_\tau = 0$.

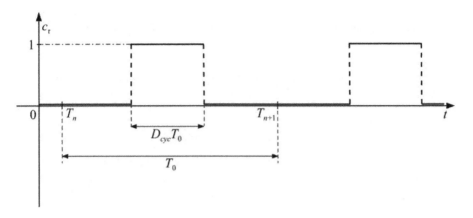

Figure 8.5. *Case of centered PWM*

8.5. Comparative study based on simulation results

The parameters of the IM are: $r_s = 0.29\ \Omega$, $r_r = 0.38\ \Omega$, $M = 47.3\ \text{mH}$, $L_s = L_r = 50\ \text{mH}$, $N_p = 2$, and $J = 0.5\ \text{Kg.m}^2$. It has the following ratings: 220 V, 10 kW, and 1,470 rpm at 50 Hz. The sampling period is fixed to $T_s = 50\ \mu s$ in both DTC approaches under study, and the load torque is equal to the nominal torque $T_l = T_N = 63.7\ \text{N.m}$.

8.5.1. *Steady-state and transient behavior analysis*

In order to highlight the performances gained by the improved DTC approach, we consider the transient behavior of the IM under a reference speed, which allows its start-up, acceleration, and then deceleration. The resulting features are compared to those obtained following the implementation of the conventional DTC approach, which is considered the case of a constant load torque characterizing electric and hybrid propulsion applications. Modulation period $T_0 = 160\ \mu s$ in the proposed DTC strategy with constant torque commutation frequency.

Referring to Figures 8.6(a) and 8.7(a), both approaches have almost the same speed control performance under the same operating conditions.

Comparing Figures 8.6(b) and 8.7(b), the second DTC approach offers a notable reduction of the electromagnetic torque ripples compared to the one using the torque hysteresis controller.

Figures 8.6(c) and 8.7(c) show that the stator flux is almost the same for the two DTC approaches.

Figures 8.6(d) and 8.7(d) show that the stator phase current is almost the same for the two DTC approaches under comparison.

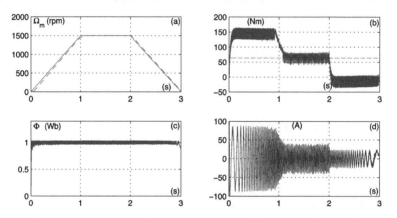

Figure 8.6. *Transient response during starting, acceleration and deceleration of an IM under DTC with variable frequency. (a) Speed and its reference, (b) electromagnetic torque, (c) stator flux, and (d) stator phase current. For a color version of this figure, see www.iste.co.uk/besbes/transport.zip*

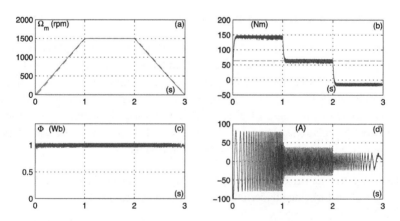

Figure 8.7. *Transient response during starting, acceleration, and deceleration of an IM under the proposed DTC using a torque controller with fixed frequency. (a) Speed and its reference, (b) electromagnetic torque, (c) stator flux, and (d) stator phase current. For a color version of this figure, see www.iste.co.uk/besbes/transport.zip*

8.5.2. *Performance criteria*

Using the same simulation parameters and different reference speed levels, we consider the ripples of the torque around its steady-state value $T_{em,n}$, for different speed levels, as performance criteria. It can be expressed as the norm of the ratio of torque ripples by the torque mean, during one period, as follows:

$$T_{RIP} = \left\| \frac{T_{em}(t) - T_{em,n}}{T_{em,n}} \right\| = \left\| \frac{T_{em}(t)}{T_{em,n}} - 1 \right\| \qquad [8.11]$$

Three norms can be considered, thus leading to three criteria describing the torque ripples, based on the three well-known norms (norm 1, norm 2, and the infinite norm):

$$T_{RIP,1} = \frac{1}{T} \int_{t_0}^{t_0+T} \left| \frac{T_{em}(t) - T_{em,n}}{T_{em,n}} \right| dt \qquad [8.12]$$

$$T_{RIP,2} = \sqrt{\frac{1}{T} \int_{t_0}^{t_0+T} \left[\frac{T_{em}(t) - T_{em,n}}{T_{em,n}} \right]^2 dt} \qquad [8.13]$$

$$T_{RIP,\infty} = \max_{t_0 \le t \le t_0 + T} \left| \frac{T_{em}(t) - T_{em,n}}{T_{em,n}} \right| \qquad [8.14]$$

The criterion $T_{RIP,2}$ represents the root-mean-square (RMS) value of the torque ripple, and $T_{RIP,1}$ represents the mean absolute (MA) value of the torque ripple. However, $T_{RIP,\infty}$ represents the maximum ripple (MR) value of the torque around its steady-state value.

T has been chosen equal to the stator period and time t_0 should be chosen in such a way that the system reaches its permanent regime for *t* larger than t_0. It is to be noted that these three criteria can be computed from t_0 to ∞ without any significant difference between the results obtained. These criteria become:

$$T_{RIP,1} = \lim_{T \to \infty} \frac{\int_{t_0}^{T} |T_{em}(t) - T_{em,n}| dt}{\int_{t_0}^{T} |T_{em,n}| dt} \qquad [8.15]$$

$$T_{RIP,2} = \lim_{T \to \infty} \sqrt{\frac{\int_{t_0}^{T} [T_{em}(t) - T_{em,n}]^2 dt}{\int_{t_0}^{T} [T_{em,n}]^2 dt}} \qquad [8.16]$$

$$T_{RIP,\infty} = \max_{t \ge t_0} \left| \frac{T_{em}(t) - T_{em,n}}{T_{em,n}} \right| \qquad [8.17]$$

The proposed DTC approach with fixed torque switching frequency gives fewer electromagnetic torque ripples. These results are confirmed by the corresponding torque ripple values as shown below. Index criteria ($T_{RIP,1}$, $T_{RIP,2}$, and $T_{RIP,\infty}$) related to torque ripples have been computed for steady-state operations for different speed levels from 100 to 1,500 rpm. The evolution of these criteria for steady-state operations for different speed levels is shown in Figure 8.8. Referring to Figure 8.8(b) and 8.8(c), it is clear that the proposed approach with constant torque switching frequency presents the lowest torque ripple criteria.

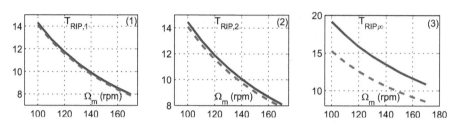

Figure 8.8. *Rate of the torque ripples. (1) $T_{RIP,1}$, (2) root-mean-square (RMS) value of the torque ripple $T_{RIP,2}$, and (3) $T_{RIP,\infty}$. For a color version of this figure, see www.iste.co.uk/besbes/transport.zip*

8.5.3. *Discussion*

Table 8.2 summarizes the results of the comparative study treated previously. In fact, from Table 8.2, we can choose the approach to be used according to the required objectives, the desired performances, and the available means.

Control approach	DTC with hysteresis controllers	DTC with proposed torque controller
Switching frequency	Variable	Fixed
Electromagnetic torque ripples	High	Low
Switching losses	High	Low
Behavior at low speeds	Bad	Good
Algorithm complexity	Low	Low

Table 8.2. *Comparison between performances of the two DTC approaches*

8.6. Conclusion

This chapter approaches for devoted to the comparative study between two is DTC based IMs for an EV propulsion system: the first one was the conventional DTC using hysteresis controllers and the second one was a proposed DTC with fixed switching strategy using a PI-PWM torque controller. These have been derived in the case of a constant load torque which characterizes automotive applications. Simulation works have clearly shown that, thanks to the improved DTC approach, the torque ripples are reduced, which is of great importance in electric propulsion applications as far as ride comfort is concerned.

8.7. References

Afroditia, A., Boilea, M., Theofanisb, S., Sdoukopoulosa, E., and Margaritis, D. (2014). Electric Vehicle Routing Problem with industry constraints: trends and insights for future research. *Transportation Research Procedia*, 3, 452–459.

Arunadevi, R., Ramesh, N., Metilda, A.J., and Sharmeela, C. (2011). Analysis of direct torque control using space vector modulation for three phase induction motor. *Recent Research in Science and Technology*, 3(7), 37–40.

Ben Hamed, M.L., Messaoudi, S.M., Kraiem, H., and Abdelkrim, M.N. (2008). A robust sensorless direct torque control of induction motor based on MRAs and extended Kalman filter. *Leonardo Journal of Sciences*, 12, 35–56.

Ben Salem, F. and Derbel, N. (2007). A sliding mode field oriented control of an induction machine operating with variable parameters. *Journal of Power and Energy Systems*, 27(2), 205–212.

Ben Salem, F. and Derbel, N. (2014). Direct torque control of induction motors based on discrete space vector modulation using adaptive sliding mode control. *Electric Power Components and Systems (EPCS)*, 42(14), 1598–1610.

Ben Salem, F. and Derbel, N. (2016). Second-order sliding-mode control approaches to improve low-speed operation of induction machine under direct torque control. *Electric Power Components and Systems (EPCS)*, 44(17), 1969–1980.

Ben Salem, F. and Masmoudi, A. (2006). On the reduction of vibration caused by DTC strategy in automotive drives: an attempt to guarantee passenger comfort. *22th International Battery, Hybrid and Fuel Cell Electric Vehicle Symposium and Exposition EVS'22*, Yokohama, Japan.

Ben Salem, F. and Masmoudi, A. (2007a). A comparative analysis of the inverter switching frequency in Takahashi DTC strategy. *International Journal for Computation and Mathematics in Electrical and Electronic Engineering*, 26(1), 148–166.

Ben Salem, F. and Masmoudi, A. (2007b). On the comparison of the performance of different DTC strategies with fixed commutation frequency. *5th International Conference and Exhibition on Ecological Vehicles and Renewable Energies*, Monte Carlo, Monaco, March–April.

Ben Salem, F. and Masmoudi, A. (2007c). On the reduction of the commutation frequency in DTC: a comparative study. *European Transactions on Electrical Power Engineering (ETEP)*, 15(6), 571–584.

Blaschke, F. (1972). The principal of field oriented applied to the new transvector closed loop control system for rotating field machines. *Siemens Revue*, 39, 217–220.

Bose, B.K. (1980). *Adjustable Speed AC Drive Systems*. IEEE Press and Wiley, New York.

Chan, T.F. and Shi, K. (2011). *Applied Intelligent Control of Induction Motor Drives*. IEEE Press and Wiley, New York.

Chlebis, P., Brandstetter, P., and Palacky, P. (2010). Direct torque control of induction motor with direct calculation of voltage vector. *Advances in Electrical and Computer Engineering Journal*, 10(4), 17–22.

Depenbrock, M. (1992). Direct self-control (DSC) of inverter-fed induction machine. *IEEE Transactions on Industry Applications*, 28(3), 581–588.

Depenbrock, M., Baader, U., and Gierse, G. (1988). Direct self-control (DSC) of inverter-fed induction machine: a basis for speed control without speed measurement. *IEEE Transactions on Power Electronics*, 3(4), 420–429.

Erdogan, S. and Miller-Hooks, E. (2012). A green vehicle routing problem. *Transportation Research Part E: Logistics and Transportation Review*, 48(1), 100–114.

Faiz, J., Sharifian, M., Keyhani, A., and Proca, A. (2003). Sensorless direct. Torque control of induction motors used in electric vehicle. *IEEE Transactions on Energy Conversion*, 18, 1–10.

Felipe, A., Ortuno, M.T., Righini, G., and Tirado, G. (2014). A heuristic approach for the green vehicle routing problem with multiple technologies and partial recharges. *Transportation Research Part E: Logistics and Transportation Review*, 71(1), 111–128.

Kang, J.K. and Sul, S.K. (2001). Analysis and prediction of inverter switching frequency in direct torque control of induction machine based on hysteresis bands and machine parameters. *IEEE Transactions on Industrial Electronics*, 48, 545–553.

Kang, J.K., Chung, D.W., and Sul, S.K. (1999). Direct torque control of induction machine with variable amplitude control of flux and torque hysteresis bands. *International Electronic Machines and Drives Conference (IEMDS'99)*, Washington, DC, USA, 640–642.

Liu, H. and Zhang, H. (2016). An improved DTC for in-wheel BLDC motors in micro all-electric vehicles. *Automatika*, 57(3), 648–659.

Meroufel, A., Wira, P.M., and Nefsi, A.M. (2012). Contrôle directe du couple de la machine asynchrone basé sur MLI vectorielle discrétisée (DSVM-DTC). *Acta Electrotehnica*, 53(1), 35–40.

Noguchi, T., Yamamoto, M., Kondo, S., and Takahashi, I. (1999). Enlarging switching frequency in direct torque-controlled inverter by means of dithering. *IEEE Transactions on Industry Applications*, 35(6), 1358–1366.

Ronanki, D., Hemasundar, A., and Parthiban, P. (2013). A small 4-wheeler EV propulsion system using DTC controlled induction motor. *Proceedings of the World Congress on Engineering 2013, WCE 2013* (Vol. 2), 3–5 July, London, UK.

Serra, J.V.F. (2013). *Electric Vehicles. Technology, Policy and Commercial Development.* Earthscan, London.

Silva, C.S., Rodriguez, K.J., Pontt J., and Miranda, H. (2004). A novel direct torque control scheme for induction machines with space vector modulation. *35th Annual IEEE Power Electronics Specialists Conference*, Aachen, Germany, 1392–1397.

Singh, B., Jain, P., Mittal, A.P., and Gupta, J.R.P. (2006). Speed sensorless electric vehicle propulsion system using DTC IM drive. *Proceedings of India International Conference on Power Electronics*, December 19–21, Chennai, India.

Struben, J. and Sterman, J.D. (2008). Transition challenges for alternative fuel vehicle and transportation systems. *Environment and Planning B: Planning and Design*, 35(6), 1070–1097.

Tabbache, B., Kheloui, A., and Benbouzid, M. (2010). Design and control of the induction motor propulsion of an electric vehicle. *IEEE Vehicle Power and Propulsion Conference*, Lille, France.

Takahashi, I. and Asakawa, S. (1987). Ultra-wide speed control of induction motor covered 10^6 range. *IEEE Transactions on Industry Applications*, 22(5), 820–827.

Takahashi, I. and Noguchi, T. (1986). A new quick-response and high-efficiency control strategy of an induction motor. *IEEE Transaction Industry Applications*, IA-22(5), 820–827.

Takahashi, I. and Ohmori, Y. (1988). High performance direct torque control of induction machine. *IEEE Power Electronics Specialists Conference (PESC'88)*, Kyoto, Japan, April, 870–876.

US Environmental Protection Agency (2016). Greenhouse gas emissions from the U.S. Transportation Section. Available at: https://www3.epa.gov/otaq/climate/420r06003.pdf [Accessed March 2016].

Xue, X.D., Cheng, K.W.E., and Cheung, N.C. (2008). Selection of electric motor drives for electric vehicles. In *Proceedings of Australasian Universities Power Engineering Conference (AUPEC)*, Padova, Australia.

9

Optimization in Multilevel Green Transportation Problems with Electrical Vehicles

Research on transport problems is widely undertaken due to its practical importance. The use of electric vehicles is being stimulated by governments and, thus, new issues are appearing. Recently, the scientific community has also been considering environmental aspects in transportation optimization problems. The main challenges include, the construction planning of all the infrastructure required to adopt electric vehicles in the transportation systems and the route optimization with capacity battery constraints. As different agents are involved (government, users, etc.), and each of them aims to solve its particular optimization problem whilst considering the other solutions, a multilevel optimization problem rises. A review and a general analysis of green transportation problems involving electric vehicles and modeled as multilevel optimization problems are presented in this chapter.

9.1. Introduction

Although research on transport problems is vast and covers several characteristics, such as fleet type (homogeneous/heterogeneous), time window, number of depots, and so on, only recently has the scientific community started to consider environmental aspects in transport models. In this new context, with regard to combustion vehicles, issues related to the emission of pollutants are the main focus and can be treated according to the type of fuel used, speed along the route, energy efficiency of the engine, and so on. On the other hand, in the search for new

Chapter written by Marcos R. LEITE, Heder S. BERNANDINO, Luciana B. GONÇALVES and Stênio SOARES.

technologies with lower emission of pollutants, the use of alternative sources of energy brought new challenges.

In this new scenario, environmental issues are increasingly present in the industry sector and are an essential element in the logistics and transportation sector, which have undergone structural changes thanks to advances in research related to the production of vehicles using "green" technology, such as hybrid vehicles and electric vehicles. Governments around the world maintain monetary and non-monetary political subsidies to encourage the purchase of electric vehicles[1,2], which has led to an increase in the fleet of hybrid and electric vehicles and a reduction in the emission of greenhouse gases. These bring new challenges, such as the need for building battery charging/swapping stations, where their location, quantity, and capacity to meet demand should be defined. Also, there are challenges related to the planning of routes according to the battery capacity of the vehicles.

In this way, an analysis of the construction planning of all the infrastructure required to adopt electric vehicles in the transportation systems is important.

Besides the reduction in the building costs, the traffic produced by the electric vehicle users should also be addressed. Therefore, several optimization problems appear with different constraints and objectives, and they can be organized in different levels, making multilevel optimization a good option to model this problem in order to meet those goals.

The multilevel optimization problems discussed here can be written as in Migdalas *et al.* (2012).

$$(P_1) \quad \min_{x^{(1)} \in X^{(1)}} f_1(x^{(1)}, \dots, x^{(k)})$$

$$s.t. \quad g_1(x^{(1)}, \dots, x^{(k)}) \leq 0$$

$$(P_2) \quad \min_{x^{(2)} \in X^{(2)}} f_2(x^{(1)}, \dots, x^{(k)}) \qquad\qquad [9.1]$$

$$s.t. \quad g_2(x^{(1)}, \dots, x^{(k)}) \leq 0$$

$$\vdots$$

1 https://www.energy.gov/eere/electricvehicles/electric-vehicles-tax-credits-and-other-incentives.

2 https://www.gov.uk/plug-in-car-van-grants.

$$(P_k) \quad \begin{matrix} min \\ x^{(k)} \in X^{(k)} \end{matrix} f_k(x^{(1)}, \dots, x^{(k)})$$

$$s.t. \quad g_k(x^{(1)}, \dots, x^{(k)}) \leq 0$$

where k is the number of levels, $x^{(i)} \in X^{(i)} \subset \mathbb{R}^{n_i}$, $i = 1, \dots, k$, are the (bound constrained) control variables of the ith level, $f_{(i)}: \mathbb{R}^{n_1 + \dots + n_k} \to \mathbb{R}$, and n_i is the number of design variables of the ith level. The problem is subject to the inequality constraints $g_{(i)}: \mathbb{R}^{n_1 + \dots + n_k} \to \mathbb{R}^{m_i}$, where m_i is the number of constraints of the ith level. An equality constraint $\mathbf{h}_{(i)} = 0$ can be translated to $\mathbf{h}_{(i)} \leq 0$ and $-\mathbf{h}_{(i)} \leq 0$. The bilevel optimization problem appears when $k = 2$ and, in this case, P_1 and P_2 can be called as leader and follower, respectively. This is currently the most common multilevel problem involving electric vehicles in the literature.

In the analyzed papers, the upper level generally models the allocation of the charging stations, while the lower-level model considers the user equilibrium and routing of electric vehicles, so each level has its restrictions and objectives to be met, and the solution process of one level influences the solution process of the other level. This influence can occur through a cyclical process of interaction between the models in the search for solutions or through a hierarchical solution process, where the top-level model is solved first and based on the solution found the lower model is solved.

One can find, in the literature, some papers where the allocation of charging stations and routing of electric vehicles are modeled and solved as multilevel optimization problems.

However, to the best of the authors' knowledge, there is no paper review regarding this subject, highlighting the most common objectives used, the practical aspects considered in the models, and discussing the search methods adopted to solve this type of problem. A general analysis of multilevel optimization problems involving electric vehicles is the objective of this chapter. We aim to fill this existing gap in the literature of electrical vehicles.

This chapter initially presents models commonly found in the literature for multilevel optimization problems, as well as details regarding the objectives and constraints involved in multilevel models. Most of them are bi-level optimization problems and involve the allocation of charging stations and users' equilibrium. In the sequence, some search techniques commonly adopted for solving multilevel optimization problems of electric vehicles are presented. The problems and search techniques, highlighting their features, are also discussed. Finally, some considerations are made regarding the difficulties found in the problems and ideas for future work in this research field.

9.2. Transportation problems with electric vehicles

Normally, the multilevel problems involving the allocation of charging stations and routing of electric vehicles have objectives that are different with respect to the strategy of allocation of the charging stations and the users' equilibrium. Among the work found in the literature, the most common objectives can be seen in Table 9.1, where we present types (maximization/minimization), short descriptions, and abbreviations/labels of the optimization problems.

Type	Description	Abbreviation
Minimization	Construction Cost of Charging Stations	CC
	Social Cost	SC
	Deviation Cost	DC
	Travel Time	TT
	Number of Failure Trips	FT
Maximization	Number of Users Using the Recharge Service	NU
	Number of Success Trips	ST

Table 9.1. *Objective functions found in the literature*

Many works presented the reduction in the cost of construction of charging stations as a target of the government, as it is considered responsible for the construction and planning of charging stations. Usually, the construction of this type of station is limited to a budget value. Also, the number of stations to be built is limited by a fixed value. The deviation cost is the number of users who must deviate from their original path in order to recharge their vehicles, and its calculation may be associated with the State of Charge (SOC) of the vehicle battery. When the battery level reaches a certain (low) value, it is not possible to complete the route without passing through a charging station on the way. The deviation cost should be small for users having the shortest travel time, which is also one of the objectives considered in some works from the literature.

The number of failed trips is the number of journeys in which the vehicle's battery ends without completing the current journey. To avoid this type of situation, one can recharge the battery during travel. On the other hand, the success trips are those in which the vehicle can complete the journey without the battery becoming empty. These objectives are similar, and some studies seek to minimize the former and others to maximize the latter. The number of users that use the charging service is important when planning the allocation of the stations. This is normally attempted by maximizing the number of charging stations.

There are several factors considered in the papers from the literature, which affect the total cost of the travel, such as the cost of charging the vehicle in the stations, the costs related to queue times, the cost caused by the congestion at charging stations, and the costs due to failures, which are the penalties applied when a failed trip occurs. There are several ways to consider these factors, and they are called social costs (SC). In this way, the social cost is a set of different factors that are calculated in different ways for each case, depending on the level of detail and characteristics addressed.

9.2.1. *Multilevel formulations*

Guo *et al.* (2018) consider in the formulation of the problem the customer's range anxiety, which is the concern that the driving range of the EV may not be sufficient to reach its destination, and this is directly related to the allocation structure and deviations from the routes. At the higher level, besides the objective of minimizing the cost of the construction of the charging stations, the objective is to minimize the cost of the deviations made by the users of electric vehicles in order to ensure that a defined proportion of the electric vehicle users is served by the charging stations and there is a reduction in the customer's range anxiety level. At the lower level, considering the influence of this anxiety factor on the route choices on the part of the users, the number of users that use the service of the charging stations should be maximized, thus maximizing the flow in each station.

Range anxiety is also considered in the work of Zang *et al.* (2018), as well as the satisfaction index, which seeks to reflect the convenience the location of charging stations brings to the users of electric vehicles. The main objective of the upper level is to maximize the trip success ratio and to perform the least amount of stops due to battery charging during a trip. Based on the solutions obtained at the top level, the lower model is applied to determine the best routes for users, considering system voltage constraints, station serviceability, social cost, and satisfaction index.

Maximizing the number of users using the charging station service, then maximizing the flow at each station, is the goal of the top level in the work of He *et al.* (2018). In the model, it is considered that users can charge their vehicles at home at night, so vehicles only need to be charged in cases of very long journeys and when users forget to take the vehicle home. The lower model is formulated as a user equilibrium traffic assignment problem, also seeking to minimize the charging time and considering the restrictions of the driving range of electric vehicles.

As in the previous case, Xiong et al. (2018) consider the possibility of charging vehicles at home at night. The problem is formulated on the basis of game theory, where the upper level is modeled as a game of allocation of charging stations, having a maximum number of possible stations to be allocated and considering the reduction in the social cost as the main objective, that is, the total charging cost of all players (users of electric vehicles), which includes the queue and travel times, the number of players, and their charging strategies. The lower level is modeled as a congestion game, and Nash equilibrium is used to meet and define the charging behavior of the players, who follow strategies for reducing their charging costs and congestion time.

The problem in the work of Liu and Wang (2017) was formulated as a tri-level problem, with the possibility of using different types of charging stations (plug-in, wireless, or dynamic charging) with the upper level in order to minimize the social cost and penalties for delays, respecting the budget limit for the construction of charging stations. The intermediate level is related to the users' choices as to the type of electric vehicle that will be used by them and the factors that influence that decision. The lower model is modeled based on the user equilibrium constraints, considering the different types of routes that can be chosen by the users according to the decisions taken at the higher levels, that is, according to the types of charging stations allocated and the type of vehicle chosen by them. The possibility of using different pumping stations is also explored in the work of He et al. (2015), which uses a tour-based model, aiming at the top level to minimize social cost and at the lower level to minimize the flow of users at the charging stations and the time of shitting.

In the work of Zheng et al. (2017), the upper level is formulated with the objective of minimizing the generalized cost that is a measure related to the social cost, allocating the charging stations according to the budget limit. The lower level is modeled as a user equilibrium problem, as in the work of Liu and Wang (2017). In the latter, the upper level considers battery exchange and charging stations, and the objective (to be minimized) is the cost of construction and operation of the charging stations.

In the work of Lee et al. (2014), the formulation of the top-level model aims to minimize the social cost and penalties for failed journeys by allocating a pre-defined number of charging stations. The lower model is also modeled in a similar way to the models of the previous case, considering that the users can be divided into two groups: those that use the charging stations during the trip and those that do not use them. The trips are also divided into a similar way using this same parameter. Minimizing the social cost is also the goal of the upper level in the work of Zhang *et al.* (2015), which calculates the social cost on an annual basis and considering the constraints of flow, voltage magnitude, and charging station transformer capacity. The lower level is modeled according to the user equilibrium models of the previous cases, also considering the demand and service radius restrictions of each station.

In the work of Jung *et al.* (2014), the main objective of the upper level is to minimize the total travel time, which includes the queue time, considering that each node generates a stochastic demand that must be met by the stations, obtained from the lower level, which is a simulation in order to generate a charging profile and queue time for each charging station, thus measuring system performance.

9.2.2. *Summary review of the literature*

As shown in the previous sections, there are several objectives present in the literature so that some objectives appear in one level in certain papers and in the other level in some other ones. We can group the references found in the literature in general according to the objectives of each level as seen in Table 9.2.

As can be seen in Table 9.2, approximately 54% of the papers have the reduction in the social cost, which encompasses a number of factors depending on the elaboration of the model, in one of the levels as their objective. The objective of reducing the travel time, which is one of the main aspects that influence the user experience, is present in the top level in 64% of the references and, except for only two papers (where it appears in both levels), in all others it appears on the lower level. In 18% of the papers, the objective of reducing the cost of construction of the charging stations is presented, which is taken as the objective of the government and all of them present that goal at the higher level. It is worth noting that all works aim to maximize the use of the charging service, and this objective is considered at the lower level as it is directly related to the user flow and route planning.

Objective	Upper level	Lower level
SC	He *et al.* (2015); Zhang *et al.* (2015); Liu and Wang (2017)*; Zheng *et al.* (2017); Xiong *et al.* (2018)	Zheng *et al.* (2017); Zang *et al.* (2018)
NU	He *et al.* (2018)	Guo *et al.* (2018) Xiong *et al.* (2018)
ST	Zang *et al.* (2018)	-
CC	Liu *et al.* (2017)	-
CC and DC	Guo *et al.* (2018)	-
FT and TT	Lee *et al.* (2014)	-
NU and TT	-	Zhang *et al.* (2015)
TT	Jung *et al.* (2014)	Jung *et al.* (2014); Lee *et al.* (2014); He *et al.* (2015); Liu and Wang (2017); Liu *et al.* (2017); He *et al.* (2018)

A three-level optimization problem is solved in the reference checked with a star (*), and we present here the objectives of the first and third levels.

Table 9.2. *Organization of the objectives of each reference according to each level*

Other important factors to consider in the literature are the possibility of partial charging, battery replacement, the use of charging stations with different types of charging technologies (such as wireless), and the application of the techniques in real-world instances. In relation to these factors, the papers present in the literature can be grouped as given in Table 9.3.

Aspects	References
Partial charging	Jung *et al.* (2014); Lee *et al.* (2014); He *et al.* (2015); Guo *et al.* (2018); Zang *et al.* (2018); He *et al.* (2018); Liu and Wang (2017); Liu *et al.* (2017)
Battery swap	Jung *et al.* (2014); Liu *et al.* (2017); Guo *et al.* (2018)
Different stations	Liu and Wang (2017)
Real case	Jung *et al.* (2014); Guo *et al.* (2018); Xiong *et al.* (2018)

Table 9.3. *Other features observed in the literature*

As can be seen in the table, about 73% of the papers consider that users can only charge a part of the battery when they visit a station. This is an important factor as it depends on the time spent by the users while charging their batteries. Only 27% of the references consider the possibility of carrying out not only the charging and the exchanging of batteries in the vehicles but also closely link this factor to the charging time spent by the users, which is one of the most important factors to consider. Another important fact is that only 9% of the papers consider the use of different charging technologies, such as static wireless, plug-in, and dynamic charging (dynamic wireless), which makes the use of different types of charging stations little explored by the models.

With respect to the problem instances, only 27% of the works solved real-world problems. Considering the artificial instances, about 67% of them use the Sioux Falls Network instance[3] or generate new instances taking this instance into account. Sioux Falls Network is formed by 24 nodes and 76 connections. As it is commonly found in the literature, the Sioux Falls Network instance is used as a base to comparatively evaluate new proposals. This instance is used in the computational experiments of the works of He *et al.* (2015), He *et al.* (2018), and Lee *et al.* (2014).

Besides the use of the original version of the Sioux Falls Network instance in the computational experiments, some works generate new instances based on it. In the work of Zheng *et al.* (2017), the new instance is generated considering only three origin nodes to keep the computational burden reasonable. In addition, smaller instances (from 3 to 18 nodes) are generated in the work of Guo *et al.* (2018) based on the nodes of the original Sioux Falls Network instance. In the work of Liu and Wang (2017), the entire instance is used, but only some nodes and connections are available to allocate a particular type of recharge infrastructure.

9.3. Search techniques

The search methods found in the literature for solving multilevel optimization problems involving electric vehicles are presented in this section. These techniques can be classified as exact or approximate methods. The approximate methods can be classified as populational-based or single-solution based approaches, where the populational methods evolve a set of candidate solutions. Simulated Annealing (SA) and Neighborhood Search (NS) can be classified as single and stochastic methods.

On the other hand, populational and stochastic techniques, such as Genetic Algorithms (GAs), Imperialism Competitive Algorithm (ICA), and Particle Swarm

---

3 https://github.com/bstabler/TransportationNetworks/tree/master/SiouxFalls.

Optimization (PSO), were also found in the literature solving the type of problem outlined here.

All these search approaches are briefly described in the following sections. Also, a summary regarding the use of these techniques on the multilevel transportation problems considered here is presented.

9.3.1. *Exact optimization techniques*

Many optimization problems in their formulation contain variables that have value restrictions that can be assumed so that some are continuous and others are discrete, which makes it difficult to search for solutions since, in many cases, it is not possible to solve the version (considering all continuous variables) and then round off the values for the variables that are integers. Thus, mixed-integer linear programming is a way of finding solutions to optimization problems, attending to its constraints of variable values, and being able to model and solve them efficiently.

There are several solvers currently available, and these methods can be used in different ways: as a tool to solve the problem as a whole, as a tool to solve part of the problem – both being used to refine a solution found by some other techniques – or just to find an initial solution that will be used as input for some other method.

Many existing solvers also implement other search techniques as their internal routines, which makes them even faster and more efficient in the search for solutions, greatly improving the performance of these tools in solving problems. So as they are considered robust and efficient, solvers are often used as an object of comparison in the works, which compare the performance of these tools with those of the methods proposed by the works in solving the problem addressed by them.

Some papers from the literature, besides modeling the problem of allocation of charging stations and routing of electric vehicles as a multilevel optimization problem, also present a single-level model usually derived from a combination of the optimization problems at different levels.

One of the techniques used for this is the use of the Karush–Kuhn–Tucker (KKT) conditions. A single-level reformulation is presented by Zheng *et al.* (2017), where the bi-level model is transformed into a single-level one by incorporating the KKT conditions of the lower-level model as constraints of the upper level. According to the authors, the objective function of the lower level (a user equilibrium problem) is strictly convex with respect to the link flows. Thus, the KKT conditions are both necessary and sufficient. These conditions generate a set of constraints, which are added to the constraints of the upper level. The constraints of the lower level are also included in the upper level (allocation of charging stations). The single-level model formulated by this procedure is then linearized (including auxiliary binary variables), simplified, and the resulting mixed-integer linear model is solved using the commercial solver CPLEX. According to Zheng *et al.* (2017), the global optimal solution was obtained by transforming the bi-level nonlinear problem into a single-level program.

9.3.2. *Genetic algorithms*

Introduced by Holland (1975), a genetic algorithm (GA) is a search technique based on evolution and genetics, which adopts concepts of the theory of biological evolution, such as population, generation, heredity, chromosomes, genes, recombination, and mutation.

GAs are implemented as a simulation of the evolution process, starting with an initial population of individuals representing a set of candidate solutions. These candidate solutions, called individuals, are commonly generated at random and are improved over generations (iterations). On each generation, the best individuals are selected. Mechanisms of recombination and mutation are applied to these individuals, and new candidate solutions (descendants) are created. A new selection procedure chooses the best solutions, considering the parents and the newly generated individuals as surviving to the next generation. The selection of the individuals is performed with respect to the fitness of the individuals, which represents their qualities and considers the objective function of the optimization problem. Thus, the best individuals are selected to compose the new population that will be used as input for the next iteration. The selection for recombination, crossover, mutation, and selection for surviving is repeated until the stop condition is reached. A pseudo-code of a GA is presented in Algorithm 9.1.

In the work of He *et al.* (2015), a MATLAB library of GAs is used for optimizing the upper level (allocation of charging stations). However, no details are presented regarding the use of that tool in the paper.

This chapter is focused on multilevel optimization problems with electric-only vehicles. However, GAs are also applied to other (but similar) types of problems. For instance, a GA approach designed for solving routing problems with a mixed fleet of conventional, electric, and hybrid vehicles can be found in the work of Hiermann *et al.* (2019). A combination of a GA with neighborhood search algorithms (local and large) for the choice of routes is proposed in that paper. The search technique selects the charging stations visited and the type of fuel used.

CPLEX is also used to obtain high-quality routes and recombine them with the other routes found.

---

1 Generate an initial random population;

2 **while** *not stop condition* **do**

3 | Select the individuals according to their fitness;

4 | Perform crossover and mutation;

5 | Calculated the fitness of each individual;

6 | Select individuals to the new population;

7 **return** The best individual;

Algorithm 9.1. *Pseudo-code of a genetic algorithm (GA)*

9.3.3. *Imperialism competitive algorithm*

The Imperialism Competitive Algorithm (ICA) was proposed by Gargari and Lucas (2007). ICA is an adaptive optimization strategy based on imperial territorial disputes, using concepts of territories, disputes, empires, and colonies. In imperialism, countries seek to increase their dominions by assimilating other territories, called colonies, so that the more powerful a country, the more colonies it can dominate. As a consequence, this makes the more powerful countries more likely to dominate territories and the weaker countries lose their territories. The colonies always seek to become more like the imperialist countries to which that they are subordinate.

The imperialist countries and their colonies together form the empire, which has its power calculated based on the power of the imperialist country and of all its colonies. In this way, the weaker empires end up being extinguished, and their territories are assimilated by the stronger empires, so that the process of dispute converges to a single great empire. During the process of competition, it is possible for a colony to take the place of an imperialist country when it acquires a power greater than that of its imperialist country. This replacement makes the colony become an imperialist country.

ICA initially generates a set of territories and calculates their power using the objective function evaluation. This is similar to the initial population and fitness function of GA. The best territories become imperialist and form the first empires, and the other ones become colonies of these empires. At each decade (iteration), the colonies move toward the imperialist country, becoming more similar to the empire's leading territory and also the weaker colonies are dominated by the stronger empires. This process is called assimilation. Territories can also undergo random changes in their characteristics; this process is called revolution and it is similar to a mutation. A colony can attain a better position and can take control of the entire empire by assuming the place of the imperialist country. When an empire has no more colonies, it collapses and is eliminated from the dispute. The processes of assimilation, revolution, and competition are repeated until the stop condition is reached. Algorithm 9.2 presents a pseudo-code of an ICA.

---

1 Generate initial random countries;
2 Form initial empires;
3 **while** *not stop condition* **do**
4   Calculated the power of each country;
5   Perform the assimilation;
6   Perform revolution;
7   **if** *the cost of a colony is better than the own imperialist* **then**
8   Swap positions of the imperialist and colony;
9 **return** The best empire;

Algorithm 9.2. *Pseudo-code of an imperialist competitive algorithm*

In the work of Zhang *et al.* (2015), an ICA is used to solve the problem of allocation of charging stations, which is the upper level of the proposed model. In that work, the empires represent the charging stations, the initial number of empires being 20, the number of colonies 12, and the number of empires at the end of the process of territorial dispute 4. The remaining parameters of the algorithm are not presented.

Although it is outside the scope of this chapter, an ICA is applied to the scheduling of charging of hybrid-electric vehicles problem in the work of Amirhosseini and Hosseini (2018). In that paper, the objective is to optimize the charging and supply of hybrid-electric vehicles in order to reduce operational costs. In addition to ICA, Particle Swarm Optimization and the Teaching-learning-based Optimization algorithms are also used, and the three techniques presented good performance in the tests. However, when comparing the results from the perspective of the objective cost function and the convergence of the methods, ICA obtained the best performance when compared to the other two methods.

9.3.4. *Particle Swarm Optimization*

Proposed by Kennedy and Eberhart (1995), the Particle Swarm Optimization (PSO) method is a metaheuristic inspired by the social and cooperative behavior of some animals, such as a flock of birds or a shoal of fish. It is implemented as a simulation of the movement of a set of particles, moving them around a search space according to mathematical formulas referring to the position and velocity of each particle. The motion of each particle is influenced by the best position of the particle, which reflects the personal experience, and the best position of the swarm, which reflects the general experience. When a better position is found, the particles are updated using this new information so that over time the particles tend to converge to the solution of the optimization problem. The process repeats until the stop criterion is satisfied. A pseudo-code of this process can be seen in Algorithm 9.3.

---

1 Generate initial swarm of particles with random velocities and positions;
2 Calculated the best position of each particle;
3 Calculated the best position of the swarm;
4 **while** *not stop condition* **do**
5 | Calculated the fitness of each particle;
6 | Select the best position of each particle and the best position of the swarm;
7 | Calculate the velocity and position of each particle;
8 | Update the best position of each particle and the best position of the swarm;
9 **return** the best particle;

Algorithm 9.3. *Pseudo-code of a Particle Swarm Optimization method*

A discrete version of PSO called DPSO is applied in the work of Zang *et al.* (2018) to solve the upper level of the problem, in which charging stations must be allocated in order to obtain a higher rate of successful trips with the smallest number of recharges. In that approach, the particles represent possible allocations of the charging stations and they are evaluated based on the user's travel pattern information, which is generated based on the problem data.

Although it is outside the scope of this chapter, another approach called discrete PSO for the vehicle routing problem with time windows (VRPTW) can be seen in the work of Gong *et al.* (2012). In that paper, the objective function of the PSO involves two objectives that reduce the number of routes and the total distance traveled by the vehicles given a set of routes. The particles represent a subset of all possible routes and they are modified by selecting and removing new arcs at each iteration to form new solutions that are evaluated based on the two aforementioned objectives.

9.3.5. *Simulated annealing*

Developed by Kirkpatrick *et al.* (1983), simulated annealing (SA) is an optimization method inspired by the annealing process used in metallurgy. In this process, a material is heated to a high temperature and then slowly cooled in order to obtain its minimum energy state.

SA is implemented as a simulation of its counterpart physical process. From a high enough initial temperature (level), which decays at each iteration, the algorithm generates several possible neighborhood solutions of the current one. The new solutions are accepted or rejected according to a probability value that decays according to the temperature. Initially, considering the system with higher temperature, the algorithm accepts many transitions in the expectation of escaping the local optima. On the other hand, a smaller number of solutions are accepted as the temperature decreases. A pseudo-code of this process can be found in Algorithm 9.4.

---

1 Initialize the system with the initial temperatures configuration;
2 **while** *not stop condition* **do**
3   Generate a solution;
4   Accept the solution according to a probability;
5   Update the system temperature;
6 **return** the current solution;

Algorithm 9.4. *Pseudo-code of simulated annealing*

In the work of Lee *et al.* (2014), an SA-based approach is used to solve the problem of allocation of charging stations where the travel time and the number of failed trips are minimized. It is not clear in that work what parameters are used by the algorithm and how the cooling schedule is performed.

An approach that uses SA for the problem of hybrid vehicle routing can be seen in the work of Yu *et al.* (2017). Although it is not the focus of this chapter, the multilevel problems considered here also solve routing problems. Two approaches were developed by Yu *et al.* (2017) based on SA, where a mechanism of restart is used to avoid being trapped in local optima. The difference in the methods is the criterion of acceptance of a new solution: to determine the acceptance probability of a worse solution, the first version uses the Boltzmann function and the second version employs the Cauchy function. The solutions represent a set of routes, composed of customers and charging or gas stations to be visited. At each iteration, new candidate solutions are generated from the current one with the application of the modification methods: insertion, removal, exchange, and reversion.

9.3.6. *Neighborhood search*

The neighborhood of a solution is defined as the set of solutions that can be reached from that solution when some change is applied. A simple neighborhood search (NS) algorithm investigates the neighborhood of a candidate solution looking for better ones. When a better solution is found, a new neighborhood is generated from this new solution, and the process is repeated until the stop criterion is met. A pseudo-code of this process is presented in Algorithm 9.5.

---

1 Generate initial solution;
2 **while** *not stop condition* **do**
3 │ Find the neighborhood of the current solution;
4 │ Select the best solution in the neighborhood;
5 └ Replace the current solution with the solution founded;
6 **return** the current solution;

Algorithm 9.5. *Pseudo-code of neighborhood search algorithm*

In order to do this search for new solutions in the neighbor of a solution, there are several strategies in the literature as proposed by Ropke and Pisinger (2006). The adaptive large neighborhood search (ALNS) is an extension of the large neighborhood search (LNS) in which the neighborhood search is done through the mechanisms of removing and inserting elements that are part of the solution to create other possible solutions that are results of the application of these mechanisms. There are several ways to implement these mechanisms and many of them can be employed in the search algorithm, unlike the LNS that uses only one mechanism of each type (removal and insertion). In this way, weights are assigned to each mechanism so that the better the performance of the mechanism, the greater its weight and the probability of it being chosen by the algorithm. A pseudo-code of this process is shown in Algorithm 9.6.

---

1 Generate initial solution;
2 **while** *not stop condition* **do**
3 │ Select an insertion and removal mechanisms;
4 │ Perform the selected mechanisms;
5 │ Replace the current solution with the new solution found if it is better;
6 └ Adjust the weights of the mechanisms;
7 **return** the current solution;

Algorithm 9.6. *Pseudo-code of adaptive large neighborhood search*

An approach based on ALNS is applied in the work of Guo *et al.* (2018) for solving a routing problem with electric vehicles, where the capacity of service of the charging stations is a constraint. In that proposal, the solutions represent complete planning of allocation of the charging stations. In order to perform the search, the following removal mechanisms are considered: random removal (RaR), customer-based removal (CBR), single-point removal (SPR), two-point removal (TPR), basic worst removal (BWR), and advanced worst removal (AWR). Also, four insertion methods are used: basic greedy insertion (BGI), advanced greedy insertion (AGI), basic regret-k insertion (BRkI), and advanced regret-k insertion (ARkI). Insertion/deletion mechanisms are selected based on a weighted roulette mechanism, where weights are assigned according to the performance of the selected method and applied at each iteration. The constraints of the problem (capacity of the charging stations) are handled using a penalty function.

A neighborhood-based implementation for the problem of routing electric vehicles with time windows can be seen in the work of Schneider *et al.* (2014). The goal is to minimize the travel length taking into account the capacity of the battery and customer time windows. The solutions represent a set of routes, formed by customers and charging or gas stations. At each iteration, new solutions are generated randomly modifying the current one. The best solutions found are recorded in order to avoid the cycling process between solutions already found and analyzed in the previous iterations.

9.3.7. *Summary review of the literature*

As explained in previous sessions, there are several techniques in the literature that can be used to solve the multilevel optimization models for the problem of allocation of charging stations and routing of electric vehicles. We can group the references found in the literature in general according to the methods used in each level as seen in Table 9.4.

Some of the papers considered here solved the Mixed Integer Linear Programming (MILP) problems using only exact methods, such as those of Zheng *et al.* (2017), He *et al.* (2018), and Xiong *et al.* (2018). Other works, such as those of Lee *et al.* (2014), He *et al.* (2015), and Zhang *et al.* (2015), use such techniques to solve only part of the model together with other techniques such as genetic algorithms, the imperialism competitive algorithm, and simulated annealing, respectively.

Some papers also use other stochastic methods to solve the problems as a whole, as in the work of Liu and Wang (2017), which treats the proposed tri-level model as a problem of classifying black-box problems, solving it using a stochastic radial base function algorithm to find and evaluate the solutions to the problem. Other works use iterative algorithms for solution search and lower model resolution such as the work of Zang *et al.* (2018), which uses an iterative procedure that has queue theory elements, and the work of Liu and Wang (2017), which uses a route/time-swapping procedure. For the top level, the first paper uses a discrete version of PSO, and the second one used another iterative algorithm for searching solutions.

Upper level	Lower level	Reference
Adaptive Large Neighborhood Search		Guo *et al.* (2018)
Neighborhood Search		Jung *et al.* (2014)
		Liu *et al.* (2017)
		Liu and Wang (2017)
Exact Method		He *et al.* (2018)
		Xiong *et al.* (2018)
		Zheng *et al.* (2017)
Genetic Algorithm	Exact Method	He *et al.* (2015)
Imperialism Competitive Algorithm		Zhang *et al.* (2015)
Simulated Annealing		Lee *et al.* (2014)
Particle Swarm Optimization	Neighborhood Search	Zang *et al.* (2018)

Table 9.4. *Characterization of the search techniques found in the literature for solving multilevel optimization problems involving electric vehicles*

In order to solve the problem, several techniques are combined: adaptive Large neighborhood search to find the proportion of users, a greedy iterative procedure for the allocation of stations, and K-shorter paths to generate a solution for the problem. In the case of Jung *et al.* (2014), an iterative procedure is used to allocate charging stations at the upper level and simulation is used for the lower level, generating a cyclic interaction process. The problem is also reformulated as a single-level problem and solved with the application of a genetic algorithm.

Some of the papers, as in the previous case, reshape the multilevel optimization model proposed in a single-level model and solve it, as in the work of Xiong *et al.* (2018), where the lower-level problem model is transformed into a set of constraints for the top level, in order to limit the space of the Nash equilibrium of the charging game (since the problem is formulated on the basis of game theory), making the resulting model a level. However, this model has a large number of variables, some of which are continuous and others are integers, with a large search space. In order to obtain a single-level model that is more easily solved, the problem is reformulated considering deviations from strategies that were not possible in the previous formulations and a specific heuristic search algorithm is used to search for solutions more quickly and easily.

In the work of He *et al.* (2018), an iterative heuristic method is used to find good solutions in an acceptable computational time due to the difficulty of finding exact solutions for the proposed model. With the addition of new constraints and variables to the proposed two-level optimization model, it is transformed into a single-level model, but just as in the previous case, the resulting model has integer and continuous variables besides not being linear and yet needs data coming from the previous two-level optimization model. Thus, a new one-level optimization model is generated by making a linear approximation of the original model: transforming objective and link travel time functions into a set of new linear variables and constraints, as well as the problem parameters that are independent of the allocation of charging stations.

With the definition and use of KKT conditions, the lower-level problem in the work of Zheng *et al.* (2017) is rephrased. By having nonlinear elements in this new formulation as in the above case, these parts are linearized and, after applying this same process in the nonlinear parts of the upper level, they are combined making the model a single level and formulated as an MILP problem standard, able to be solved by any commercial solver available in the market.

The performance of metaheuristics is affected by its parameters (Smith and Fogarty 1997). Preliminary experiments are commonly performed in order to reduce the negative impact caused by an inappropriate choice of the parameters. Also, adaptive techniques have become very popular in the metaheuristics literature as they alleviate the parameter tuning process. About 82% of the works from the literature contain the parameters used by the techniques. However, they do not present a justification for them or show how these parameters were defined. In addition, no paper was found where the parameters of the metaheuristics are adapted during the search.

It is also important to highlight that, considering the papers in this review, only the works of Jung *et al.* (2014), Guo *et al.* (2018), and Xiong *et al.* (2018) comparatively evaluate search techniques. These papers represent about 27% of those considered here. Despite this small percentage, we observed about 78% of the papers considered here used the Sioux Falls Network instance or another one generated based on that. However, it is important to highlight that the objectives and the constraints in each work are different, making it hard to compare the results.

In the work of Guo *et al.* (2018), new instances are generated by selecting nodes (from 3 to 18) from the Sioux Falls Network instance. In order to compare with CPLEX, the bi-level model is reformulated to a concentrated decision-making model by relaxing the concern about costumers' decay with their range anxiety. Based on this previous reformulation of the bi-level model, a comparison is also made with the results obtained in the work of Li and Huang (2014), in which the multipath recharging location model is developed considering the effects of vehicle range and multiple deviation paths.

A comparison of the two versions (continuous and discrete) of the proposed algorithm is provided in the work of Xiong *et al.* (2018). As the continuous version obtained the best results, they are also compared to those found by the other three methods from the literature for the assignment of the number of chargers in each zone.

A comparison between the solutions obtained by the bi-level and single-level formulations of the problem is presented in the work of Jung *et al.* (2014). The single-level problem is solved using a genetic algorithm without the cyclic interaction between the upper and lower levels. The proposed method consists in evaluating different charge station allocation schemes and using GA to improve the fitness of the population of solutions.

One can see that different search techniques are used for solving the optimization problems considered here. Thus, we also analyzed the features of these methods with respect to the type of problem being solved. Table 9.5 presents the objective functions used in the multilevel optimization with electric vehicles and the search techniques adopted. According to this table, 85% of the papers presented the use of an exact method or a neighborhood search when the objective function involves travel time (TT). Only in the work of Lee *et al.* (2014), when the objective function is a combination of travel time and the number of failure trips (FT), is the search technique different. Also, one can observe that an exact method is used in half of the papers considered here. In addition, neighborhood search is used in 38% of the papers. Despite this tendency, other search methods are also considered. For instance, four different methods (imperialism competitive algorithm, genetic algorithm, exact method, and neighborhood search) can be found in the literature when the social cost is optimized. In general, all the papers displayed in Table 9.5 presented the use of a neighborhood search (45%) or an exact method (55%) in the lower level. On the other hand, populational metaheuristics were also adopted when solving the higher level.

Finally, the exact methods can be used to find the optimal numerical solutions, especially in the optimization problems of the lower level. However, there are situations in which this type of technique cannot be used, and metaheuristics are adopted. There is no guarantee of finding the global optimal solution when using these methods, but normally a good result is obtained.

Objective	Search Technique	Reference
SC	Imperialism Competitive Algorithm	Zhang *et al.* (2015)
	Genetic Algorithm	He *et al.* (2015)
	Exact Method	Xiong *et al.* (2018) and Zheng *et al.* (2017)
	Neighborhood Search	Zang *et al.* (2018) and Liu and Wang (2017)
NU	Exact Algorithm	Xiong *et al.* (2018) and He *et al.* (2018)
	Adaptive Large Neighborhood Search	Guo *et al.* (2018)
ST	Particle Swarm Optimization	Zang *et al.* (2018)
CC	Neighborhood Search	Liu *et al.* (2017)
CC and DC	Adaptive Large Neighborhood Search	Guo *et al.* (2018)
FT and TT	Simulated Annealing	Lee *et al.* (2014)
NU and TT	Exact Method	Zhang *et al.* (2015)
TT	Neighborhood Search	Jung *et al.* (2014), Liu *et al.* (2017), and Liu and Wang (2017)
	Exact Method	Lee *et al.* (2014), He *et al.* (2015), and He *et al.* (2018)

Table 9.5. *Search techniques used to solve each objective function*

9.4. Tendencies and challenges

It is important to consider, in the models, the congestion factors (queue times in stations and routes), distance anxiety (which is related to the users' fear of the battery running out of power), the number of stops for charging the battery (several charging stops may harm the user), the consumption of the battery (must be modeled as accurately as possible), the possibility of changing batteries (which can be an alternative to speed up the operation in the stations), and the deviations of the routes for charging the battery (they must happen as often as possible and be as small as possible), as these factors are present in daily life, may intensify at peak times and significantly influence user satisfaction and satisfaction with the service.

Other factors besides the reduction in the cost of construction of the charging stations, which in the great majority of the references is considered as the responsibility and the main objective of the government, can be considered, such as a rate of minimum adoption of electric vehicles by companies, once it is cheaper and more viable for companies to start exchanging only part of the fleet, thus forming a mixed fleet and ensuring a minimum use of the built structure for the government. Other forms of partnership between government and business can also be explored.

An issue that can also be considered is the size of the areas intended for the construction of the charging stations, thus allowing the construction of larger and larger capacity stations in areas with greater flows of electric vehicles and smaller and simpler stations at points where the volume of traffic is smaller, including being able to consider different prices for charging the batteries in each station.

The technological advances in the field of electric vehicle charging, which enable other forms of charging, such as wireless charging, for example, can also be considered in the design of the model, to contemplate the largest number of options available and make the models as up to date as possible. Another option to consider is the exchange of batteries in conjunction with the charging, as it is an option that can directly impact the time spent by the user and, consequently, their satisfaction with the service.

The heuristics and other methods presented are efficient in solving the models, and an interesting point for the evaluation of these proposals is the application of them to instances of real problems, which are considerably larger and more complex, thus providing a notion of the applicability of the model to real problems. Hybrid algorithms that combine two or more methods to solve the problem are also an option to be considered, and performance analyses of the hybrid algorithm as a whole and of each part can be conducted by exploring the best of the combined techniques to solve the problem.

Most of the search algorithms, especially the heuristic methods, have parameters that directly affect their performance. As shown previously, most of the papers considered here present the parameters used by the search techniques; however, the parameter selection procedure is not adequately explored. Considering the great importance of this topic, it is necessary that the papers present more details on the choice of these parameters. Were the parameters empirically selected? Were the choices based on the literature? Was a parameter selection tool used? Also, adaptive techniques can be investigated in order to alleviate the user from choosing the parameters.

It is also important to make available the source codes of the proposed methods and the data of the instances used in the computational experiments. As an alternative way to provide the instances of the problems, a detailed procedure for generating them can be presented. With these artifacts, it is possible to compare (currently and newly proposed) search techniques.

9.5. Concluding remarks

As it has been shown throughout the chapter, the current topic is a subject of great importance and must be studied, since increasingly governments and companies have sought to meet the requirements of sustainability, seeking to form partnerships for the elaboration and implementation of these technologies in order to improve social well-being and preserve the environment.

In this chapter, we presented some of the main techniques found in the literature for the multilevel problem involving the allocation of charging stations and routing of electric vehicles. We also discussed the main features that are considered in the formulation of the models. Ideas for future research were shown in order to make the models even closer to reality, considering the various aspects that affect users' daily lives.

This chapter focused on the literature of search techniques to solve multilevel problems involving the allocation of charging stations, routing, and electric vehicles. Another important research avenue involved including classic electric vehicle routing problems present in the literature in the multilevel optimization. As examples, we can cite the electric traveling salesman problem with time windows (ETSPTW) (Roberti and Wen 2016), the electric vehicle scheduling problem (EVSP) in the context of mobility-on-demand (MoD) (Rigas *et al.* 2018), and the dial-a-ride problem (DARP) with electric vehicles (Masmoudi *et al.* 2018). With the adoption of electric vehicles becoming more widespread, these and other problems are increasingly present in the context of electric vehicles, and these are the problems not yet explored in the context of multilevel optimization.

Acknowledgments

This study was financed in part by the Coordenação de Aperfeiçoamento de Pessoal de Nível Superior – Brasil (CAPES) – Finance Code 001. The authors also thank FAPEMIG (APQ-00337-18) and CNPq (312682/2018-2). Finally, we would like to thank the reviewers for their suggestions that have helped us to improve this chapter.

9.6. References

Amirhosseini, B. and Hosseini, S. M. H. (2018). Scheduling charging of hybrid-electric vehicles according to supply and demand based on particle swarm optimization, imperialist competitive and teaching-learning algorithms. *Sustainable Cities and Society*, 43, 339–349.

Gargari, E. A. and Lucas, C. (2007). Imperialist competitive algorithm: an algorithm for optimization inspired by imperialistic competition. *IEEE Congress on Evolutionary Computation*, Singapore, 4661–4667.

Gong, Y., Zhang, J., Liu, O., Huang, R., Chung, H. S., and Shi, Y. (2012). Optimizing the vehicle routing problem with time windows: a discrete particle swarm optimization approach. *IEEE Transactions on Systems, Man, and Cybernetics, Part C (Applications and Reviews)*, 42(2), 254–267.

Guo, F., Yang, J., and Lu, J. (2018). The battery charging station location problem: impact of users' range anxiety and distance convenience. *Transportation Research Part E: Logistics and Transportation Review*, 114, 1–18.

He, F., Yin, Y., and Zhou, J. (2015). Deploying public charging stations for electric vehicles on urban road networks. *Transportation Research Part C: Emerging Technologies*, 60, 227–240.

He, J., Yang, H., Tang, T. O., and Huang, H. J. (2018). An optimal charging station location model with the consideration of electric vehicle's driving range. *Transportation Research Part C: Emerging Technologies*, 86, 641–654.

Hiermann, G., Richard, F. H., Puchinger, J., and Vidal, T. (2019). Routing a mix of conventional, plug-in hybrid, and electric vehicles. *European Journal of Operational Research*, 272(1), 235–248.

Holland, J. H. (1975). *Adaptation in Natural and Artificial Systems: An Introductory Analysis with Applications to Biology, Control and Artificial Intelligence*. University of Michigan Press, Cambridge.

Jung, J., Chow, J. Y. J., Jayakrishnan, R., and Park, J. Y. (2014). Stochastic dynamic itinerary interception refueling location problem with queue delay for electric taxi charging stations. *Transportation Research Part C: Emerging Technologies*, 40, 123–142.

Kennedy, J. and Eberhart, R. (1995). Particle swarm optimization. *Proceedings of ICNN'95 – International Conference on Neural Networks*, 4, 1942–1948.

Kirkpatrick, S., Gelatt, D., and Vecchi, M. P. (1983). Optimization by simulated annealing. *Science*, 220, 671–680.

Lee, Y. G., Kim, H. S., Kho, S. Y., and Lee, C. (2014). UE-based location model of rapid charging stations for EVs with batteries that have different states-of-charge. *Proceedings of the Annual Meeting on Transportation Research Board*, 12–16.

Li, S. and Huang, Y. (2014). Heuristic approaches for the flow-based set covering problem with deviation paths. *Transportation Research Part E: Logistics and Transportation Review*, 72, 144–158.

Liu, X., Guo, R.-Y., and Zhang, C.-Y. (2017). Bi-level programming model of locating public charging stations for electric vehicles. In *COTA International Conference of Transportation Professionals*, July 7–9, Shanghai, China, 3465–3474. https://ascelibrary.org/doi/abs/10.1061/9780784480915.362.

Liu, H. and Wang, D. Z. W. (2017). Locating multiple types of charging facilities for battery electric vehicles. *Transportation Research Part B: Methodological*, 103, 30–55.

Masmoudi, M. A., Hosny, M., Demir, E., Genikomsakis, K. N., and Cheikhrouhou, N. (2018). The dial-a-ride problem with electric vehicles and battery swapping stations. *Transportation Research Part E: Logistics and Transportation Review*, 118, 392–420.

Migdalas, A., Pardalos, P. M., and Värbrand, P. (2012). *Multilevel Optimization: Algorithms and Applications*. Springer, Berlin.

Rigas, E. S., Ramchurn, S. D., and Bassiliades, N. (2018). Algorithms for electric vehicle scheduling in large-scale mobility-on-demand schemes. *Artificial Intelligence*, 262, 248–278.

Roberti, R. and Wen, M. (2016). The electric traveling salesman problem with time windows. *Transportation Research Part E: Logistics and Transportation Review*, 89, 32–52.

Ropke, S. and Pisinger, D. (2006). An adaptive large neighborhood search heuristic for the pickup and delivery problem with time windows. *Transportation Science*, 40, 455–472.

Schneider, M., Stenger, A., and Goeke, D. (2014). The electric vehicle-routing problem with time windows and recharging stations. *Transportation Science*, 48(4), 500–520.

Smith, J. E. and Fogarty, T. C. (1997). Operator and parameter adaptation in genetic algorithms. *Soft Computing*, 1(2), 81–87.

Xiong, Y., Gan, J., An, B., Miao, C., and Bazzan, A. L. C. (2018). Optimal electric vehicle fast charging station placement based on game theoretical framework. *IEEE Transactions on Intelligent Transportation Systems*, 19(8), 2493–2504.

Yu, V. F., Perwira Redi, A. A. N., Hidayat, Y. A., and Wibowo, O. J. (2017). A simulated annealing heuristic for the hybrid vehicle routing problem. *Applied Soft Computing*, 53, 119–132.

Zang, H., Fu, Y., Chen, M., Shen, H., Miao, L., Zhang, S., Wei, Z., and Sun, G. (2018). Bi-level planning model of charging stations considering the coupling relationship between charging stations and travel route. *Applied Sciences*, 8(7), 1–25, Article 1130. http://www.mdpi.com/2076-3417/8/7/1130.

Zhang, G., Yang, H., and Dong, J. (2015). Electric vehicle charging stations layout research based on bi-level programming. *5th International Conference on Electric Utility Deregulation and Restructuring and Power Technologies (DRPT)*, November, Changsha, China, 609–614. doi: 10.1109/DRPT.2015.7432302.

Zheng, H., He, X., Li, Y., and Peeta, S. (2017). Traffic equilibrium and charging facility locations for electric vehicles. *Networks and Spatial Economics*, 17(2), 435–457.

List of Authors

Mohamed Haykal AMMAR
LOGIQ
University of Sfax
Tunisia

Fatma BEN SALEM
CEMLab
University of Sfax
Tunisia

Heder S. BERNANDINO
Federal University of Juiz de Fora
Brazil

Walid BESBES
CIT College
Taif University
Kingdom of Saudi Arabia
and
LOGIQ
University of Sfax
Tunisia

Emrah DEMIR
Panalpina Centre for Manufacturing
and Logistics Research
Cardiff Business School
Cardiff University
United Kingdom

Diala DHOUIB
LOGIQ
University of Sfax
Tunisia
Moez FEKI
CEMLab
University of Sfax
Tunisia

Angus FURNEAUX
Kent Business School
University of Kent
Canterbury
United Kingdom

Olivier GALLAY
HEC
University of Lausanne
Switzerland

Luciana B. GONÇALVES
Federal University of Juiz de Fora
Brazil

Nouha HAMMAMI
LOGIQ
University of Sfax
Tunisia

Manar HOSNY
CCIS
King Saud University
Riyadh
Kingdom of Saudi Arabia

Marcos R. LEITE
Federal University of Juiz de Fora
Brazil

Emna MARREKCHI
LOGIQ
University of Sfax
Tunisia

Mohamed Amine MASMOUDI
Department of Management
Information Science
University of Siegen
Germany

Said SALHI
Kent Business School
University of Kent
Canterbury
United Kingdom

Lina SIMEONOVA
Kent Business School
University of Kent
Canterbury
United Kingdom

Stênio SOARES
Federal University of Juiz de Fora
Brazil

Naveed WASSAN
Sukkur IBA University
Pakistan

Niaz WASSAN
Kent Business School
University of Kent
Canterbury
United Kingdom
and
Department of Operations
Management and Business Statistics
College of Economics and Political
Sciences
Sultan Qaboos University
Muscat
Oman

Alaeddine ZOUARI
LOGIQ
University of Sfax
Tunisia

Nicolas ZUFFEREY
GSEM
University of Geneva
Switzerland

Index

Other titles from

in

Computer Engineering

2019

CLERC Maurice
Iterative Optimizers: Difficulty Measures and Benchmarks

GHLALA Riadh
Analytic SQL in SQL Server 2014/2016

TOUNSI Wiem
Cyber-Vigilance and Digital Trust: Cyber Security in the Era of Cloud Computing and IoT

2018

ANDRO Mathieu
*Digital Libraries and Crowdsourcing
(Digital Tools and Uses Set – Volume 5)*

ARNALDI Bruno, GUITTON Pascal, MOREAU Guillaume
Virtual Reality and Augmented Reality: Myths and Realities

BERTHIER Thierry, TEBOUL Bruno
From Digital Traces to Algorithmic Projections

CARDON Alain
Beyond Artificial Intelligence: From Human Consciousness to Artificial Consciousness

HOMAYOUNI S. Mahdi, FONTES Dalila B.M.M.
Metaheuristics for Maritime Operations
(Optimization Heuristics Set – Volume 1)

JEANSOULIN Robert
JavaScript and Open Data

PIVERT Olivier
NoSQL Data Models: Trends and Challenges
(Databases and Big Data Set – Volume 1)

SEDKAOUI Soraya
Data Analytics and Big Data

SALEH Imad, AMMI Mehdi, SZONIECKY Samuel
Challenges of the Internet of Things: Technology, Use, Ethics
(Digital Tools and Uses Set – Volume 7)

SZONIECKY Samuel
Ecosystems Knowledge: Modeling and Analysis Method for Information and Communication
(Digital Tools and Uses Set – Volume 6)

2017

BENMAMMAR Badr
Concurrent, Real-Time and Distributed Programming in Java

HÉLIODORE Frédéric, NAKIB Amir, ISMAIL Boussaad, OUCHRAA Salma, SCHMITT Laurent
Metaheuristics for Intelligent Electrical Networks
(Metaheuristics Set – Volume 10)

MA Haiping, SIMON Dan
Evolutionary Computation with Biogeography-based Optimization
(Metaheuristics Set – Volume 8)

PÉTROWSKI Alain, BEN-HAMIDA Sana
Evolutionary Algorithms
(Metaheuristics Set – Volume 9)

PAI G A Vijayalakshmi
Metaheuristics for Portfolio Optimization
(Metaheuristics Set – Volume 11)

2016

BLUM Christian, FESTA Paola
Metaheuristics for String Problems in Bio-informatics
(Metaheuristics Set – Volume 6)

DEROUSSI Laurent
Metaheuristics for Logistics
(Metaheuristics Set – Volume 4)

DHAENENS Clarisse and JOURDAN Laetitia
Metaheuristics for Big Data
(Metaheuristics Set – Volume 5)

LABADIE Nacima, PRINS Christian, PRODHON Caroline
Metaheuristics for Vehicle Routing Problems
(Metaheuristics Set – Volume 3)

LEROY Laure
Eyestrain Reduction in Stereoscopy

LUTTON Evelyne, PERROT Nathalie, TONDA Albert
Evolutionary Algorithms for Food Science and Technology
(Metaheuristics Set – Volume 7)

MAGOULÈS Frédéric, ZHAO Hai-Xiang
Data Mining and Machine Learning in Building Energy Analysis

RIGO Michel
Advanced Graph Theory and Combinatorics

2015

BARBIER Franck, RECOUSSINE Jean-Luc
COBOL Software Modernization: From Principles to Implementation with the BLU AGE® Method

CHEN Ken
Performance Evaluation by Simulation and Analysis with Applications to Computer Networks

CLERC Maurice
Guided Randomness in Optimization
(Metaheuristics Set – Volume 1)

DURAND Nicolas, GIANAZZA David, GOTTELAND Jean-Baptiste, ALLIOT Jean-Marc
Metaheuristics for Air Traffic Management
(Metaheuristics Set – Volume 2)

MAGOULÈS Frédéric, ROUX François-Xavier, HOUZEAUX Guillaume
Parallel Scientific Computing

MUNEESAWANG Paisarn, YAMMEN Suchart
Visual Inspection Technology in the Hard Disk Drive Industry

2014

BOULANGER Jean-Louis
Formal Methods Applied to Industrial Complex Systems

BOULANGER Jean-Louis
Formal Methods Applied to Complex Systems:
Implementation of the B Method

GARDI Frédéric, BENOIST Thierry, DARLAY Julien, ESTELLON Bertrand, MEGEL Romain
Mathematical Programming Solver based on Local Search

KRICHEN Saoussen, CHAOUACHI Jouhaina
Graph-related Optimization and Decision Support Systems

DELAHAYE Daniel, PUECHMOREL Stéphane
Modeling and Optimization of Air Traffic

FRANCOPOULO Gil
LMF — Lexical Markup Framework

GHÉDIRA Khaled
Constraint Satisfaction Problems

ROCHANGE Christine, UHRIG Sascha, SAINRAT Pascal
Time-Predictable Architectures

WAHBI Mohamed
Algorithms and Ordering Heuristics for Distributed Constraint Satisfaction
Problems

ZELM Martin *et al.*
Enterprise Interoperability

2012

ARBOLEDA Hugo, ROYER Jean-Claude
Model-Driven and Software Product Line Engineering

BLANCHET Gérard, DUPOUY Bertrand
Computer Architecture

BOULANGER Jean-Louis
Industrial Use of Formal Methods: Formal Verification

BOULANGER Jean-Louis
Formal Method: Industrial Use from Model to the Code

CALVARY Gaëlle, DELOT Thierry, SÈDES Florence, TIGLI Jean-Yves
Computer Science and Ambient Intelligence

MAHOUT Vincent
*Assembly Language Programming: ARM Cortex-M3 2.0: Organization,
Innovation and Territory*

MARLET Renaud
Program Specialization

SOTO Maria, SEVAUX Marc, ROSSI André, LAURENT Johann
Memory Allocation Problems in Embedded Systems: Optimization Methods

2011

BICHOT Charles-Edmond, SIARRY Patrick
Graph Partitioning

BOULANGER Jean-Louis
Static Analysis of Software: The Abstract Interpretation

CAFERRA Ricardo
Logic for Computer Science and Artificial Intelligence

HOMES Bernard
Fundamentals of Software Testing

KORDON Fabrice, HADDAD Serge, PAUTET Laurent, PETRUCCI Laure
Distributed Systems: Design and Algorithms

KORDON Fabrice, HADDAD Serge, PAUTET Laurent, PETRUCCI Laure
Models and Analysis in Distributed Systems

LORCA Xavier
Tree-based Graph Partitioning Constraint

TRUCHET Charlotte, ASSAYAG Gerard
Constraint Programming in Music

VICAT-BLANC PRIMET Pascale *et al.*
Computing Networks: From Cluster to Cloud Computing

2010

AUDIBERT Pierre
Mathematics for Informatics and Computer Science

BABAU Jean-Philippe *et al.*
Model Driven Engineering for Distributed Real-Time Embedded Systems

BOULANGER Jean-Louis
Safety of Computer Architectures

MONMARCHE Nicolas *et al.*
Artificial Ants

PANETTO Hervé, BOUDJLIDA Nacer
Interoperability for Enterprise Software and Applications 2010

SIGAUD Olivier *et al.*
Markov Decision Processes in Artificial Intelligence

SOLNON Christine
Ant Colony Optimization and Constraint Programming

AUBRUN Christophe, SIMON Daniel, SONG Ye-Qiong *et al.*
Co-design Approaches for Dependable Networked Control Systems

2009

FOURNIER Jean-Claude
Graph Theory and Applications

GUEDON Jeanpierre
The Mojette Transform / Theory and Applications

JARD Claude, ROUX Olivier
Communicating Embedded Systems / Software and Design

LECOUTRE Christophe
Constraint Networks / Targeting Simplicity for Techniques and Algorithms

2008

BANÂTRE Michel, MARRÓN Pedro José, OLLERO Hannibal, WOLITZ Adam
Cooperating Embedded Systems and Wireless Sensor Networks

MERZ Stephan, NAVET Nicolas
Modeling and Verification of Real-time Systems

PASCHOS Vangelis Th
Combinatorial Optimization and Theoretical Computer Science: Interfaces and Perspectives

WALDNER Jean-Baptiste
Nanocomputers and Swarm Intelligence

2007

BENHAMOU Frédéric, JUSSIEN Narendra, O'SULLIVAN Barry
Trends in Constraint Programming

JUSSIEN Narendra
A TO Z OF SUDOKU

2006

BABAU Jean-Philippe *et al.*
From MDD Concepts to Experiments and Illustrations – DRES 2006

HABRIAS Henri, FRAPPIER Marc
Software Specification Methods

MURAT Cecile, PASCHOS Vangelis Th
Probabilistic Combinatorial Optimization on Graphs

PANETTO Hervé, BOUDJLIDA Nacer
Interoperability for Enterprise Software and Applications 2006 / IFAC-IFIP I-ESA'2006

2005

GÉRARD Sébastien *et al.*
Model Driven Engineering for Distributed Real Time Embedded Systems

PANETTO Hervé
Interoperability of Enterprise Software and Applications 2005